300 Classic Blocks
for Crochet Projects

300 Classic Blocks
for Crochet Projects

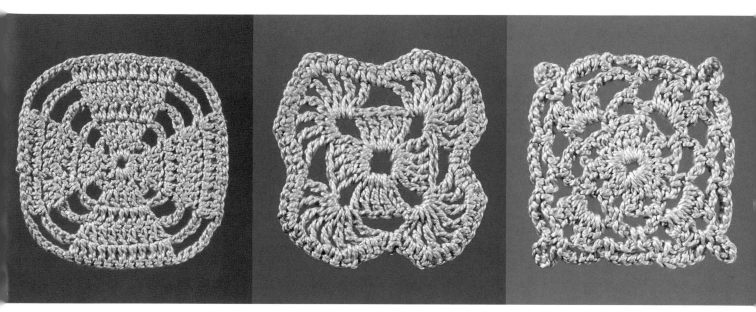

Revised Edition

Linda P. Schapper

LARK BOOKS

A Division of Sterling Publishing Co., Inc.
New York / London

Editor: Susan Mowery Kieffer
Technical Editor: Karen Manthey
Art Director: Shannon Yokeley
Cover Designer: Cindy LaBreacht
Photographer: Steve Mann
Illustrator: Orrin Lundgren
Diagrams: Karen Manthey

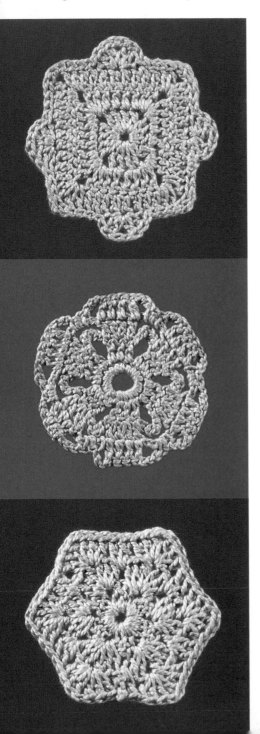

Library of Congress Cataloging-in-Publication Data

Schäpper, Linda.
    300 classic blocks for crochet projects / Linda P. Schapper. -- Rev. ed.
        p. cm.
    Includes index.
    ISBN-13: 978-1-57990-913-0 (hbk. : alk. paper)
    ISBN-10: 1-57990-913-2 (hbk. : alk. paper)
    1. Crocheting--Patterns. I. Title. II. Title: Three hundred classic
blocks for crochet projects.
    TT820.S277 2007
    746.43'4041--dc22

                                    2007046181

10 9 8 7 6 5 4 3 2 1

Revised Edition

Published by Lark Books, A Division of
Sterling Publishing Co., Inc.
387 Park Avenue South, New York, N.Y. 10016

Text © 2008, Linda P. Schapper
Photography © 2008, Lark Books
Illustrations © 2008, Lark Books unless otherwise specified
First published in 1987 by Sterling Publishing Co., Inc.

Distributed in Canada by Sterling Publishing,
c/o Canadian Manda Group, 165 Dufferin Street
Toronto, Ontario, Canada M6K 3H6

Distributed in the United Kingdom by GMC Distribution Services,
Castle Place, 166 High Street, Lewes, East Sussex, England BN7 1XU

Distributed in Australia by Capricorn Link (Australia) Pty Ltd.,
P.O. Box 704, Windsor, NSW 2756 Australia

If you have questions or comments about this book, please contact:
Lark Books
67 Broadway
Asheville, NC 28801
828-253-0467

Manufactured in China

ISBN 13: 978-1-57990-913-0
ISBN 10: 1-57990-913-2

For information about custom editions, special sales, premium and corporate
purchases, please contact Sterling Special Sales Department at 800-805-5489
or specialsales@sterlingpub.com.

Contents

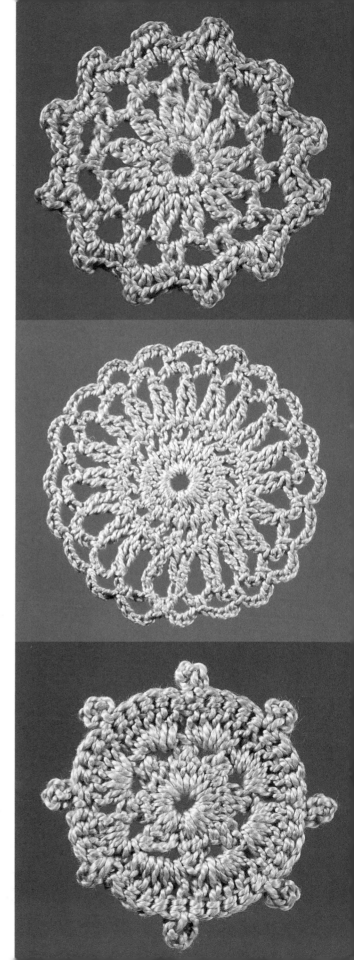

■ Introduction ■

Very little has survived in the way of a written record about the early history of crochet. However, we believe that the craft dates back to the Stone Age, when a crude hook was used to join sections of clothing. In all probability, we adopted the French word for hook—*crochet*—as the name of the craft because the French did more than any other group to record crochet patterns.

As with many handcrafts, crochet developed and flourished, taught from generation to generation without written instructions. Patterns survived by being handed down through families. New patterns were copied by examining designs with a magnifying glass. In the 19th century, written instructions became more popular as the reading level of women improved. Instructions, however, can be often long and tedious and, although perfectly clear to the writer, frequently difficult for the crocheter.

Here in *Crochet Blocks* I provide written instructions for each pattern as well as instruction in the International Crochet Symbols system. The diagrams for these symbols are easy to read after you have memorized a few of the basic stitches. This system enables you to see the whole pattern in proportion, and it is an enjoyable experience to pick up a crochet book written for a Russian, French, or Japanese audience and be able to understand the crochet symbols. The symbols themselves look a great deal like the actual crochet stitches and, as you will see, are not at all difficult to follow.

Crochet begins with a chain, and the way the stitches are formed determines the pattern. You need only a hook, your hand, and the thread. It is a portable craft and can be done almost anywhere, and it is difficult to make a mistake that cannot be corrected immediately. Crochet is versatile. You can make lace patterns, both large and small, mimic knitting, patchwork, or weaving, and you can create any number of textile patterns.

This book focuses on blocks and includes an extensive variety of shapes and sizes. Patterns range from small to large, and from circles and squares to triangles and hexagons. Some of the patterns are sculptured, while some are in the shape of rosettes and other floral patterns.

When I first discovered crochet blocks 20 years ago, I was enchanted with the sheer number of different patterns that could be made with a simple crochet hook and the same white thread. It brought to mind all the infinite possibilities we have with our lives. The slow build up of the pattern, block-by-block, suggested to me that, with small steps, we can get through anything. A close friend had died, and I was going through a particularly sad time in my life, and crocheting the blocks was a comforting exercise. Since then, my life has gone through many highs and more lows and, all these years later, I am still enchanted by the beautiful patterns we can make with a little bit of organization and determination.

With the resurgence of interest in crochet today, it has become popular with both newcomers to the craft and veteran crocheters alike. My hope is that with this book, you, too, will discover or perhaps even rediscover the joy of crochet.

Notes for those using the written instructions
- The abbreviations used throughout are ones used in the United States. A list of basic terms used in the U.K. and Australia is on page 255.
- Learn to read the diagrams, as they are much easier to follow than the instructions. When in doubt about the written instructions, check them against the diagrams.
- To make the motifs reversible, turn at the end of each round, and work the wrong-side rows in reverse—clockwise—following the diagram. Many of the motifs were worked this way to make them reversible.
- The division of stitches into chapters is somewhat arbitrary because many of the patterns can fit into several chapters. I tried to place them where they were most typical.

■ Basic Stitches ■

SLIP KNOT

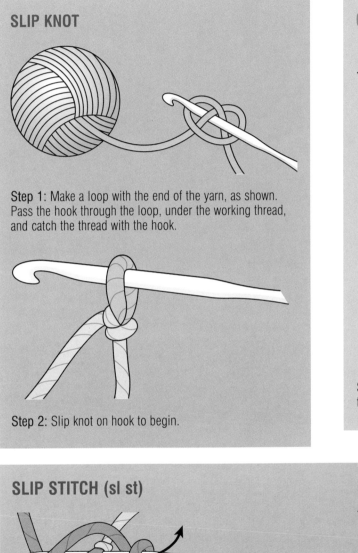

Step 1: Make a loop with the end of the yarn, as shown. Pass the hook through the loop, under the working thread, and catch the thread with the hook.

Step 2: Slip knot on hook to begin.

CHAIN (ch)

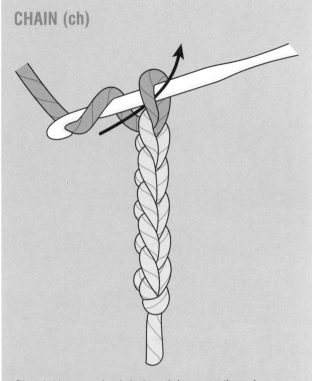

Step 1: Yarn over hook (yo), and draw yarn through the loop on hook (ch made). Repeat as required.

SLIP STITCH (sl st)

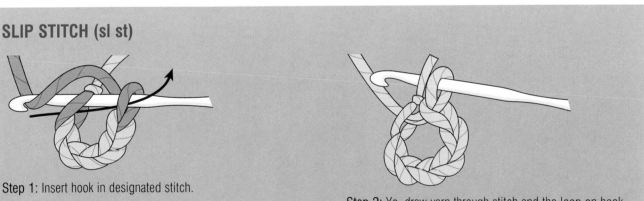

Step 1: Insert hook in designated stitch.

Step 2: Yo, draw yarn through stitch and the loop on hook (sl st made).

SINGLE CROCHET (sc)
This is a short, tight stitch.

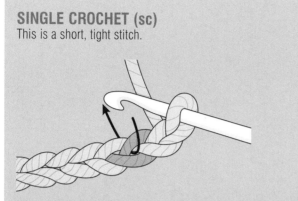

Make a chain of desired length.
Step 1: Insert hook in designated st (2nd ch from hook for first sc).

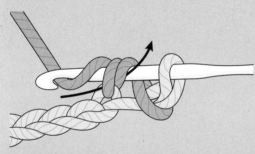

Step 2: Draw yarn through stitch.

Step 3: Yo, draw yarn through 2 loops on hook (sc made).

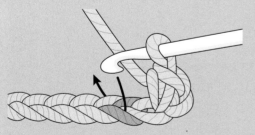

Step 4: Insert hook in next chain, and repeat steps to create another single crochet.

HALF DOUBLE CROCHET (hdc)
This stitch gives a lot of body and structure and resembles knitting.

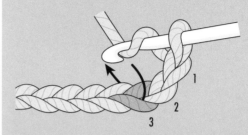

Make a chain of desired length.
Step 1: Yo, insert hook in designated st (3rd ch from hook for first hdc).

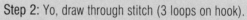

Step 2: Yo, draw through stitch (3 loops on hook).

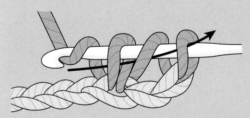

Step 3: Yo, draw yarn through 3 loops on hook (hdc made).

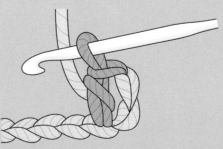

Step 4: You will have one loop left on the hook. Yo, insert hook in next ch, and repeat sequence across row.

DOUBLE CROCHET (dc)

This is perhaps the most popular and frequently used crochet stitch.

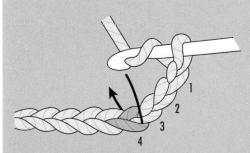

Make a chain of desired length.
Step 1: Yo, insert hook in designated st (4th ch from hook for first dc).

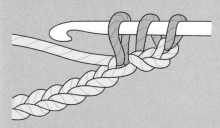

Step 2: Yo, draw through stitch (3 loops on hook).

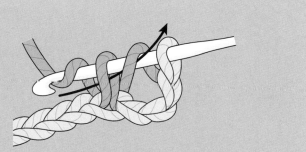

Step 3: Yo, draw yarn through first 2 loops on hook.

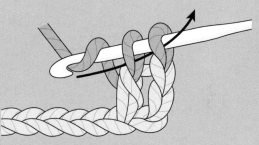

Step 4: Yo, draw yarn through last 2 loops on hook (dc made).

Step 5: Yo, insert hook in next st, and repeat steps to continue across row. Repeat steps 2–4 to work next dc.

TREBLE CROCHET (tr)

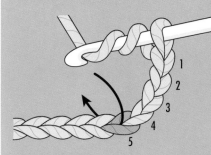

Make a chain of desired length.
Step 1: Yo twice, insert hook in designated st (5th ch from hook for first tr).

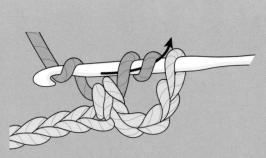

Step 4: Yo, draw yarn through 2 loops on hook (2 loops on hook).

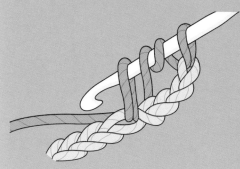

Step 2: Yo, draw through stitch (4 loops on hook).

Step 5: Yo, draw yarn through 2 loops on hook (tr made).

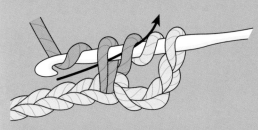

Step 3: Yo, draw yarn through 2 loops on hook (3 loops on hook).

Step 6: Yo twice, and repeat steps in next ch st.

BOBBLE

Can be made with 2 to 6 loops. Shown for 4 loops.

Step 1: Yo, insert hook in designated st.

Step 2: Yo, draw yarn through st and up to level of work (first loop).

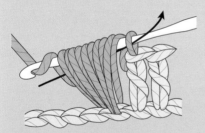

Step 3: (Yo, insert hook in same st, yo, draw yarn through st) as many times as required (3 more times for 4-looped bobble st—11 loops on hook).

Step 4: Yo, draw yarn through all loops on hook (bobble made).

PUFF STITCH

Can be made with 2 to 6 sts. Shown for 3 dc.

Step 1: Yo, insert hook in designated st (4th ch from hook for first puff st), yo, draw yarn through st, yo, draw yarn through 2 loops on hook (half-closed dc made—2 loops remain on hook).

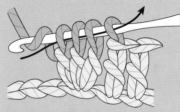

Step 2: Yo, insert hook in same st, yo, draw yarn through st, yo, draw yarn through 2 loops on hook for each additional dc required (2 more times for 3-dc puff stitch—4 loops on hook).

Step 3: Yo, draw yarn through all loops on hook (puff stitch made).

POPCORN (pop)

Can be made with 2 to 6 sts. Shown with 5 dc.

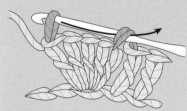

Pop on RS rows:

Step 1: Work 5 dc in designated st (4th ch from hook for first pop).

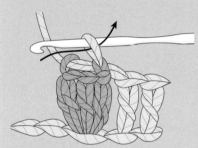

Step 2: Drop loop from hook, insert hook from front to back in top of first dc of group, pick up dropped loop, and draw through st, ch 1 tightly to secure (pop made).

Pop on WS rows:

Step 1: Work 5 dc in designated st (4th ch from hook for first pop).

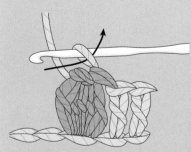

Step 2: Drop loop from hook, insert hook from back to front in top of first dc of group, pick up dropped loop, and draw through st, ch 1 tightly to secure (pop made).

CLUSTER

Shown for 4-dc cluster.

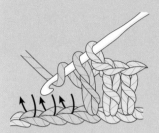

Step 1: Yo, insert hook in designated st, yo, draw yarn through st, yo, draw yarn through 2 loops on hook (half-closed dc made—2 loops remain on hook).

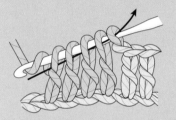

Step 2: (Yo, insert hook in next designated st, yo, draw yarn through st, yo, draw yarn through 2 loops on hook) as many times as required (3 more times for 4-dc cluster—4 half-closed dc made—5 loops on hook).

Step 3: Yo, draw yarn through all loops on hook (cluster made).

PICOT
Shown for ch-3 picot.

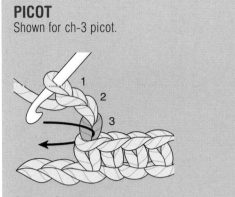

Step 1: Ch 3.

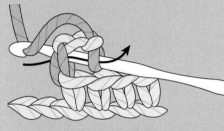

Step 2: Sl st in 3rd ch from hook (picot made).

CROSSED STITCH (CROSSED tr SHOWN)

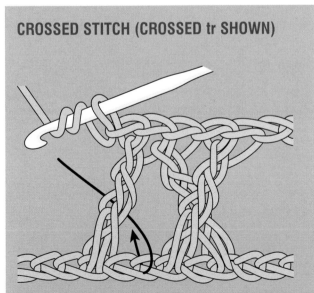

Step 1: Skip required number of sts (skip 2 sts shown), tr in next st, ch required number of sts (ch 1 shown), working behind tr just made, tr in first skipped st.

V-STITCH (V-st), OR SHELL
A designated number of stitches (frequently worked with double crochet stitches) worked in same stitch (shown for 4-dc shell). V-sts are comprised of 2 dc (with or without a ch space). Shells can be made with 3 or more dc (with or without ch spaces).

Work 4 dc in designated st (shell made).

Y-STITCH (OPEN VERSION SHOWN)

Step 1: Work tr in designated st.

Step 2: Ch required number of sts (ch 3 shown), yo, work dc in 2 strands at center of tr just made (Y-st made).

FRONT POST DOUBLE CROCHET (FPDC)
Stitch is raised to front side of work.

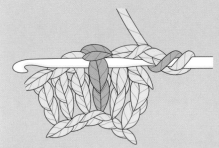

Step 1: Yo, insert hook from front to back to front again, around the post of next designated st.

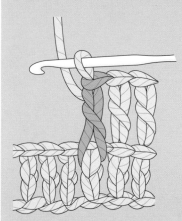

Step 2: Yo, draw yarn through st, (yo, draw yarn through 2 loops on hook) twice (FPdc made).

BACK POST DOUBLE CROCHET (BPDC)
Stitch is raised to back side of work.

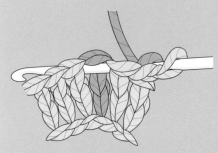

Step 1: Yo, insert hook from back to front to back again, around the post of next designated st.

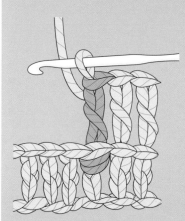

Step 2: Yo, draw yarn through st, (yo, draw yarn through 2 loops on hook) twice (BPdc made).

JOINING BLOCKS

Blocks such as squares, triangles, and hexagons, and even some other designs can be joined together directly without using a different shape to fill out the pattern. Others, such as circular or floral blocks, must be alternated, sometimes with a pattern of a different shape. This provides an opportunity to use your imagination in the selection of a complementary pattern. There is no right or wrong way. Whatever looks good to you can be used.

Illustrations © Karen Manthey

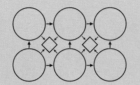

TRIANGLES

CIRCLES WITH SQUARE INSERTS

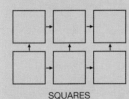

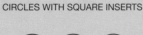

SQUARES

CIRCLES WITH CIRCLE INSERTS

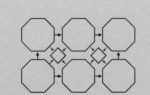

HEXAGONS

OCTAGONS WITH SQUARE INSERTS

JOINING MOTIFS TOGETHER

There are several methods for joining motifs together. Sewing and crocheting are the most popular methods. Sewn seams are the least bulky, but if you prefer to avoid sewing, I've included two methods of crocheting seams.

Joinings can be worked with right sides or wrong sides facing. Worked with the wrong sides facing, the joining will stand out on the front of the piece. Placing the motifs with right sides of the motifs facing, the joining will be on the back and less noticeable. Use whichever method you prefer, just be consistent throughout.

Joinings can be worked through both loops of stitches for a sturdy join or through only the back loops of both pieces for a flexible seam. Illustrations show sewing and slip stitching through back loops of stitches and single crocheting through both loops of stitches. Always work joining stitches as loosely as the crocheted pieces to avoid tight seams that distort the fabric.

SEWN OR WHIPSTITCHED SEAMS

Place motifs together with right (or wrong) sides facing. Using a yarn needle and matching yarn, insert needle through back loop only of corner stitches of both pieces, draw yarn through and secure with a knot, *insert needle from top to bottom through the back loop 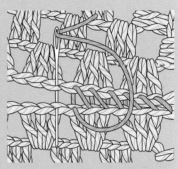 of the next stitch of each piece, then draw yarn through; repeat from * across side to be joined, to next corner stitch. Fasten off.

SLIP STITCHED SEAMS

Place motifs together with right (or wrong) sides facing. Using crochet hook and matching yarn, make a slip knot with yarn. Insert hook 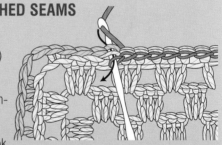 through back loop only of corner stitches of both pieces, place slip knot on hook, *insert hook through back loop of next stitch of each piece, yo, draw yarn through all three loops on hook; repeat from * across side to be joined, to next corner stitch. Fasten off.

SINGLE CROCHETED SEAMS

Place motifs together with right (or wrong) sides facing. Using crochet hook and matching yarn, make a slip knot with yarn. Insert hook through both loops of corner stitches of both pieces, place slip knot on hook, ch 1, insert hook through same two stitches, yo, draw yarn through stitches, yo, draw yarn through 2 loops on hook, *insert hook through both loops of next stitch of each piece, yo, draw yarn through stitches, yo, draw yarn through two loops on hook; repeat from * across side to be joined, to next corner stitch. Fasten off.

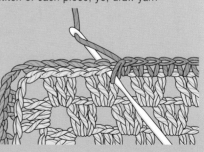

■ International Crochet Symbols ■

chain stitch (ch)	⬯	⬯⬯⬯⬯
slip stitch (sl st)	•	• • • • •
single crochet (sc)	X	X X X X X
half double crochet (hdc)	T	T T T T T
double crochet (dc)	⊤	⊤ ⊤ ⊤ ⊤ ⊤
treble crochet (tr)	⊤	⊤ ⊤ ⊤ ⊤ ⊤
double treble crochet (dtr)	⊤	⊤ ⊤ ⊤ ⊤ ⊤
triple treble crochet (trtr)	⊤	⊤ ⊤ ⊤ ⊤ ⊤
Front Post double crochet (FPdc)	⌐	⌐⌐⌐⌐⌐
Back Post double crochet (BPdc)	⌐	⌐⌐⌐⌐⌐
ch-3 picot	⬠	⬠ ⬠ ⬠ ⬠ ⬠
ch-4 picot	⬡	⬡ ⬡ ⬡ ⬡ ⬡
3-dc popcorn (pop)	⬭	⬭ ⬭ ⬭ ⬭ ⬭
4-dc popcorn (pop)	⬭	⬭ ⬭ ⬭ ⬭ ⬭
5-dc popcorn (pop)	⬭	⬭ ⬭ ⬭ ⬭ ⬭
2-looped bobble	⬭	⬭ ⬭ ⬭ ⬭ ⬭
3-looped bobble	⬭	⬭ ⬭ ⬭ ⬭ ⬭
4-looped bobble	⬭	⬭ ⬭ ⬭ ⬭ ⬭
5-looped bobble	⬭	⬭ ⬭ ⬭ ⬭ ⬭

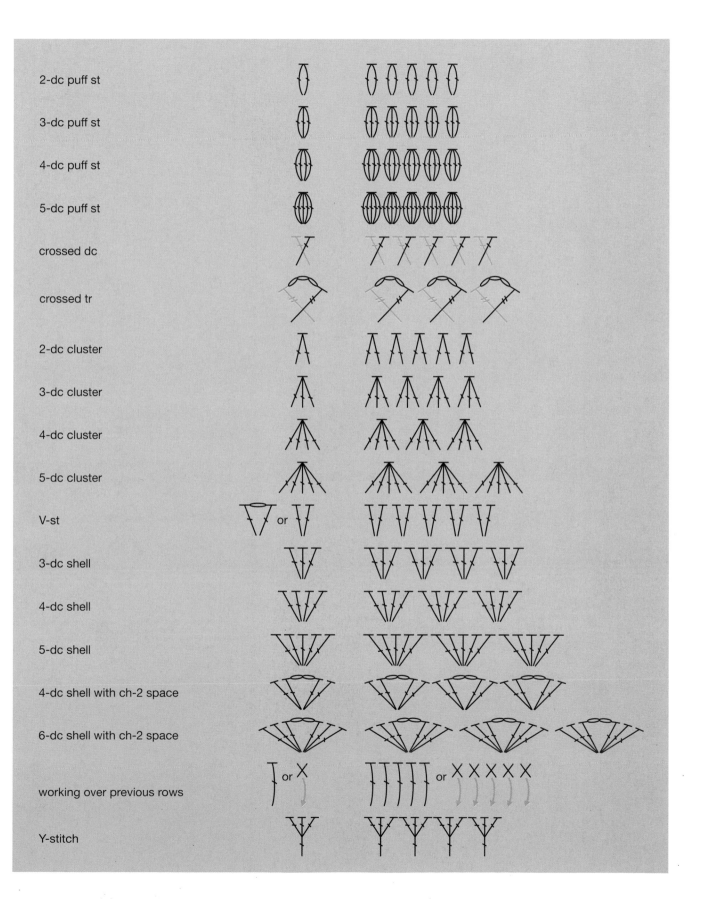

2-dc puff st

3-dc puff st

4-dc puff st

5-dc puff st

crossed dc

crossed tr

2-dc cluster

3-dc cluster

4-dc cluster

5-dc cluster

V-st

3-dc shell

4-dc shell

5-dc shell

4-dc shell with ch-2 space

6-dc shell with ch-2 space

working over previous rows

Y-stitch

.1.
Single Crochets & Chains

1 **Ch** 6 and sl st in first ch to form a ring.

Rnd 1: Ch 1, 6 sc in ring, sl st in first sc to join.

Rnd 2: Ch 1, 2 sc in each sc around, sl st in first sc to join.

Rnd 3: Ch 1, *sc in sc, 3 sc in next sc, sc in next sc; rep from * around, sl st in first sc to join.

Rnd 4: Ch 1, sc in each sc around, sl st in first sc to join.

Rnd 5: Ch 1, *sc in each of next 2 sc, 3 sc in next sc, sc in each of next 2 sc; rep from * around, sl st in first sc to join.

Rnd 3: Ch 1, *sc in each of next 3 sc, 3 sc in next sc, sc in each of next 3 sc; rep from * around, sl st in first sc to join. Fasten off.

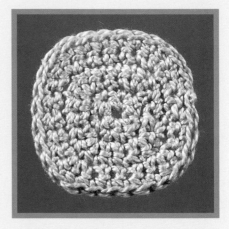

2 **Ch** 20 and sl st in first ch to form a ring.

Rnd 1: Ch 1, 36 sc in ring, sl st in first sc to join.

Rnd 2: *Ch 7, skip next 2 sc, sl st in next sc; rep from * around, ending with sl st in first sl st. Fasten off.

3 **Ch** 18 and sl st in first ch to form a ring.

Rnd 1: Ch 7, sl st to opposite side of ring, ch 1, 11 sc in first half of ring, 11 sc in 2nd half of ring, sl st in first sc to join. Fasten off.

4 **Ch** 8 and sl st in first ch to form a ring.

Rnd 1: Ch 1, 16 sc in ring, sl st in first sc to join.

Rnd 2: Ch 1, (sc, ch 5) in each sc around, sl st in first sc to join. Fasten off.

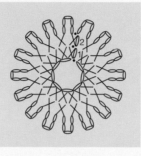

5 **Ch** 8 and sl st in first ch to form a ring.

Rnd 1: Ch 1, (sc, ch 2) 8 times in ring, sl st in first sc to join.

Rnd 2: Sl st in next ch-2 space, ch 1, (sc, ch 3) in each ch-2 space around, sl st in first sc to join.

Rnd 3: Sl st to center of next ch-3 loop, ch 1, (sc, ch 4) in each ch-3 loop around, sl st in first sc to join.

Rnd 4: Sl st to center of next ch-4 loop, ch 1, (sc, ch 5) in each ch-4 loop around, sl st in first sc to join. Fasten off.

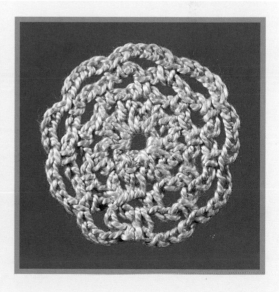

6

Ch 6 and sl st in first ch to form a ring.

Rnd 1: Ch 1, 12 sc in ring, sl st in first sc to join.

Rnd 2: Ch 1, (sc, ch 3) in each sc around, sl st in first sc to join.

Rnd 3: Sl st to center of next ch-3 loop, ch 1, (sc, ch 4) in each ch-3 loop around, sl st in first sc to join.

Rnd 4: Sl st to center of next ch-4 loop, ch 1, (sc, ch 5) in each ch-4 loop around, sl st in first sc to join.

Rnd 5: Sl st to center of next ch-5 loop, ch 1, (sc, ch 6) in each ch-5 loop around, sl st in first sc to join.

Rnd 6: Sl st to center of next ch-6 loop, ch 1, (sc, ch 7) in each ch-6 loop around, sl st in first sc to join. Fasten off.

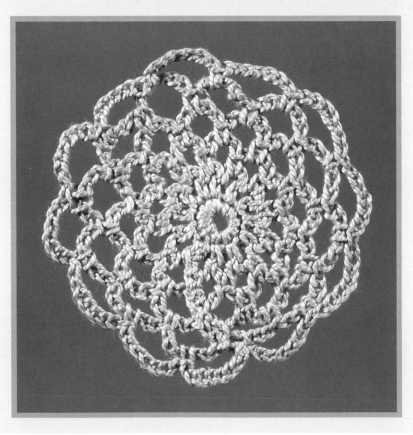

7

Ch 6 and sl st in first ch to form a ring.

Rnd 1: Ch 3 (counts as dc), 17 dc in ring, sl st in 3rd ch of beg ch to join.

Rnd 2: Ch 1, sc in first st, ch 5, skip next 2 dc, *sc in next dc, ch 5, skip next 2 dc; rep from * around, sl st in first sc to join.

Rnd 3: Ch 1, *sc in sc, ch 7, skip next loop; rep from * around, sl st in first sc to join.

Rnd 4: Ch 1, *sc in sc, ch 9, skip next loop; rep from * around, sl st in first sc to join.

Rnd 5: Ch 1, *sc in sc, ch 11, skip next loop; rep from * around, sl st in first sc to join.

Rnd 6: Ch 1, *sc in sc, ch 13, skip next loop; rep from * around, sl st in first sc to join. Fasten off.

8 Ch 6 and sl st in first ch to form a ring.

Rnd 1: Ch 1, 12 sc in ring, sl st in first sc to join.

Rnd 2: Ch 1, *sc in sc, ch 5, skip next sc; rep from * around, sl st in first sc to join.

Rnd 3: Sl st to center of first ch-5 loop, ch 1, (sc, ch 5, sc, ch 5) in each ch-5 loop around, sl st in first sc to join.

Rnd 4: Sl st to center of next ch-5 loop, ch 1, *(sc, ch 5, sc) in ch-5 loop, ch 5, sc in next ch-5 loop, ch 5; rep from * around, sl st in first sc to join.

Rnd 5: Sl st to center of next ch-5 loop, ch 1, *(sc, ch 5, sc) in ch-5 loop, (ch 5, sc) in each of next 2 ch-5 loops, ch 5; rep from * around, sl st in first sc to join.

Rnd 6: Sl st to center of next ch-5 loop, ch 1, *(sc, ch 5, sc) in ch-5 loop, (ch 5, sc) in each of next 3 ch-5 loops, ch 5; rep from * around, sl st in first sc to join. Fasten off.

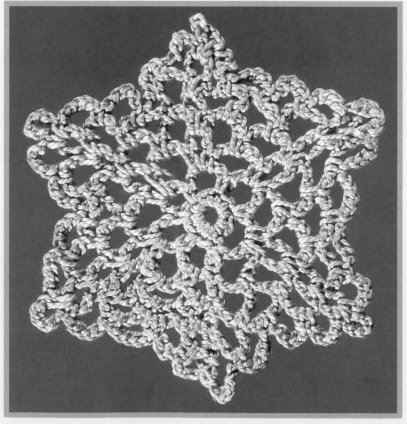

▪2▪
Double Crochets
& Filet

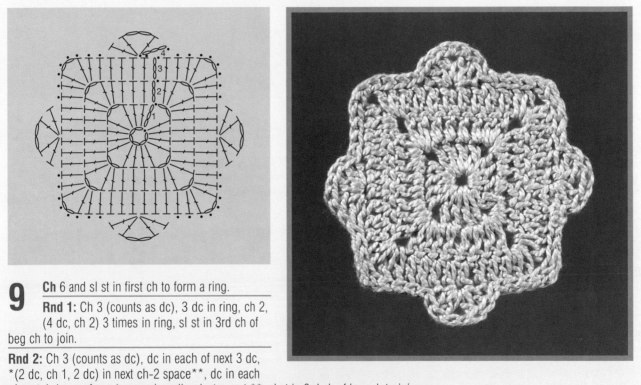

9 **Ch** 6 and sl st in first ch to form a ring.

Rnd 1: Ch 3 (counts as dc), 3 dc in ring, ch 2, (4 dc, ch 2) 3 times in ring, sl st in 3rd ch of beg ch to join.

Rnd 2: Ch 3 (counts as dc), dc in each of next 3 dc, *(2 dc, ch 1, 2 dc) in next ch-2 space**, dc in each of next 4 dc; rep from * around, ending last rep at **, sl st in 3rd ch of beg ch to join.

Rnd 3: Ch 3 (counts as dc), dc in each of next 5 dc, *(2 dc, ch 1, 2 dc) in next ch-2 space**, dc in each of next 8 dc; rep from * around, ending last rep at **, dc in next 2 dc, sl st in 3rd ch of beg ch to join.

Rnd 4: Sl st in next dc, sl st bet last dc and next dc, ch 3 (counts as dc), (dc, ch 2, 2 dc) in same space, *skip next 3 dc, sl st in each of next 3 dc, sl st in each of next 2 ch, sl st in each of next 3 dc**, skip next 3 dc, (2 dc, ch 2, 2 dc) bet last skipped and next dc; rep from * around, ending last rep at **, sl st in 3rd ch of beg ch to join. Fasten off.

10 **Ch** 6 and sl st in first ch to form a ring.

Rnd 1: Ch 3 (counts as dc), 11 dc in ring, sl st in 3rd ch of beg ch to join.

Rnd 2: Ch 4 (counts as dc, ch 1), dc in first dc, *dc in each of next 2 dc**, (dc, ch 1, dc) in next dc; rep from * around, ending last rep at **, sl st in 3rd ch of beg ch to join.

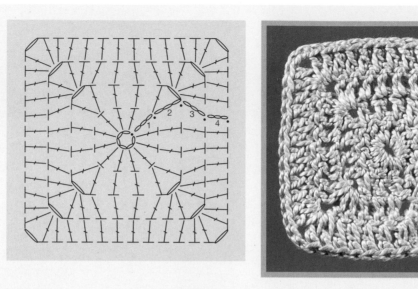

Rnd 3: Ch 3 (counts as dc), *(2 dc, ch 1, 2 dc) in next ch-1 space, dc in each of next 4 dc; rep from * around, omitting last dc, sl st in 3rd ch of beg ch to join.

Rnd 4: Ch 3 (counts as dc), dc in each of next 2 dc, *(2 dc, ch 1, 2 dc) in next ch-1 space**, dc in each of next 8 dc; rep from * around, ending last rep at **, dc in each of next 5 dc, sl st in 3rd ch of beg ch to join. Fasten off.

11 **Ch** 6 and sl st in first ch to form a ring.

Rnd 1: Ch 4 (counts as dc, ch 1), *4 dc in ring, ch 1, dc in ring, ch 1; rep from * twice, 4 dc in ring, ch 1, sl st in 3rd ch of beg ch to join.

Rnd 2: Ch 3 (counts as dc), (dc, ch 1, 2 dc) in first st, *skip next ch-1 space, dc in each of next 4 dc, skip next ch-1 space**, (2 dc, ch 1, 2 dc) in next dc; rep from * around, ending last rep at **, sl st in 3rd ch of beg ch to join.

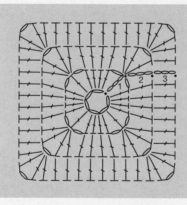

Rnd 3: Ch 3 (counts as dc), dc in next dc, *(2 dc, ch 1, 2 dc) in next ch-1 space**, dc in each of next 8 dc; rep from * around, ending last rep at **, dc in each of next 6 dc, sl st in 3rd ch of beg ch to join. Fasten off.

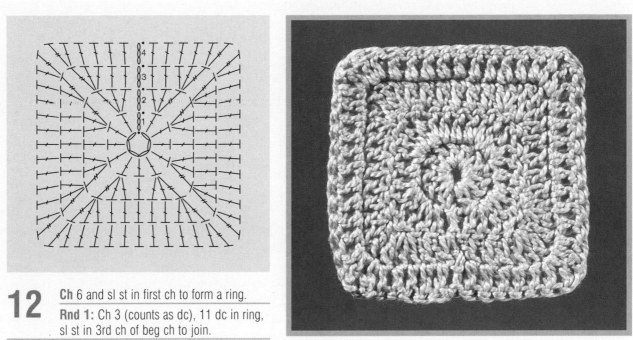

12 Ch 6 and sl st in first ch to form a ring.

Rnd 1: Ch 3 (counts as dc), 11 dc in ring, sl st in 3rd ch of beg ch to join.

Rnd 2: Ch 3 (counts as dc), *(2 dc, tr) in next dc, (tr, 2 dc) in next dc, dc in next dc; rep from * around, omitting last dc, sl st in 3rd ch of beg ch to join.

Rnd 3: Ch 3 (counts as dc), *dc in each of next 2 dc, (2 dc, tr) in next tr, (tr, 2 dc) in next tr, dc in each of next 3 dc; rep from * around, omitting last dc, sl st in 3rd ch of beg ch to join.

Rnd 4: Ch 3 (counts as dc), *dc in each of next 4 dc, (dc, tr) in next tr, (tr, dc) in next tr, dc in each of next 5 dc; rep from * around, omitting last dc, sl st in 3rd ch of beg ch to join. Fasten off.

13 Ch 3 and sl st in first ch to form a ring.

Rnd 1: Ch 8 (counts as dc, ch 5), (dc, ch 5) 3 times in ring, sl st in 3rd ch of beg ch to join. Fasten off.

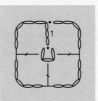

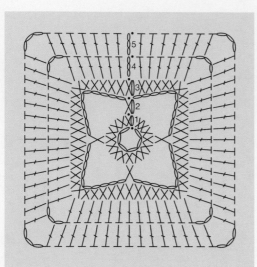

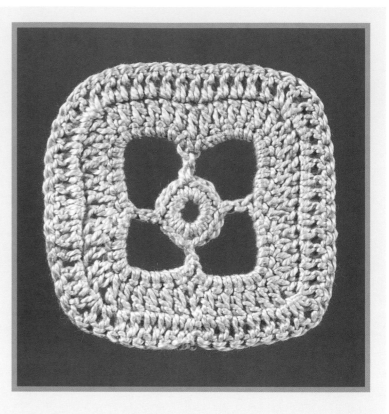

14

Ch 6 and sl st in first ch to form a ring.

Rnd 1: Ch 1, 16 sc in ring, sl st in first sc to join.

Rnd 2: Ch 1, *sc in sc, ch 10, skip next 3 sc; rep from * around, sl st in first sc to join.

Rnd 3: Ch 1, *sc in sc, 11 sc in next ch-10 loop; rep from * around, sl st in first sc to join.

Rnd 4: Ch 3 (counts as dc), *dc in each of next 5 sc, (dc, ch 3, dc) in next sc, dc in each of next 6 sc; rep from * around, omitting last dc, sl st in 3rd ch of beg ch to join.

Rnd 5: Ch 3 (counts as dc), *dc in each of next 6 dc, (dc, ch 3, dc) in next ch-3 loop, dc in each of next 7 dc; rep from * around, omitting last dc, sl st in 3rd ch of beg ch to join. Fasten off.

15

Ch 6 and sl st in first ch to form a ring.

Rnd 1: Ch 3 (counts as dc), 2 dc in ring, ch 3, (3 dc, ch 3) 3 times in ring, sl st in 3rd ch of beg ch to join.

Rnd 2: Ch 3 (counts as dc), dc in each of next 2 dc, *(dc, ch 5, dc) in next ch-3 loop**, dc in each of next 3 dc; rep from * around, ending last rep at **, sl st in 3rd ch of beg ch to join.

Rnd 3: Ch 3 (counts as dc), dc in each of next 3 dc, *(dc, ch 7, dc) in next ch-5 loop**, dc in each of next 5 dc; rep from * around, ending last rep at **, dc in next dc, sl st in 3rd ch of beg ch to join. Fasten off.

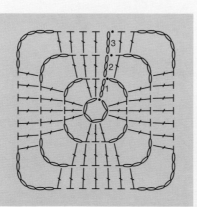

16

Ch 13 and sl st in first ch to form a ring.

Rnd 1: Ch 5 (counts as dc, ch 2), (dc, ch 5, dc, ch 2) 3 times in ring, dc in ring, ch 5, sl st in 3rd ch of beg ch to join.

Rnd 2: Ch 3 (counts as dc), *2 dc in next ch-2 space, dc in next dc, (3 dc, ch 5, 3 dc) in next ch-5 loop**, dc in next dc; rep from * around, ending last rep at **, sl st in 3rd ch of beg ch to join. Fasten off.

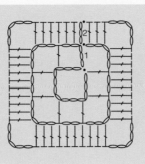

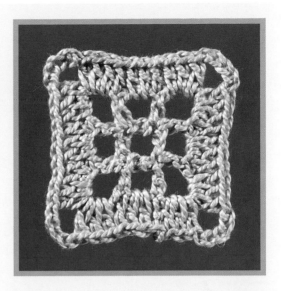

17

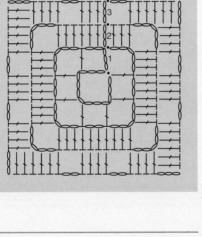

Ch 13 and sl st in first ch to form a ring.

Rnd 1: Ch 5 (counts as dc, ch 2), (dc, ch 5, dc, ch 2) 3 times in ring, dc in ring, ch 5, sl st in 3rd ch of beg ch to join.

Rnd 2: Ch 3 (counts as dc), *2 dc in next ch-2 space, dc in next dc, (3 dc, ch 5, 3 dc) in next ch-5 loop**, dc in next dc; rep from * around, ending last rep at **, sl st in 3rd ch of beg ch to join.

Rnd 3: Ch 3 (counts as dc), *dc in each of next 3 dc, ch 2, skip next 2 dc, dc in next dc, 3 dc in next ch-5 loop, ch 3, 2 dc in side of last dc made, 3 dc in same ch-5 loop already holding 3 dc, dc in next dc, ch 2, skip next 2 dc**, dc in next dc; rep from * around, ending last rep at **, sl st in 3rd ch of beg ch to join. Fasten off.

18

Ch 8 and sl st in first ch to form a ring.

Rnd 1: Ch 4 (counts as dc, ch 1), (dc, ch 5, dc, ch 1) 3 times in ring, dc in ring, ch 5, sl st in 3rd ch of beg ch to join.

Rnd 2: Ch 3 (counts as dc), *dc in next ch-1 space, dc in next dc, ch 1, 5 dc in next ch-5 loop, ch 1**, dc in next dc; rep from * around, ending last rep at **, sl st in 3rd ch of beg ch to join.

Rnd 3: Ch 4 (counts as dc, ch 1), *skip next dc, dc in next dc, dc in next ch-1 space, dc in next dc, ch 1, skip next dc, 5 dc in next dc, ch 1, skip next dc, dc in next dc, dc in next ch-1 space**, dc in next dc; rep from * around, ending last rep at **, sl st in 3rd ch of beg ch to join. Fasten off.

19

Ch 12 and sl st in first ch to form a ring.

Rnd 1: Ch 8 (counts as dc, ch 5), (dc, ch 2, dc, ch 5) 3 times in ring, dc in ring, ch 2, sl st in 3rd ch of beg ch to join.

Rnd 2: Ch 3 (counts as dc), *(3 dc, ch 5, 3 dc) in next ch-5 loop, dc in next dc, 2 dc in next ch-2 space**, dc in next dc; rep from * around, ending last rep at **, sl st in 3rd ch of beg ch to join.

Rnd 3: Ch 3 (counts as dc), *dc in each of next 3 dc, (3 dc, ch 5, 3 dc) in next ch-5 loop, dc in each of next 4 dc, ch 2, skip next 2 dc**, dc in next dc; rep from * around, ending last rep at **, sl st in 3rd ch of beg ch to join. Fasten off.

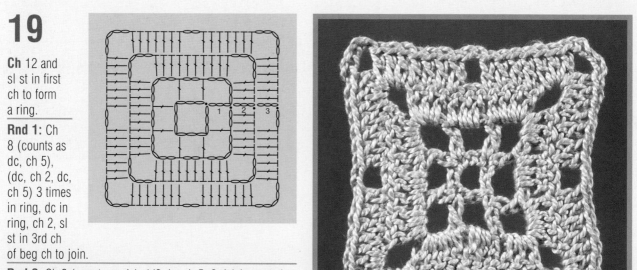

20

Ch 10 and sl st in first ch to form a ring.

Rnd 1: Ch 1, 16 sc in ring, sl st in first sc to join.

Rnd 2: Ch 6 (counts as dc, ch 3), *skip next sc, sc in next sc, ch 3**, skip next sc, dc in next sc, ch 3; rep from * around, ending last rep at **, sl st in 3rd ch of beg ch to join.

Rnd 3: Ch 3 (counts as dc), *4 dc in next ch-3 loop, dc in next sc, 4 dc in next ch-3 loop**, dc in next dc; rep from * around, ending last rep at **, sl st in 3rd ch of beg ch to join. Fasten off.

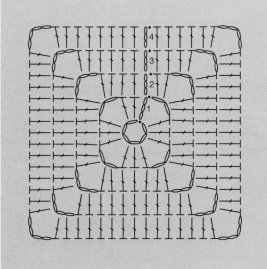

21

Ch 6 and sl st in first ch to form a ring.

Rnd 1: Ch 3 (counts as dc), 2 dc in ring, ch 2, (3 dc, ch 2) 3 times in ring, sl st in 3rd ch of beg ch to join.

Rnd 2: Ch 3 (counts as dc), *dc in each of next 2 dc, (2 dc, ch 4, 2 dc) in next ch-2 space, dc in next dc; rep from * around, omitting last dc, sl st in 3rd ch of beg ch to join.

Rnd 3: Ch 3 (counts as dc), *dc in each of next 4 dc, (2 dc, ch 4, 2 dc) in next ch-4 loop, dc in each of next 3 dc; rep from * around, omitting last dc, sl st in 3rd ch of beg ch to join.

Rnd 4: Ch 3 (counts as dc), *dc in each of next 6 dc, (2 dc, ch 4, 2 dc) in next ch-4 loop, dc in each of next 5 dc; rep from * around, omitting last dc, sl st in 3rd ch of beg ch to join. Fasten off.

22

Ch 6 and sl st in first ch to form a ring.

Rnd 1: Ch 6 (counts as dc, ch 3), (dc, ch 2, dc, ch 3) 3 times in ring, dc in ring, ch 2, sl st in 3rd ch of beg ch to join.

Rnd 2: Sl st in next ch-3 loop, ch 3 (counts as dc), (2 dc, ch 3, 3 dc) in same ch-3 loop, *ch 2, dc in next ch-2 space, ch 2**, (3 dc, ch 3, 3 dc) in next ch-3 loop; rep from * around, ending last rep at **, sl st in 3rd ch of beg ch to join.

Rnd 3: Ch 5 (counts as dc, ch 2), *skip next 2 dc, (3 dc, ch 3, 3 dc) in next ch-3 loop, ch 2, skip next 2 dc, dc in next dc, ch 2, skip next ch-2 space, dc in next dc, ch 2, skip next ch-2 space**, dc in next dc, ch 2; rep from * around, ending last rep at **, sl st in 3rd ch of beg ch to join.

Rnd 4: Ch 5 (counts as dc, ch 2), *skip next ch-2 space, dc in next dc, ch 2, skip next 2 dc, (3 dc, ch 3, 3 dc) in next ch-3 loop, ch 2, skip next 2 dc, dc in next dc, (ch 2, skip next ch-2 space, dc in next dc) twice, ch 2, skip next ch-2 space**, dc in next dc, ch 2; rep from * around, ending last rep at **, sl st in 3rd ch of beg ch to join.

Rnd 5: Ch 5 (counts as dc, ch 2), *skip next ch-2 space, dc in next dc, ch 2, skip next ch-2 space, dc in next dc, ch 2, skip next 2 dc, (3 dc, ch 3, 3 dc) in next ch-3 loop, ch 2, skip next 2 dc, dc in next dc, (ch 2, skip next ch-2 space, dc in next dc) 3 times, ch 2**, dc in next dc, ch 2; rep from * around, ending last rep at **, sl st in 3rd ch of beg ch to join. Fasten off.

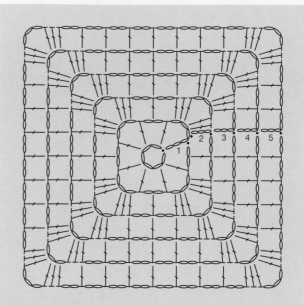

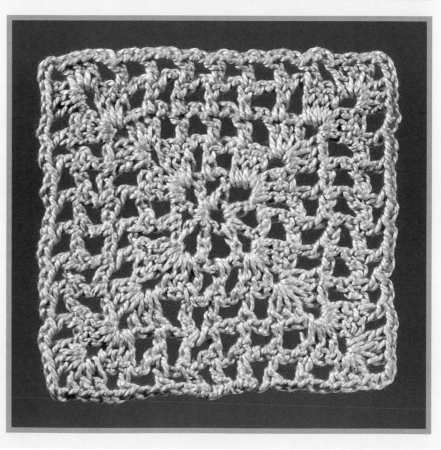

23

Ch 6 and sl st in first ch to form a ring.

Rnd 1: Ch 3 (counts as dc), 2 dc in ring, ch 3, (3 dc, ch 3) 3 times in ring, sl st in 3rd ch of beg ch to join.

Rnd 2: Ch 3 (counts as dc), dc in each of next 2 dc, *(dc, ch 1, dc, ch 1, dc) in next ch-3 loop**, dc in each of next 3 dc; rep from * around, ending last rep at **, sl st in 3rd ch of beg ch to join.

Rnd 3: Ch 3 (counts as dc), *dc in each of next 3 dc, 2 dc in next ch-1 space, ch 1, dc in next dc, ch 1, 2 dc in next ch-1 space, dc in each of next 2 dc; rep from * around, omitting last dc, sl st in 3rd ch of beg ch to join.

Rnd 4: Ch 3 (counts as dc), *dc in each of next 5 dc, 2 dc in next ch-1 space, ch 1, dc in next dc, ch 1, 2 dc in next ch-1 space, dc in each of next 4 dc; rep from * around, omitting last dc, sl st in 3rd ch of beg ch to join.

Rnd 5: Ch 3 (counts as dc), *dc in each of next 7 dc, 2 dc in next ch-1 space, ch 1, dc in next dc, ch 1, 2 dc in next ch-1 space, dc in each of next 6 dc; rep from * around, omitting last dc, sl st in 3rd ch of beg ch to join.

Rnd 6: Ch 3 (counts as dc), *dc in each of next 9 dc, 2 dc in next ch-1 space, ch 1, dc in next dc, ch 1, 2 dc in next ch-1 space, dc in each of next 8 dc; rep from * around, omitting last dc, sl st in 3rd ch of beg ch to join.

Rnd 7: Ch 3 (counts as dc), *dc in each of next 11 dc, 2 dc in next ch-1 space, ch 1, dc in next dc, ch 1, 2 dc in next ch-1 space, dc in each of next 10 dc; rep from * around, omitting last dc, sl st in 3rd ch of beg ch to join. Fasten off.

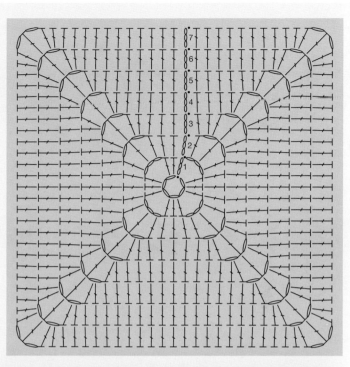

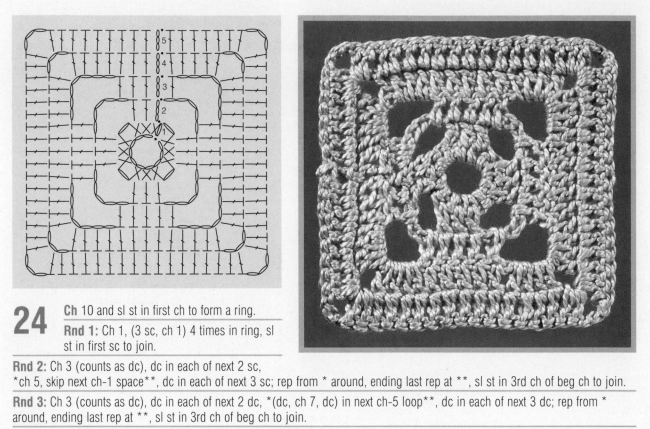

24

Ch 10 and sl st in first ch to form a ring.

Rnd 1: Ch 1, (3 sc, ch 1) 4 times in ring, sl st in first sc to join.

Rnd 2: Ch 3 (counts as dc), dc in each of next 2 sc, *ch 5, skip next ch-1 space**, dc in each of next 3 sc; rep from * around, ending last rep at **, sl st in 3rd ch of beg ch to join.

Rnd 3: Ch 3 (counts as dc), dc in each of next 2 dc, *(dc, ch 7, dc) in next ch-5 loop**, dc in each of next 3 dc; rep from * around, ending last rep at **, sl st in 3rd ch of beg ch to join.

Rnd 4: Ch 3 (counts as dc), *dc in each of next 3 dc, (4 dc, ch 3, 4 dc) in next ch-7 loop, dc in each of next 2 dc; rep from * around, omitting last dc, sl st in 3rd ch of beg ch to join.

Rnd 5: Ch 3 (counts as dc), *dc in each of next 7 dc, (2 dc, ch 3, 2 dc) in next ch-3 loop, dc in each of next 6 dc; rep from * around, omitting last dc, sl st in 3rd ch of beg ch to join. Fasten off.

25

Ch 6 and sl st in first ch to form a ring.

Rnd 1: Ch 3 (counts as dc), 2 dc in ring, ch 2, (3 dc, ch 2) 3 times in ring, sl st in 3rd ch of beg ch to join.

Rnd 2: Ch 3 (counts as dc), dc in first st, *dc in next dc, 2 dc in next dc, ch 3, skip next ch-2 space**, 2 dc in next dc; rep from * around, ending last rep at **, sl st in 3rd ch of beg ch to join.

Rnd 3: Ch 3 (counts as dc), dc in first st, *dc in each of next 3 dc, 2 dc in next dc, ch 5, skip next ch-3 loop**, 2 dc in next dc; rep from * around, ending last rep at **, sl st in 3rd ch of beg ch to join.

Rnd 4: Ch 3 (counts as dc), dc in first st, *dc in each of next 5 dc, 2 dc in next dc, ch 6, skip next ch-5 loop**, 2 dc in next dc; rep from * around, ending last rep at **, sl st in 3rd ch of beg ch to join.

Rnd 5: Ch 3 (counts as dc), dc in first st, *dc in each of next 7 dc, 2 dc in next dc, ch 8, skip next ch-6 loop**, 2 dc in next dc; rep from * around, ending last rep at **, sl st in 3rd ch of beg ch to join. Fasten off.

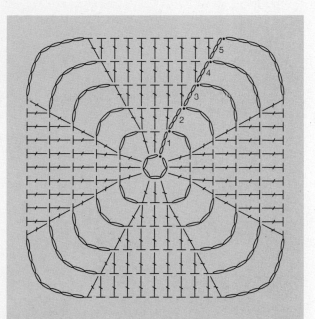

26

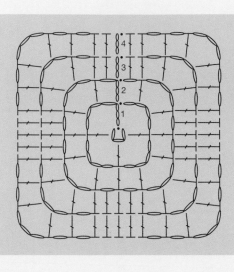

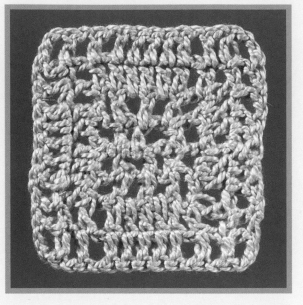

Ch 3 and sl st in first ch to form a ring.

Rnd 1: Ch 7 (counts as dc, ch 4), (dc, ch 4) 3 times in ring, sl st in 3rd ch of beg ch to join.

Rnd 2: Ch 4 (counts as dc, ch 1), *(dc, ch 3, dc) in next ch-4 loop, ch 1**, dc in next dc, ch 1; rep from * around, ending last rep at **, sl st in 3rd ch of beg ch to join.

Rnd 3: Ch 3 (counts as dc), *dc in next ch-1 space, dc in next dc, ch 1, (dc, ch 3, dc) in next ch-3 loop, ch 1, dc in next dc, dc in next ch-1 space**, dc in next dc; rep from * around, ending last rep at **, sl st in 3rd ch of beg ch to join.

Rnd 4: Ch 3 (counts as dc), *dc in each of next 2 dc, ch 1, skip next ch-1 space, dc in next dc, ch 1, (dc, ch 3, dc) in next ch-3 loop, ch 1, dc in next dc, ch 1, skip next ch-1 space, dc in next 2 dc**, dc in next dc; rep from * around, ending last rep at **, sl st in 3rd ch of beg ch to join. Fasten off.

27

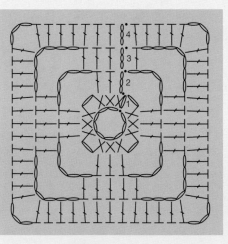

Ch 9 and sl st in first ch to form a ring.

Rnd 1: Ch 1, (3 sc, ch 1) 4 times in ring, sl st in first sc to join.

Rnd 2: Ch 3 (counts as dc), dc in each of next 2 sc, *ch 5, skip next ch-1 space**, dc in each of next 3 sc; rep from * around, ending last rep at **, sl st in 3rd ch of beg ch to join.

Rnd 3: Ch 3 (counts as dc), dc in each of next 2 dc, *(dc, ch 7, dc) in next ch-5 loop**, dc in each of next 3 dc; rep from * around, ending last rep at **, sl st in 3rd ch of beg ch to join.

Rnd 4: Ch 3 (counts as dc), dc in each of next 3 dc, *(4 dc, ch 3, 4 dc) in next ch-7 loop**, dc in each of next 5 dc; rep from * around, ending last rep at **, dc in next dc sl st in 3rd ch of beg ch to join. Fasten off.

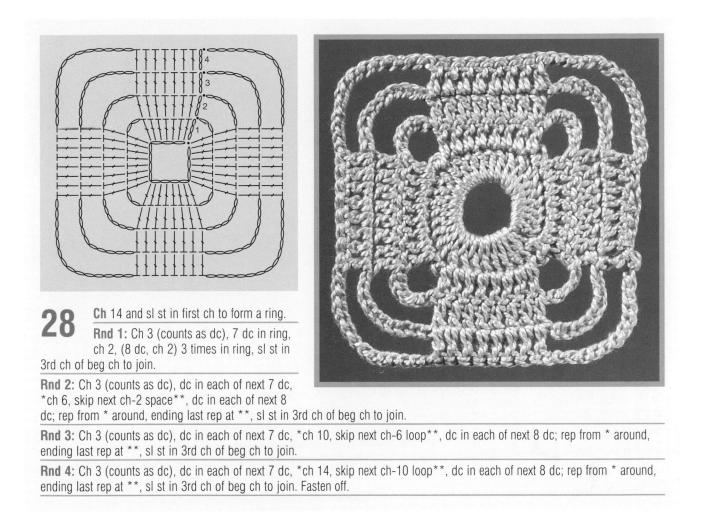

28 Ch 14 and sl st in first ch to form a ring.

Rnd 1: Ch 3 (counts as dc), 7 dc in ring, ch 2, (8 dc, ch 2) 3 times in ring, sl st in 3rd ch of beg ch to join.

Rnd 2: Ch 3 (counts as dc), dc in each of next 7 dc, *ch 6, skip next ch-2 space**, dc in each of next 8 dc; rep from * around, ending last rep at **, sl st in 3rd ch of beg ch to join.

Rnd 3: Ch 3 (counts as dc), dc in each of next 7 dc, *ch 10, skip next ch-6 loop**, dc in each of next 8 dc; rep from * around, ending last rep at **, sl st in 3rd ch of beg ch to join.

Rnd 4: Ch 3 (counts as dc), dc in each of next 7 dc, *ch 14, skip next ch-10 loop**, dc in each of next 8 dc; rep from * around, ending last rep at **, sl st in 3rd ch of beg ch to join. Fasten off.

.3.
Double Crochets & Chains

29 **Ch** 6 and sl st in first ch to form a ring.

Rnd 1: Ch 3 (counts as dc), 11 dc in ring, sl st in 3rd ch of beg ch to join.

Rnd 2: Ch 4 (counts as dc, ch 1), (dc, ch 1) in each dc around, sl st in 3rd ch of beg ch to join.

Rnd 3: Ch 3 (counts as dc), *skip next ch-1 space, dc in next dc, 6 dc in next ch-1 space, dc in next dc, skip next ch-1 space**, dc in next dc; rep from * around, ending last rep at **, sl st in 3rd ch of beg ch to join. Fasten off.

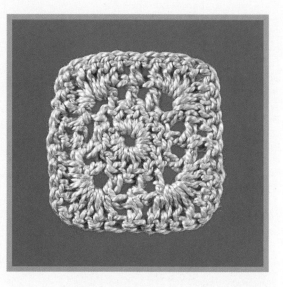

30 **Ch** 4 and sl st in first ch to form a ring.

Rnd 1: Ch 3 (counts as dc), 2 dc in ring, ch 2, (3 dc, ch 2) 3 times in ring, sl st in 3rd ch of beg ch to join.

Rnd 2: Ch 3 (counts as dc), dc in each of next 2 dc, *5 dc in next ch-2 space**, dc in each of next 3 dc; rep from * around, ending last rep at **, sl st in 3rd ch of beg ch to join.

Rnd 3: Ch 1, *([sc, ch 1] bet next 2 dc) 5 times, (sc, ch 2, sc) in next dc, ch 1, ([sc, ch 1] bet next 2 dc) 3 times; rep from * around, sl st in first sc to join. Fasten off.

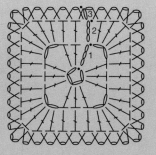

31 **Ch** 6 and sl st in first ch to form a ring.

Rnd 1: Ch 3 (counts as dc), 15 dc in ring, sl st in 3rd ch of beg ch to join.

Rnd 2: Ch 1, *sc in dc, ch 3, skip next dc; rep from * around, sl st in first sc to join.

Rnd 3: Sl st in first ch-3 loop, ch 3 (counts as dc), dc in same ch-3 loop, *(3 dc, ch 3, 3 dc) in next ch-3 loop**, 2 dc in next ch-3 loop; rep from * around, ending last rep at **, sl st in 3rd ch of beg ch to join.

Rnd 4: Ch 1, sc in first 5 dc, *3 sc in next ch-3 loop**, sc in each of next 8 dc; rep from * around, ending last rep at **, sc in each of next 3 dc, sl st in first sc to join. Fasten off.

32 **Ch** 6 and sl st in first ch to form a ring.

Rnd 1: Ch 3 (counts as dc), 11 dc in ring, sl st in 3rd ch of beg ch to join.

Rnd 2: Ch 1, (sc, ch 3) in each dc around, sl st in first sc to join.

Rnd 3: Sl st in first ch-3 loop, ch 3 (counts as dc), dc in same ch-3 loop, *2 dc in next ch-3 loop, (3 dc, ch 3, 3 dc) in next ch-3 loop**, 2 dc in next ch-3 loop; rep from * around, ending last rep at **, sl st in 3rd ch of beg ch to join.

Rnd 4: Ch 1, sc in first 7 dc, *3 sc in next ch-3 loop**, sc in each of next 10 dc; rep from * around, ending last rep at **, sc in each of next 3 dc, sl st in first sc to join. Fasten off.

33

Ch 6 and sl st in first ch to form a ring.

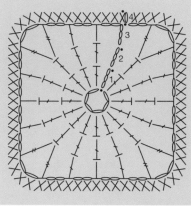

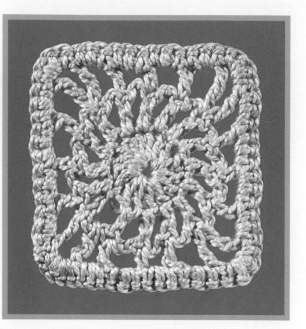

Rnd 1: Ch 3 (counts as dc), 15 dc in ring, sl st in 3rd ch of beg ch to join.

Rnd 2: Ch 3 (counts as dc), dc in each dc around, sl st in 3rd ch of beg ch to join.

Rnd 3: Ch 5 (counts as dc, ch 2), *hdc in next dc, ch 2, dc in next dc, ch 2, (tr, ch 2, tr) in next dc, ch 2**, dc in next dc, ch 2; rep from * around, ending last rep at **, sl st in 3rd ch of beg ch to join.

Rnd 4: Ch 1, *sc in dc, 2 sc in next ch-2 space, sc in next hdc, 2 sc in next ch-2 space, sc in next dc, 2 sc in next ch-2 space, sc in next tr, 3 sc in next ch-2 space, sc in next tr, 2 sc in next ch-2 space; rep from * around, sl st in first sc to join. Fasten off.

34

Ch 6 and sl st in first ch to form a ring.

Rnd 1: Ch 6 (counts as dc, ch 3), (dc, ch 3) 7 times in ring, sl st in 3rd ch of beg ch to join.

Rnd 2: Sl st in next ch-3 loop, ch 3 (counts as dc), 3 dc in same ch-3 loop, ch 2, (4 dc, ch 2) in each ch-3 loop around, sl st in 3rd ch of beg ch to join.

Rnd 3: Ch 5 (counts as dc, ch 2), (6 dc, ch 2) in each of next 7 ch-2 spaces, 5 dc in last ch-2 space, sl st in 3rd ch of beg ch to join.

Rnd 4: Sl st in next ch-2 space, ch 1, *sc in ch-2 space, ch 3, skip next 3 dc, sc bet last skipped and next dc, ch 3, sc in next ch-2 space, ch 3, skip next 3 dc, (2 dc, ch 3, 2 dc) bet last skipped and next dc, ch 3; rep from * around, sl st in first sc to join. Fasten off.

35 Ch 6 and sl st in first ch to form a ring.

Rnd 1: Ch 3 (counts as dc), 15 dc in ring, sl st in 3rd ch of beg ch to join.

Rnd 2: Ch 4 (counts as dc, ch 1), (dc, ch 1) in each dc around, sl st in 3rd ch of beg ch to join.

Rnd 3: Ch 3 (counts as dc), *2 dc in next ch-1 space**, dc in next dc; rep from * around, ending last rep at **, sl st in 3rd ch of beg ch to join.

Rnd 4: Ch 1, *sc in dc, ch 3, skip next 2 dc, sc in next dc, ch 2, skip next 2 dc, sc in next dc, ch 5, skip next 2 dc, sc in next dc, ch 2, skip next 2 dc; rep from * around, sl st in first sc to join.

Rnd 5: Sl st in next ch-3 loop, ch 3 (counts as dc), 4 dc in same ch-3 loop, *sc in next ch-2 space, (5 dc, ch 3, 5 dc) in next ch-5 loop, sc in next ch-2 space**, 5 dc in next ch-3 loop; rep from * around, ending last rep at **, sl st in 3rd ch of beg ch to join. Fasten off.

36 Ch 10 and sl st in first ch to form a ring.

Rnd 1: Ch 1, (sc, ch 10) 11 times in ring, sc in ring, ch 4, dtr in in first sc to join and form last loop.

Rnd 2: Ch 2 (counts as hdc), 2 hdc in same loop, *3 hdc in next ch-10 loop, (3 dc, ch 2, 3 dc) in next ch-10 loop**, 3 hdc in next ch-10 loop; rep from * around, ending last rep at **, sl st in 2nd ch of beg ch to join. Fasten off.

37 Ch 6 and sl st in first ch to form a ring.

Rnd 1: Ch 3 (counts as dc), 15 dc in ring, sl st in 3rd ch of beg ch to join.

Rnd 2: Ch 5 (counts as dc, ch 2), (dc, ch 2) in each dc around, sl st in 3rd ch of beg ch to join.

Rnd 3: Sl st in next ch-2 space, ch 1, sc in same ch-2 space, ch 2, (sc, ch 2) in each of next 2 ch-2 spaces, *(2 dc, ch 3, 2 dc) in next ch-2 space, ch 2**, (sc, ch 2) in each of next 4 ch-2 spaces; rep from * around, ending last rep at **, sl st in first sc to join.

Rnd 4: Sl st in next ch-2 space, ch 1, sc in same ch-2 space, ch 2, (sc, ch 2) in each of next 2 ch-2 spaces, *(2 dc, ch 3, 2 dc) in next ch-3 space, ch 2**, (sc, ch 2) in each of next 4 ch-2 spaces; rep from * around, ending last rep at **, sc in next ch-2 space, ch 2, sl st in first sc to join.

Rnd 5: Sl st in next ch-2 space, ch 3 (counts as dc), dc in same ch-2 space, ch 1, (2 dc, ch 1) in each of next 2 ch-2 spaces, *(3 dc, ch 2, 3 dc) in next ch-3 loop, ch 1**, (2 dc, ch 1) in each of next 5 ch-2 spaces; rep from * around, ending last rep at **, (2 dc, ch 1) in each of next 2 ch-2 spaces, sl st in 3rd ch of beg ch to join. Fasten off.

38

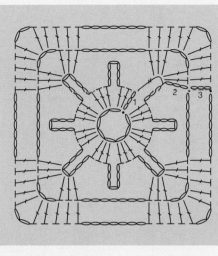

Ch 8 and sl st in first ch to form a ring.

Rnd 1: Ch 3 (counts as dc), 2 dc in ring, *ch 5, 3 dc in ring; rep from * 6 times, ch 3, tr in 3rd ch of beg ch to join and form last loop.

Rnd 2: Ch 3 (counts as dc), (2 dc, ch 3, 3 dc) in same loop, ch 7, *skip next ch-5 loop, (3 dc, ch 3, 3 dc) in next ch-5 loop, ch 7; rep from * around, skip next ch-5 loop, sl st in 3rd ch of beg ch to join.

Rnd 3: Ch 3 (counts as dc), *dc in each of next 2 dc, (2 dc, ch 2, 2 dc) in next ch-3 loop, dc in each of next 3 dc, ch 7 skip next ch-7 loop**, dc in next dc; rep from * around, ending last rep at **, sl st in 3rd ch of beg ch to join. Fasten off.

39

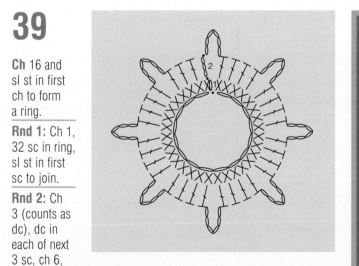

Ch 16 and sl st in first ch to form a ring.

Rnd 1: Ch 1, 32 sc in ring, sl st in first sc to join.

Rnd 2: Ch 3 (counts as dc), dc in each of next 3 sc, ch 6, *dc in each of next 4 sc, ch 6; rep from * around, sl st in 3rd ch of beg ch to join. Fasten off.

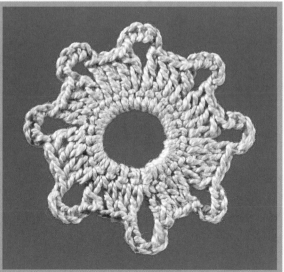

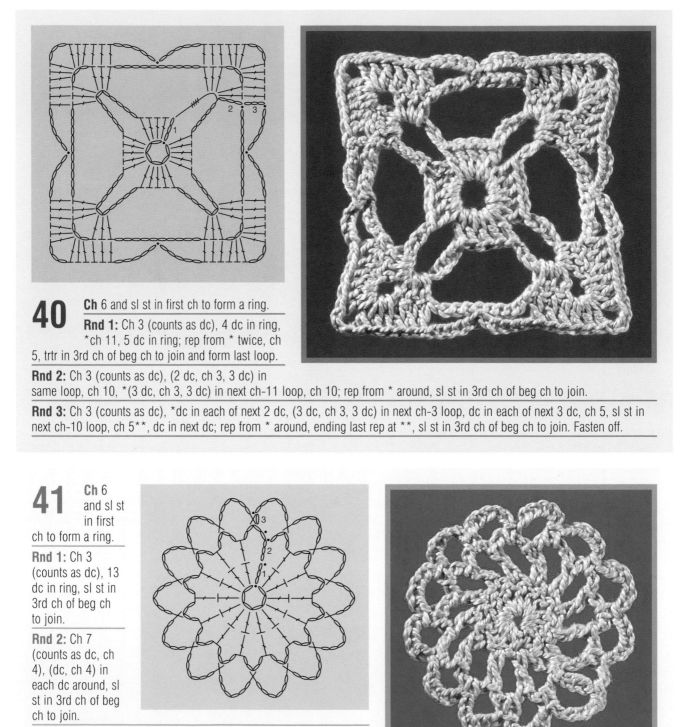

40 Ch 6 and sl st in first ch to form a ring.

Rnd 1: Ch 3 (counts as dc), 4 dc in ring, *ch 11, 5 dc in ring; rep from * twice, ch 5, trtr in 3rd ch of beg ch to join and form last loop.

Rnd 2: Ch 3 (counts as dc), (2 dc, ch 3, 3 dc) in same loop, ch 10, *(3 dc, ch 3, 3 dc) in next ch-11 loop, ch 10; rep from * around, sl st in 3rd ch of beg ch to join.

Rnd 3: Ch 3 (counts as dc), *dc in each of next 2 dc, (3 dc, ch 3, 3 dc) in next ch-3 loop, dc in each of next 3 dc, ch 5, sl st in next ch-10 loop, ch 5**, dc in next dc; rep from * around, ending last rep at **, sl st in 3rd ch of beg ch to join. Fasten off.

41 Ch 6 and sl st in first ch to form a ring.

Rnd 1: Ch 3 (counts as dc), 13 dc in ring, sl st in 3rd ch of beg ch to join.

Rnd 2: Ch 7 (counts as dc, ch 4), (dc, ch 4) in each dc around, sl st in 3rd ch of beg ch to join.

Rnd 3: Sl st to center of next ch-4 loop, ch 1, (sc, ch 6) in in each ch-4 loop around, sl st in first sc to join. Fasten off.

42

Center Square:

Ch 17.

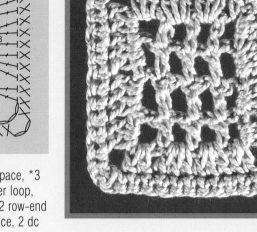

Row 1: Dc in 8th ch from hook, *ch 2, skip next 2 ch, dc in next ch; rep from * across, turn.

Rows 2-4: Ch 5 (counts as dc, ch 2), skip next ch-2 space, (dc, ch 2) in each of next 3 dc, dc in 3rd ch of turning ch, turn.

Edging:

Rnd 1: Ch 3 (counts as dc), working across top edge of Center Square, dc in next ch-2 space, *3 dc in each of next 2 ch-2 spaces, (2 dc, ch 3, 2 dc) in next corner loop, working across side edge of Center Square, 3 dc in each of next 2 row-end sts**, (2 dc, ch 3, 2 dc) in next corner loop; rep from * to ** once, 2 dc in next row-end st of corner, ch 3, sl st in 3rd ch of beg ch to join.

Rnd 2: Ch 1, *sc in each of next 10 dc, (sc, ch 2, sc) in next ch-3 loop; rep from * around, sl st in first sc to join. Fasten off.

43

Ch 6 and sl st in first ch to form a ring.

Rnd 1: Ch 3 (counts as dc), 19 sc in ring, sl st in 3rd ch of beg ch to join.

Rnd 2: Ch 6 (counts as dc, ch 3), skip next dc, *dc in next dc, ch 3, skip next dc; rep from * around, sl st in 3rd ch of beg ch to join.

Rnd 3: Ch 3 (counts as dc), *4 dc in next ch-3 loop**, dc in next dc; rep from * around, ending last rep at **, sl st in 3rd ch of beg ch to join.

Rnd 4: Ch 1, *sc in dc, ch 4, skip next dc; rep from * around, sl st in first sc to join. Fasten off.

44 **Ch** 10 and sl st in first ch to form a ring.

Rnd 1: Ch 3 (counts as dc), dc in ring, (ch 5, 2 dc) 9 times in ring, ch 2, dc in 3rd ch of beg ch to join and form last loop.

Rnd 2: Ch 1, (sc, ch 5) in each loop around, sl st in first sc to join.

Rnd 3: Ch 1, 6 sc in each ch-5 loop around, sl st in first sc to join.

Rnd 4: Ch 1, *sc in sc, ch 6, skip next 2 sc; rep from * around, sl st in first sc to join.

Rnd 5: Sl st to center of next ch-6 loop, ch 1, (sc, ch 7) in each ch-6 loop around, sl st in first sc to join.

Rnd 6: Sl st to center of next ch-7 loop, ch 1, (sc, ch 7, 3 dc) in each ch-7 loop around, sl st in first sc to join. Fasten off.

45

Ch 8 and sl st in first ch to form a ring.

Rnd 1: Ch 3 (counts as dc), 2 dc in ring, *ch 7, 3 dc in ring; rep from * 6 times, ch 3, tr in 3rd ch of beg ch to join and form last loop.

Rnd 2: Ch 3 (counts as dc), (2 dc, ch 3, 3 dc) in same loop, ch 7, *(3 dc, ch 3, 3 dc) in next ch-7 loop, ch 7; rep from * around, sl st in 3rd ch of beg ch to join.

Rnd 3: Ch 3 (counts as dc), *dc in each of next 2 dc, (2 dc, ch 2, 2 dc) in next ch-3 loop, dc in each of next 3 dc, ch 7**, dc in next dc; rep from * around, ending last rep at **, sl st in 3rd ch of beg ch to join.

Rnd 4: Ch 3 (counts as dc), *dc in each of next 4 dc, (2 dc, ch 2, 2 dc) in next ch-2 space, dc in each of next 5 dc, ch 4, sc over next next 3 ch-7 loops in 3 rnds below, ch 4**, dc in next dc; rep from * around, ending last rep at **, sl st in 3rd ch of beg ch to join. Fasten off.

46

2-dc cluster:
Yo, insert hook in next st, yo, draw yarn through st, yo, draw yarn through 2 loops on hook, skip next ch-3 loop, yo, insert hook in next st, yo, draw yarn through st, yo, draw yarn through 2 loops on hook, yo, draw yarn through 3 loops on hook.

Ch 6 and sl st in first ch to form a ring.

Rnd 1: Ch 6 (counts as dc, ch 3), (dc, ch 3) 5 times in ring, sl st in 3rd ch of beg ch to join.

Rnd 2: Ch 5 (counts as dc, ch 2), work 2-dc cluster, working first half-closed dc in first st, skip next ch-3 loop, work 2nd half-closed dc in next dc, yo, complete cluster, ch 2, *dc in same dc already holding 2nd leg of last cluster, ch 2, work 2-dc cluster, working first half-closed dc in same dc holding last dc, skip next ch-3 loop, work 2nd half-closed dc in next dc, yo, complete cluster, ch 2; rep from * around, sl st in 3rd ch of beg ch to join.

Rnd 3: Ch 1, *sc in dc, ch 5, skip next ch-2 space, sc in next cluster, ch 5; rep from * around, sl st in first sc to join. Fasten off.

47

Ch 6 and sl st in first ch to form a ring.

Rnd 1: Ch 4 (counts as dc, ch 1), (dc, ch 1) 13 times in ring, sl st in 3rd ch of beg ch to join.

Rnd 2: Sl st in next ch-1 space, ch 5 (counts as dc, ch 2), (dc, ch 2) in each ch-1 space around, sl st in 3rd ch of beg ch to join.

Rnd 3: Sl st in first ch-2 space, ch 3 (counts as dc), 2 dc in same ch-2 space, ch 1, (3 dc, ch 1) in each ch-2 space around, sl st in 3rd ch of bet ch to join.

Rnd 4: Turn, sl st in next ch-1 space, ch 1, turn, (sc, ch 6) in each ch-1 space around, sl st in first sc to join.

Rnd 5: Sl st to center of next ch-6 loop, ch 1, (sc, ch 6) in each ch-1 space around, sl st in first sc to join.

Rnd 6: Sl st in next ch-6 loop, ch 1, 6 sc in each ch-6 loop around, sl st in first sc to join. Fasten off.

48

Ch 10 and sl st in first ch to form a ring.

Rnd 1: Ch 3 (counts as dc), 23 dc in ring, sl st in 3rd ch of beg ch to join.

Rnd 2: Ch 4 (counts as dc, ch 1), (dc, ch 1) in each dc around, sl st in 3rd ch of beg ch to join.

Rnd 3: Sl st in next ch-1 space, ch 10 (counts as tr, ch 6), ch 6, skip next ch-1 space, *tr in next ch-1 space, ch 6, skip next ch-1 space; rep from * around, sl st in 4th ch of beg ch to join.

Rnd 4: Ch 1, *sc in tr, ch 3, (dc, ch 2, dc) in next ch-6 loop, ch 3; rep from * around, sl st in first sc to join.

Rnd 5: Ch 1, *sc in sc, ch 2, skip next ch-3 loop, dc in next dc, ch 2, dc in next ch-2 space, ch 2, dc in next dc, ch 2; rep from * around, sl st in first sc to join. Fasten off.

49

Ch 6 and sl st in first ch to form a ring.

Rnd 1: Ch 4 (counts as dc, ch 1), (dc, ch 1) 11 times in ring, sl st in 3rd ch of beg ch to join.

Rnd 2: Sl st in next ch-1 space, ch 1, (sc, ch 5) in each ch-1 space around, sl st in first sc to join.

Rnd 3: Sl st to center of next ch-5 loop, ch 1, (sc, ch 6) in each ch-5 loop around, sl st in first sc to join.

Rnd 4: Sl st to center of next ch-6 loop, ch 1, (sc, ch 7) in each ch-6 loop around, sl st in first sc to join.

Rnd 5: Sl st to center of next ch-7 loop, ch 3 (counts as dc), (dc, ch 2, 2 dc) in same ch-7 loop, *ch 3, (dc, ch 5, dc) in next ch-7 loop, ch 3**, (2 dc, ch 2, 2 dc) in next ch-7 loop; rep from * around, ending last rep at **, sl st in 3rd ch of beg ch to join. Fasten off.

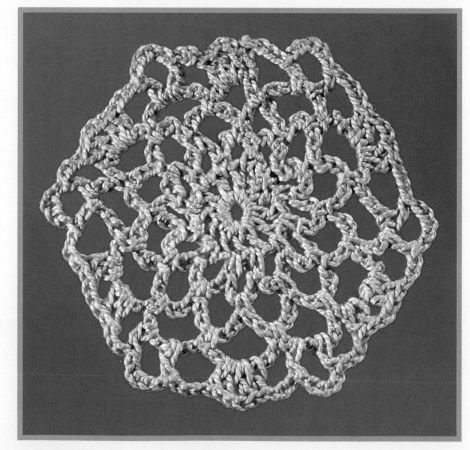

50

Ch 6 and sl st in first ch to form a ring.

Rnd 1: Ch 6 (counts as dc, ch 3), (dc, ch 3) 5 times in ring, sl st in 3rd ch of beg ch to join.

Rnd 2: Sl st in next ch-3 loop, ch 3 (counts as dc), (dc, ch 2, 2 dc) in same ch-3 loop, ch 2, *(2 dc, ch 2, 2 dc) in next ch-3 loop, ch 2; rep from * around, sl st in 3rd ch of beg ch to join.

Rnd 3: Sl st to next ch-2 space, ch 1, (sc, ch 5) in in each ch-2 space around, sl st in first sc to join. Fasten off.

51

Ch 6 and sl st in first ch to form a ring.

Rnd 1: Ch 3 (counts as dc), 23 sc in ring, sl st in 3rd ch of beg ch to join.

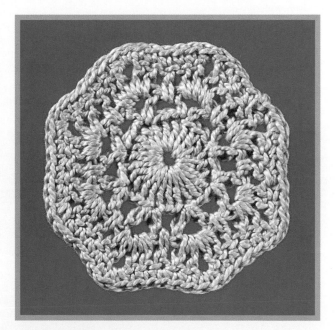

Rnd 2: Ch 5 (counts as dc, ch 2), dc in first st, ch 1, skip next 2 dc, *(dc, ch 2, dc) in next dc, ch 1, skip next 2 dc; rep from * around, sl st in 3rd ch of beg ch to join.

Rnd 3: Sl st in next ch-2 space, ch 3 (counts as dc), (dc, ch 2, 2 dc) in same ch-2 space, dc in next ch-1 space, *(2 dc, ch 2, 2 dc) in next ch-2 space, dc in next ch-1 space; rep from * around, sl st in 3rd ch of beg ch to join.

Rnd 4: Ch 1, sc in first 2 dc, *2 sc in next ch-2 space**, sc in each of next 5 dc; rep from * around, ending last rep at **, sc in each of last 3 dc, sl st in first sc to join. Fasten off.

52

Ch 6 and sl st in first ch to form a ring.

Rnd 1: Ch 4 (counts as dc, ch 1), (dc, ch 1) 15 times in ring, sl st in 3rd ch of beg ch to join.

Rnd 2: Sl st in next ch-1 space, ch 3 (counts as dc), dc in same ch-1 space, ch 2, (2 dc, ch 2) in each ch-1 space around, sl st in 3rd ch of beg ch to join.

Rnd 3: Ch 3 (counts as dc), dc in same st, dc in next dc, ch 7, skip next ch-2 space, *2 dc in next dc, dc in next dc, ch 7, skip next ch-2 space; rep from * around, sl st in 3rd ch of bet ch to join.

Rnd 4: Sl st in next dc, ch 1, *sc in dc, ch 3, sc in next ch-7 loop, ch 3, skip next dc; rep from * around, sl st in first sc to join.

Rnd 5: Ch 1, *sc in sc, ch 3, skip next ch-3 loop, (sc, ch 5, sc) in next sc, ch 3, skip next ch-3 loop; rep from * around, sl st in first sc to join. Fasten off.

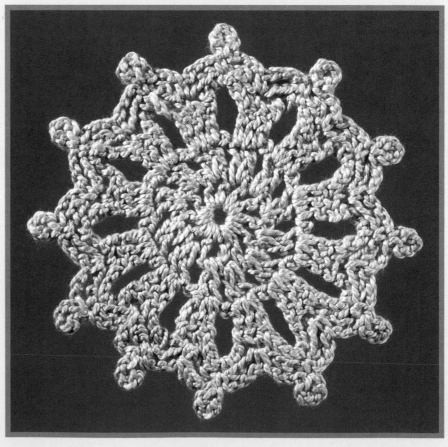

53

Ch 6 and sl st in first ch to form a ring.

Rnd 1 (RS): Ch 1, (2 sc, ch 12) 8 times in ring, sl st in first sc to join. Fasten off.

Rnd 2: With RS facing rejoin yarn in any ch-12 loop, ch 3 (counts as dc), (2 dc, ch 3, 3 dc) in same ch-12 loop, *ch 2, 3 dc in next ch-12 loop, ch 2**, (3 dc, ch 3, 3 dc) in next ch-12 loop; rep from * around, ending last rep at **, sl st in 3rd ch of beg ch to join.

Rnd 3: Sl st to next ch-3 loop, ch 3 (counts as dc), (2 dc, ch 3, 3 dc) in same ch-3 loop, *ch 2, (3 dc, ch 2) in each of next 2 ch-2 spaces**, (3 dc, ch 3, 3 dc) in next ch-3 loop; rep from * around, ending last rep at **, sl st in 3rd ch of beg ch to join.

Rnd 4: Ch 3 (counts as dc), dc in each of next 2 dc, *(2 dc, ch 2, 2 dc) in next ch-3 loop, (dc in each of next 3 dc, 2 dc in next ch-2 space) 3 times**, dc in each of next 3 dc; rep from * around, ending last rep at **, sl st in 3rd ch of beg ch to join. Fasten off.

.4.
Treble Crochets &
Double Treble Crochets

54 Ch 8.

Row 1: Tr in 5th ch from hook, tr in each of next 3 ch, *ch 4, 4 tr around the post of last tr made; rep from * twice, sl st in 4th ch of beg ch to join. Fasten off.

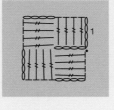

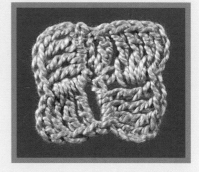

55 Ch 8 and sl st in first ch to form a ring.

Rnd 1: Ch 5 (counts as dtr), 3 dtr in ring, ch 5, (4 dtr, ch 5) 3 times in ring, sl st in 5th ch of beg ch to join. Fasten off.

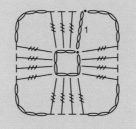

56 Ch 15 and sl st in first ch to form a ring.

Rnd 1: Ch 4 (counts as tr), 4 tr in ring, ch 7, (5 tr, ch 7) 3 times in ring, sl st in 4th ch of beg ch to join. Fasten off.

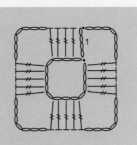

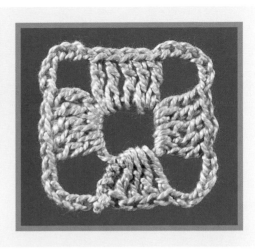

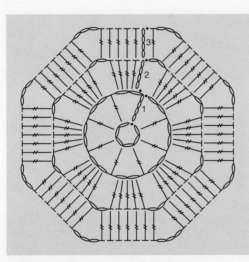

57 Ch 6 and sl st in first ch to form a ring.

Rnd 1: Ch 6 (counts as tr, ch 2), (tr, ch 2) 7 times in ring, sl st in 4th ch of beg ch to join.

Rnd 2: Sl st in next ch-2 space, ch 4 (counts as tr), 4 tr in same space, ch 2, (5 tr, ch 2) in each ch-2 space around, sl st in 4th ch of beg ch to join.

Rnd 3: Ch 4 (counts as tr), tr in each of next 4 tr, *(tr, ch 3, tr) in next ch-2 space**, tr in each of next 5 tr; rep from * around, ending last rep at **, sl st in 4th ch of beg ch to join. Fasten off.

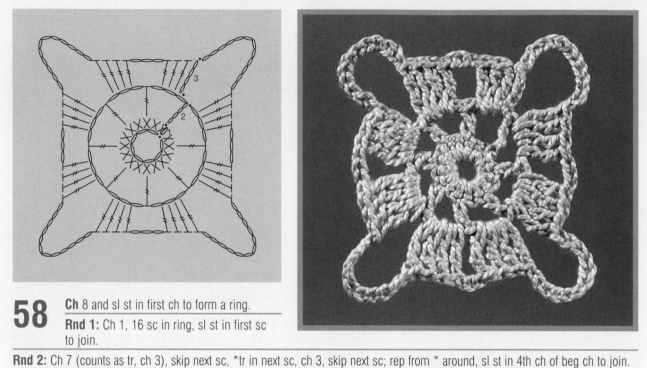

58 **Ch** 8 and sl st in first ch to form a ring.

Rnd 1: Ch 1, 16 sc in ring, sl st in first sc to join.

Rnd 2: Ch 7 (counts as tr, ch 3), skip next sc, *tr in next sc, ch 3, skip next sc; rep from * around, sl st in 4th ch of beg ch to join.

Rnd 3: Sl st in next ch-3 loop, ch 4 (counts as tr), 3 tr in same ch-3 loop, *ch 3, 4 tr in next ch-3 loop, ch 12**, 4 tr in next ch-3 loop; rep from * around, ending last rep at **, sl st in 4th ch of beg ch to join. Fasten off.

59 **Ch** 6 and sl st in first ch to form a ring.

Rnd 1: Ch 4 (counts as dc, ch 1), (4 dc, ch 1) 3 times in ring, 3 dc in ring, sl st in 3rd ch of beg to join.

Rnd 2: Sl st in next ch-1 space, ch 3 (counts as dc), (2 dc, ch 2, 3 dc) in same ch-1 space, (3 dc, ch 2, 3 dc) in each ch-1 space around, sl st in 3rd ch of beg ch to join.

Rnd 3: Sl st to next ch-2 space, ch 4 (counts as tr), (3 tr, ch 3, 4 tr) in same ch-2 space, (4 tr, ch 3, 4 tr) in each ch-2 space around, sl st in 4th ch of beg ch to join.

Rnd 4: Ch 1, *sc in each of next 4 tr, 3 sc in next ch-3 loop, sc in each of next 4 tr; rep from * around, sl st in first sc to join. Fasten off.

60

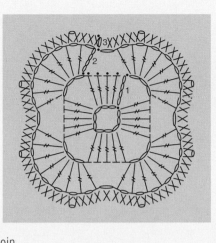

Ch 10 and sl st in first ch to form a ring.

Rnd 1: Ch 4 (counts as tr), 4 tr in ring, ch 3, (5 tr, ch 3) 3 times in ring, sl st in 4th ch of beg ch to join.

Rnd 2: Sl st to next ch-3 loop, ch 5 (counts as tr, ch 1), (tr, ch 1) 7 times in same ch-2 space, (tr, ch 1) 8 times in each ch-3 loop around, sl st in 4th ch of beg ch to join.

Rnd 3: Ch 1, *sc in tr, sc in next ch-1 space, sc in next tr, (sc, ch 1, sc) in next ch-1 space, (sc in next tr, sc in next ch-1 space) 3 times, sc in next tr, (sc, ch 1, sc) in next ch-1 space, (sc in next tr, sc in next ch-1 space) twice; rep from * around, sl st in first sc to join. Fasten off.

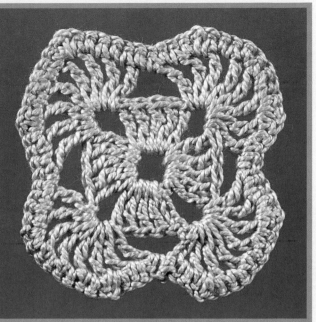

61

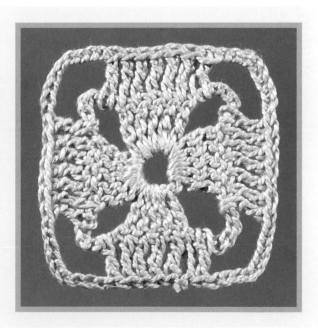

Ch 16 and sl st in first ch to form a ring.

Rnd 1: Ch 4 (counts as tr), 4 tr in ring, ch 7, (5 tr, ch 7) 3 times in ring, sl st in 4th ch of beg ch to join.

Rnd 2: Ch 4 (counts as tr), *tr in each of next 4 tr, (tr, ch 9, tr) in next ch-7 loop**, tr in next tr; rep from * around, ending last rep at **, sl st in 4th ch of beg ch to join. Fasten off.

62

Ch 10 and sl st in first ch to form a ring.

Rnd 1: Ch 4 (counts as tr), 3 tr in ring, ch 7, (4 tr, ch 7) 3 times in ring, sl st in 4th ch of beg ch to join.

Rnd 2: Ch 1, *sc in each of next 4 tr, 6 sc in next ch-7 loop; rep from * around, sl st in first sc to join.

Rnd 3: Ch 4 (counts as tr), tr in each of next 6 sc, *(tr, ch 5, tr) bet next 2 sc**, tr in each of next 10 sc; rep from * around, ending last rep at **, tr in each of next 3 sc, sl st in 4th ch of beg ch to join.

Rnd 4: Ch 1, *sc in each of next 8 tr, 6 sc in next ch-5 loop, sc in each of next 4 tr; rep from * around, sl st in first sc to join.

Rnd 5: Ch 4 (counts as tr), tr in each of next 10 sc, *3 tr bet next 2 sc**, tr in each of next 18 sc; rep from * around, ending last rep at **, tr in each of next 7 sc, sl st in 4th ch of beg ch to join. Fasten off.

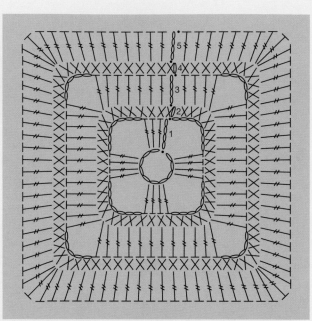

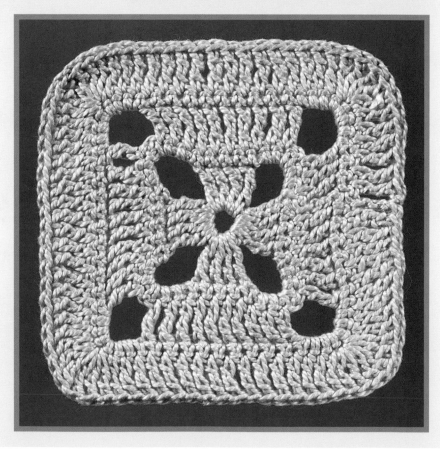

63

Ch 6 and sl st in first ch to form a ring.

Rnd 1: Ch 3 (counts as dc), 15 dc in ring, sl st in 3rd ch of beg ch to join.

Rnd 2: Ch 4 (counts as tr), 6 tr in same st, *skip next dc, dc in next dc, skip next dc**, 7 tr in next dc; rep from * around, ending last rep at **, sl st in 4th ch of beg ch to join.

Rnd 3: Sl st in each of next 3 tr, ch 5 (counts as tr, ch 1), (tr, ch 1) 6 times in same tr, *5 tr in next ch-3 loop, ch 1**, skip next 3 tr, (tr, ch 1) 7 times in next tr; rep from * around, ending last rep at **, sl st in 4th ch of beg ch to join. Fasten off.

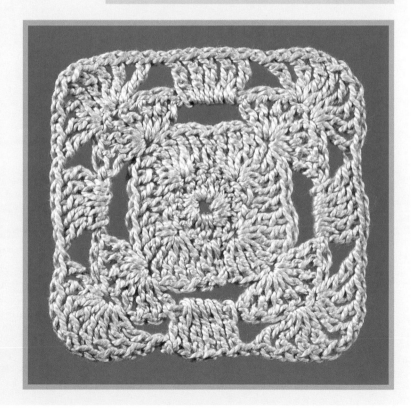

.5.
Clusters

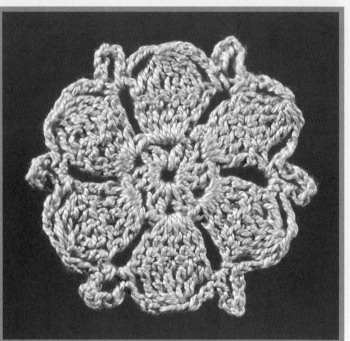

64 **4-tr cluster:** *(Yo [twice], insert hook in next st, yo, draw yarn through st, [yo, draw yarn through 2 loops on hook] twice) 4 times, yo, draw yarn through 5 loops on hook.*

5-tr cluster: *(Yo [twice], insert hook in next st, yo, draw yarn through st, [yo, draw yarn through 2 loops on hook] twice) 5 times, yo, draw yarn through 6 loops on hook.*

Ch 6 and sl st in first ch to form a ring.

Rnd 1: Ch 3 (counts as dc), dc in ring, ch 2, (2 dc, ch 2) 5 times in ring, sl st in 3rd ch of beg ch to join.

Rnd 2: Sl st to next ch-2 space, ch 4 (counts as tr), 4 tr in same ch-2 space, ch 3, (5 tr, ch 3) in each ch-2 space around, sl st in 4th ch of beg ch to join.

Rnd 3: Ch 4 (counts as tr), 4-tr cluster worked across next 4 tr, *ch 4, (sc, ch 7, sc) in next ch-3 loop, ch 4**, 5-tr cluster worked across next 5 tr; rep from * around, ending last rep at **, sl st in first cluster to join. Fasten off.

65

4-tr cluster: (Yo [twice], insert hook in next st, yo, draw yarn through st, [yo, draw yarn through 2 loops on hook] twice) 4 times, yo, draw yarn through 5 loops on hook.

Ch 8 and sl st in first ch to form a ring.

Rnd 1: Ch 1, (sc, ch 3, 4 tr, ch 3) 4 times in ring, sl st in first sc to join.

Rnd 2: Sl st to top of first ch-3 loop, ch 1, *sc in ch-3 loop, ch 3, 4-tr cluster worked across next 4 tr, ch 3, sc in next ch-3 loop, ch 2; rep from * around, sl st in first sc to join.

Rnd 3: Sl st to first cluster, *ch 4, skip next ch-3 loop, working over ch-2 space in last rnd, work (dc, ch 2, dc) in next corresponding sc 2 rnds below, ch 4, skip next ch-3 loop, sl st in next cluster; rep from * around, ending with sl st in first sl st to join.

Rnd 4: Ch 1, *2 sc in ch-4 loop, (4 dc, ch 3, 4 dc) in next ch-2 space, 2 sc in next ch-4 loop; rep from * around, sl st in first sc to join. Fasten off.

66

Y-st: Tr in next space, 2 dc in 2 strands at center of tr just made.

2-dc cluster: (Yo, insert hook in next st, yo, draw yarn through st, yo, draw yarn through 2 loops on hook) twice, yo, draw yarn through 3 loops on hook.

3-dc cluster: (Yo, insert hook in next st, yo, draw yarn through st, yo, draw yarn through 2 loops on hook) 3 times, yo, draw yarn through 4 loops on hook.

Ch 6 and sl st in first ch to form a ring.

Rnd 1: Ch 4, 2 dc in 3rd ch from hook (counts as first Y-st), ch 3, (Y-st, ch 3) 4 times in ring, sl st in 4th ch of beg ch to join.

Rnd 2: Ch 3, 2 dc cluster worked across next 2 dc, ch 5, skip next ch-3 loop, *3-dc cluster worked across next 3 sts of Y-st, ch 5, skip next ch-3 loop; rep from * around, sl st in first cluster to join.

Rnd 3: Ch 8 (counts as dc, ch 5), *sc in over next 2 loops in 2 rnds below, ch 5**, dc in next cluster, ch 5; rep from * around, ending last rep at **, sl st in 3rd ch of beg ch to join. Fasten off.

67

Y-st: Tr in next space, 2 dc in 2 strands at center of tr just made.

2-dc cluster: (Yo, insert hook in next st, yo, draw yarn through st, yo, draw yarn through 2 loops on hook) twice, yo, draw yarn through 3 loops on hook.

3-dc cluster: (Yo, insert hook in next st, yo, draw yarn through st, yo, draw yarn through 2 loops on hook) 3 times, yo, draw yarn through 4 loops on hook.

Ch 6 and sl st in first ch to form a ring.

Rnd 1: Ch 4, 2 dc in 3rd ch from hook (counts as first Y-st), ch 3, (Y-st, ch 3) 5 times in ring, sl st in 4th ch of beg ch to join.

Rnd 2: Ch 3, 2 dc cluster worked across next 2 dc, ch 5, skip next ch-3 loop, *3-dc cluster worked across next 3 sts of Y-st, ch 5, skip next ch-3 loop; rep from * around, sl st in first cluster to join.

Rnd 3: Ch 8 (counts as dc, ch 5), *sc in over next 2 loops in 2 rnds below, ch 5**, dc in next cluster, ch 5; rep from * around, ending last rep at **, sl st in 3rd ch of beg ch to join. Fasten off.

68

2-dc cluster: (Yo, insert hook in next st, yo, draw yarn through st, yo, draw yarn through 2 loops on hook) twice, yo, draw yarn through 3 loops on hook.

3-dc cluster: (Yo, insert hook in next st, yo, draw yarn through st, yo, draw yarn through 2 loops on hook) 3 times, yo, draw yarn through 4 loops on hook.

Ch 6 and sl st in first ch to form a ring.

Rnd 1: Ch 3 (counts as dc), 2 dc in ring, ch 5, (3 dc, ch 5) 5 times in ring, sl st in 3rd ch of beg ch to join.

Rnd 2: Ch 3 (counts as dc), 2-dc cluster worked across next 2 dc, *ch 4, (sc, ch 1, sc) in next ch-5 loop, ch 4**, 3-dc cluster worked across next 3 dc; rep from * around, ending last rep at **, sl st in first cluster to join. Fasten off.

69 *4-tr cluster: (Yo [twice], insert hook in next st, yo, draw yarn through st, [yo, draw yarn through 2 loops on hook] twice) 4 times, yo, draw yarn through 5 loops on hook.*

5-tr cluster: (Yo [twice], insert hook in next st, yo, draw yarn through st, [yo, draw yarn through 2 loops on hook] twice) 5 times, yo, draw yarn through 6 loops on hook.

Picot: Ch 4, sl st in 4th ch from hook.

Ch 6 and sl st in first ch to form a ring.

Rnd 1: Ch 3 (counts as dc), dc in ring, ch 2, (2 dc, ch 2) 5 times in ring, sl st in 3rd ch of beg ch to join.

Rnd 2: Sl st to next ch-2 space, ch 4 (counts as tr), 4 tr in same ch-2 space, ch 3, (5 tr, ch 3) in each ch-2 space around, sl st in 4th ch of beg ch to join.

Rnd 3: Ch 4 (counts as tr), 4-tr cluster worked across next 4 tr, picot, *ch 4, (sc, ch 8, sc) in next ch-3 loop, ch 4**, 5-tr cluster worked across next 5 tr, picot; rep from * around, ending last rep at **, sl st in first cluster to join. Fasten off.

70

6-dc cluster: (Yo, insert hook in next st, yo, draw yarn through st, yo, draw yarn through 2 loops on hook) 6 times, yo, draw yarn through 7 loops on hook.

7-dc cluster: (Yo, insert hook in next st, yo, draw yarn through st, yo, draw yarn through 2 loops on hook) 7 times, yo, draw yarn through 8 loops on hook.

Ch 11 and sl st in first ch to form a ring.

Rnd 1: Ch 3 (counts as dc), 4 dc in ring, ch 9, (5 dc, ch 9) 3 times in ring, sl st in 3rd ch of beg ch to join.

Rnd 2: Ch 3 (counts as dc), dc in first st, *dc in each of next 3 dc, 2 dc in next dc, ch 2, (3 dc, ch 5, 3 dc) in next ch-9 loop, ch 2**, 2 dc in next dc; rep from * around, ending last rep at **, sl st in 3rd ch of beg ch to join.

Rnd 3: Ch 3 (counts as dc), 6-dc cluster worked across next 6 dc, *ch 4, skip next ch-2 space, (dc, ch 3, 2 dc, ch 2, 2 dc, ch 3, dc) in next ch-5 loop, ch 4, skip next ch-2 space**, 7-dc cluster worked across next 7 dc; rep from * around, ending last rep at **, sl st in first cluster to join.

Rnd 4: Ch 1, *sc in cluster, 3 sc in next ch-4 loop, sc in next dc, 3 sc in next ch-3 loop, sc in each of next 2 dc, 3 sc in next ch-2 space, sc in each of next 2 dc, 3 sc in next ch-3 loop, sc in next dc, 3 sc in next ch-4 loop; rep from * around, sl st in first sc to join.

Rnd 5: Ch 1, *sc in each of next 11 sc, 2 sc in next sc, sc in each of next 10 sc; rep from * around, sl st in first sc to join. Fasten off.

71

4-dc cluster: (Yo, insert hook in next st, yo, draw yarn through st, yo, draw yarn through 2 loops on hook) 4 times, yo, draw yarn through 5 loops on hook.

5-dc cluster: (Yo, insert hook in next st, yo, draw yarn through st, yo, draw yarn through 2 loops on hook) 5 times, yo, draw yarn through 6 loops on hook.

3-dc puff st: (Yo, insert hook in next space, yo, draw yarn through space, yo, draw yarn through 2 loops on hook) 3 times in same space, yo, draw yarn through 4 loops on hook.

4-dc puff st: (Yo, insert hook in next space, yo, draw yarn through space, yo, draw yarn through 2 loops on hook) 4 times in same space, yo, draw yarn through 5 loops on hook.

Ch 10 and sl st in first ch to form a ring.

Rnd 1: Ch 3 (counts as dc), 4 dc in ring, ch 2, (5 dc, ch 2) 5 times in ring, sl st in 3rd ch of beg ch to join.

Rnd 2: Ch 3 (counts as dc), 4-dc cluster worked across next 4 dc, ch 6, dc in next ch-2 space, ch 6**, 5-dc cluster worked across next 5 dc; rep from * around, ending last rep at **, sl st in first cluster to join.

Rnd 3: Sl st to center of first ch-6 loop, ch 1, (2 sc, ch 6) in each ch-6 loop around, sl st in first sc to join.

Rnd 4: Sl st to next ch-6 loop, ch 3 (counts as dc), (3-dc puff st, ch 9, 4-dc puff st) in same ch-6 loop, (4-dc puff st, ch 9, 4-dc puff st) in each ch-6 loop around, sl st in first puff st to join. Fasten off.

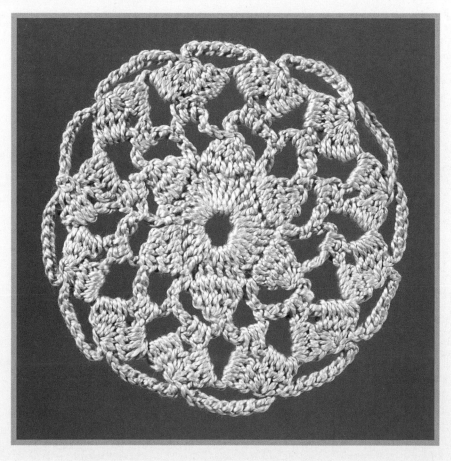

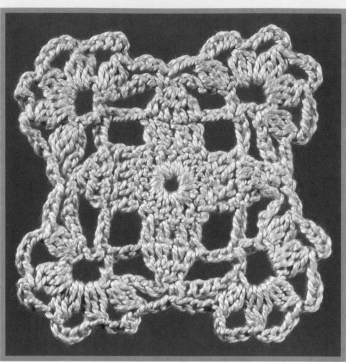

72   *3-dc cluster: (Yo, insert hook in next st, yo, draw yarn through st, yo, draw yarn through 2 loops on hook) 3 times, yo, draw yarn through 4 loops on hook.*

4-dc cluster: (Yo, insert hook in next st, yo, draw yarn through st, yo, draw yarn through 2 loops on hook) 4 times, yo, draw yarn through 5 loops on hook.

Puff st: (Yo, insert hook in next st, yo, draw yarn through st, yo, draw yarn through 2 loops on hook) 3 times in same st, yo, draw yarn through 4 loops on hook.

Ch 6 and sl st in first ch to form a ring.

Rnd 1: Ch 3 (counts as dc), 15 dc in ring, sl st in 3rd ch of beg ch to join.

Rnd 2: Ch 3 (counts as dc), dc in each of next 3 dc, ch 7, *dc in each of next 4 dc, ch 7; rep from * around, sl st in 3rd ch of beg ch to join.

Rnd 3: Ch 3 (counts as dc), 3-dc cluster worked across next 3 dc, *ch 5, (dc, ch 5, dc) in center ch of next ch-7 loop, ch 5**, 4-dc cluster worked across next 4 dc; rep from * around, ending last rep at **, sl st in first cluster to join.

Rnd 4: Ch 1, *sc in cluster, ch 3, skip next ch-5 loop, puff st in next dc, ch 5 (puff st, ch 5, puff st, ch 5, puff st) in next ch-5 loop, ch 5, puff st in next dc, ch 3; rep from * around, sl st in first sc to join. Fasten off.

73

2-tr cluster: *(Yo [twice], insert hook in next st, yo, draw yarn through st, [yo, draw yarn through 2 loops on hook] twice) twice, yo, draw yarn through 3 loops on hook.*

3-tr puff st: *(Yo [twice], insert hook in next st, yo, draw yarn through st, [yo, draw yarn through 2 loops on hook] twice) 3 times in same st, yo, draw yarn through 4 loops on hook.*

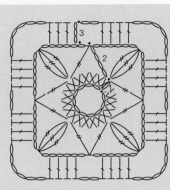

Ch 11 and sl st in first ch to form a ring.

Rnd 1: Ch 1, 20 sc in ring, sl st in first sc to join.

Rnd 2: Ch 4 (counts as tr), skip next 4 sc, tr in next sc, ch 6, *3-tr puff st in same sc holding last tr, ch 6**, 2-tr cluster, working first half-closed tr in same sc holding last puff st, skip next 4 sc, work 2nd half-closed tr in next sc, yo, complete cluster; rep from * around, ending last rep at **, sl st in 4th ch of beg ch to join.

Rnd 3: Sl st in next ch-6 loop, ch 3 (counts as dc), 3 dc in same ch-6 loop, *ch 6, 4 dc in next ch-6 loop, ch 2**, 4 dc in next ch-6 loop; rep from * around, ending last rep at **, sl st in 3rd ch of beg ch to join. Fasten off.

74

3-tr cluster: *(Yo [twice], insert hook in next st, yo, draw yarn through st, [yo, draw yarn through 2 loops on hook] twice) 3 times, yo, draw yarn through 4 loops on hook.*

4-tr cluster: *(Yo [twice], insert hook in next st, yo, draw yarn through st, [yo, draw yarn through 2 loops on hook] twice) 4 times, yo, draw yarn through 5 loops on hook.*

Ch 6 and sl st in first ch to form a ring.

Rnd 1: Ch 4 (counts as tr), 5 tr in ring, ch 5, (6 tr, ch 5) 3 times in ring, sl st in 4th ch of beg ch to join.

Rnd 2: Sl st in next tr, ch 4 (counts as tr), 3-tr cluster worked across next 3 tr, ch 6, sc in next ch-5 loop, ch 6, skip next tr**, 4-tr cluster worked across next 4 tr; rep from * around, ending last rep at **, sl st in first cluster to join. Fasten off.

75

2-dc cluster: (Yo, insert hook in next st, yo, draw yarn through st, yo, draw yarn through 2 loops on hook) twice, yo, draw yarn through 3 loops on hook.

3-dc cluster: (Yo, insert hook in next st, yo, draw yarn through st, yo, draw yarn through 2 loops on hook) 3 times, yo, draw yarn through 4 loops on hook.

Ch 10 and sl st in first ch to form a ring.

Rnd 1: Ch 3 (counts as dc), 23 dc in ring, sl st in 3rd ch of beg ch to join.

Rnd 2: Ch 3 (counts as dc), dc in next dc, ch 3, *2-dc cluster worked across next 2 dc, ch 3; rep from * around, sl st in 3rd ch of beg ch to join.

Rnd 3: Ch 3 (counts as dc), *4 dc in next ch-3 loop**, dc in next cluster; rep from * around, ending last rep at **, sl st in 3rd ch of beg ch to join.

Rnd 4: Ch 3 (counts as dc), 2-dc cluster worked across next 2 dc, *ch 7, skip next 2 dc**, 3-dc cluster worked across next 3 dc; rep from * around, ending last rep at **, sl st in first cluster to join.

Rnd 5: Ch 3 (counts as dc), *7 dc in next ch-7 loop**, dc in next cluster; rep from * around, ending last rep at **, sl st in 3rd ch of beg ch to join. Fasten off.

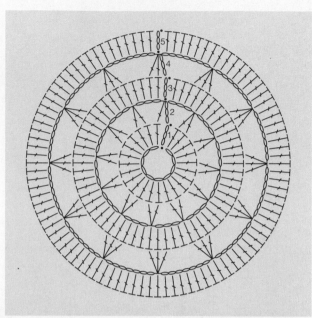

76

2-dtr puff st: *(Yo [3 times], insert hook in next space, yo, draw yarn through space, [yo, draw yarn through 2 loops on hook] 3 times) twice in same space, yo, draw yarn through 3 loops on hook.*

Ch 8 and sl st in first ch to form a ring.

Rnd 1: Ch 5 (counts as dtr), dtr in ring, ch 1, (2-dtr puff st, ch 1) 15 times in ring, sl st in 5th ch of beg ch to join.

Rnd 2: Sl st in next ch-1 space, ch 1, sc in same ch-1 space, ch 3, sc in next ch-1 space, ch 3, *(2 dc, ch 3, 2 dc) in next ch-1 space, ch 3**, (sc, ch 3) in each of next 3 ch-1 spaces; rep from * around, ending last rep at **, sc in next ch-1 space, ch 3, sl st in first sc to join.

Rnd 3: Sl st in next ch-3 loop, ch 3 (counts as dc), 2 dc in same ch-3 loop, ch 2, *skip next ch-3 loop, (3 dc, ch 2, 3 dc) in next ch-3 loop, ch 2, skip next ch-3 loop**, (3 dc, ch 2) in each of next 2 ch-3 loops; rep from * around, ending last rep at **, 3 dc in next ch-3 loop, ch 2, sl st in 3rd ch of beg ch to join.

Rnd 4: Sl st to next ch-2 space, ch 3 (counts as dc), 2 dc in same ch-2 space, ch 2, *(3 dc, ch 2, 3 dc) in next ch-2 space, ch 2**, (3 dc, ch 2) in each of next 3 ch-2 spaces; rep from * around, ending last rep at **, (3 dc, ch 2) in each of next 2 ch-2 spaces, sl st in 3rd ch of beg to join.

Rnd 5: Sl st to next ch-2 space, ch 3 (counts as dc), 2 dc in same ch-2 space, *(3 dc, ch 2, 3 dc) in next ch-2 space**, 3 dc in each of next 4 ch-2 spaces; rep from * around, ending last rep at **, 3 dc in each of next 3 ch-2 spaces, sl st in 3rd ch of beg to join. Fasten off.

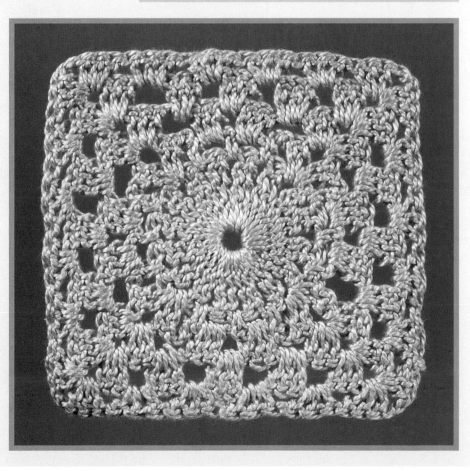

77 *3-tr cluster:* (Yo [twice], insert hook in next st, yo, draw yarn through st, [yo, draw yarn through 2 loops on hook] twice) 3 times, yo, draw yarn through 4 loops on hook.

4-tr cluster: (Yo [twice], insert hook in next st, yo, draw yarn through st, [yo, draw yarn through 2 loops on hook] twice) 4 times, yo, draw yarn through 5 loops on hook.

Ch 10 and sl st in first ch to form a ring.

Rnd 1: Ch 3 (counts as dc), 31 dc in ring, sl st in 3rd ch of beg ch to join.

Rnd 2: Ch 4 (counts as tr), tr in each of next 3 dc, ch 3, *tr in each of next 4 dc, ch 3; rep from * around, sl st in 4th ch of beg ch to join.

Rnd 3: Ch 4 (counts as tr), 3-tr cluster worked across next 3 tr, ch 8, skip next ch-3 loop, *4-tr cluster worked across next 4 tr, ch 8, skip next ch-3 loop; rep from * around, sl st in first cluster to join. Fasten off.

78 ***3-dtr puff st:*** *(Yo [3 times], insert hook in next space, yo, draw yarn through space, [yo, draw yarn through 2 loops on hook] 3 times) 3 times in same space, yo, draw yarn through 4 loops on hook.*

4-dtr puff st: *(Yo [3 times], insert hook in next space, yo, draw yarn through space, [yo, draw yarn through 2 loops on hook] 3 times) 4 times in same space, yo, draw yarn through 5 loops on hook.*

4-tr puff st: *(Yo [twice], insert hook in next space, yo, draw yarn through space, [yo, draw yarn through 2 loops on hook] twice) 4 times in same space, yo, draw yarn through 5 loops on hook.*

Ch 6 and sl st in first ch to form a ring.

Rnd 1: Ch 5 (counts as dtr), 3-dtr puff st in ring, ch 5, (4-dtr puff st, ch 5) 9 times in ring, sl st in first puff st to join.

Rnd 2: Ch 1, *sc in puff st, ch 4, 4-tr puff st in next ch-5 loop, ch 4; rep from * around, sl st in first sc to join. Fasten off.

.6.
Bobbles

79 *4-looped bobble: (Yo, insert hook in next st, yo, draw yarn through st and up to level of work) 4 times in same st, yo, draw yarn through 9 loops on hook.*

5-looped bobble: (Yo, insert hook in next st, yo, draw yarn through st and up to level of work) 5 times in same st, yo, draw yarn through 11 loops on hook.

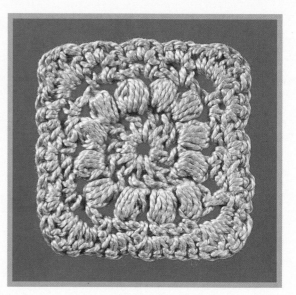

Ch 6 and sl st in first ch to form a ring.

Rnd 1: Ch 4 (counts as dc, ch 1), (dc, ch 1) 11 times in ring, sl st in 3rd ch of beg ch to join.

Rnd 2: Ch 3, 4-looped bobble in first st, ch 3, *5-looped bobble in next dc, ch 2, skip next ch-1 space, 5-looped bobble in next dc, ch 3, skip next ch-1 space**, 5-looped bobble in next dc, ch 3, skip next ch-1 space; rep from * around, ending last rep at **, sl st in first bobble to join.

Rnd 3: Sl st in next ch-3 loop, ch 1, *(sc, ch 2, sc) in each of next 3 loops, ch 3; rep from * around, sl st in first sc to join.

Rnd 4: Sl st in next ch-2 space, ch 1, *3 sc in each of next 3 ch-2 spaces, (hdc, 3 dc, hdc) in next ch-3 loop; rep from * around, sl st in first sc to join. Fasten off.

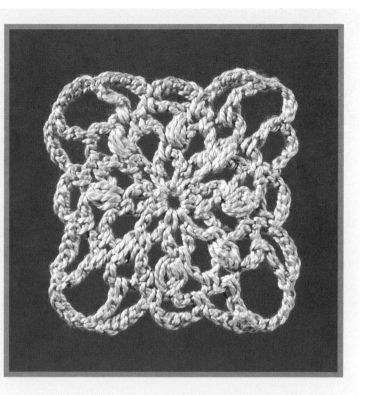

80 *3-looped bobble:* (Yo, insert hook in next st, yo, draw yarn through st and up to level of work) 3 times in same st, yo, draw yarn through 7 loops on hook.

Ch 6 and sl st in first ch to form a ring.

Rnd 1: Ch 1, (sc, ch 5) 8 times in ring, sl st in first sc to join.

Rnd 2: Sl st to center of next ch-5 loop, ch 1, (sc, ch 5) in each ch-5 loop around, around, sl st in first sc to join.

Rnd 3: Sl st to center of next ch-5 loop, ch 1, *sc in ch-5 loop, ch 3, 3-looped bobble in next sc, ch 3; rep from * around, sl st in first sc to join.

Rnd 4: Sl st to center of next ch-3 loop, ch 1, *(sc, ch 5) in each of next 2 ch-3 loops, (tr, ch 5) in each of next 2 ch-3 loops; rep from * around, sl st in first sc to join. Fasten off.

81 *3-looped bobble:*
(Yo, insert hook in next space, yo, draw yarn through space and up to level of work) 3 times in same space, yo, draw yarn through 7 loops on hook.

4-looped bobble: (Yo, insert hook in next space, yo, draw yarn through space and up to level of work) 4 times in same space, yo, draw yarn through 9 loops on hook.

Ch 6 and sl st in first ch to form a ring.

Rnd 1: Ch 4 (counts as dc, ch 1), (dc, ch 1) 11 times in ring, sl st in 3rd ch of beg ch to join.

Rnd 2: Sl st in next ch-1 space, ch 3, 3-looped bobble in same ch-1 space, ch 2, *4-looped bobble in next ch-1 space, ch 3, tr in next dc, ch 3, 4-looped bobble in next ch-1 space, ch 2**, 4-looped bobble in next ch-1 space; rep from * around, ending last rep at **, sl st in first bobble to join.

Rnd 3: Ch 1, *sc in bobble, ch 2, skip next ch-2 space, 4 dc in next ch-3 loop, ch 2, tr in next tr, ch 2, 4 dc in next ch-3 loop, ch 2; rep from * around, sl st in first sc to join. Fasten off.

82 *2-looped bobble: (Yo, insert hook in next space, yo, draw yarn through space and up to level of work) twice in same space, yo, draw yarn through 5 loops on hook.*

3-looped bobble: (Yo, insert hook in next space, yo, draw yarn through space and up to level of work) 3 times in same space, yo, draw yarn through 7 loops on hook.

Ch 6 and sl st in first ch to form a ring.

Rnd 1: Ch 5 (counts as tr, ch 1), (tr, ch 1) 11 times in ring, sl st in 4th ch of beg ch to join.

Rnd 2: Sl st in next ch-1 space, ch 3, 2-looped puff st in same ch-1 space, ch 1, (3-looped puff st, ch 1, 3 looped puff st, ch 1) in each of next 11 ch-1 spaces, 3-looped bobble in first ch-1 space, ch 1, sl st in first bobble to join.

Rnd 3: Sl st in next ch-1 space, ch 1, *sc in ch-1 space, ch 1, hdc in next ch-1 space, ch 1, dc in next ch-1 space, ch 1, (dc, ch 1, dc) in next ch-1 space, ch 1, dc in next ch-1 space, ch 1, hdc in next ch-1 space, ch 1; rep from * around, sl st in first sc to join. Fasten off.

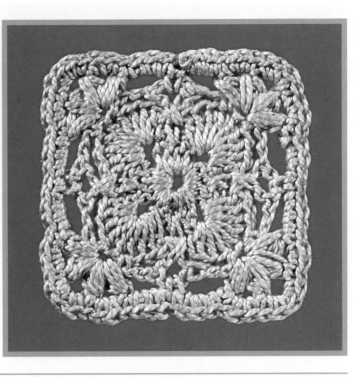

83 **Bobble:** *(Yo, insert hook in next space, yo, draw yarn through space and up to level of work) 3 times in same space, yo, draw yarn through 7 loops on hook.*

Ch 6 and sl st in first ch to form a ring.

Rnd 1: Ch 3 (counts as dc), 3 dc in ring, ch 2, (4 dc, ch 2) 3 times in ring, sl st in 3rd ch of beg ch to join.

Rnd 2: Sl st in next dc, ch 1, *sc bet next 2 dc, 9 dc in next ch-2 space, skip next 2 dc; rep from * around, sl st in first sc to join.

Rnd 3: Sl st in next dc, ch 5 (counts as dc, ch 2), working behind ch-5 beg ch, skip 1 sc to the right, dc in next dc to the right, *ch 2, skip next 3 dc, sc bet next 2 dc, ch 2, sc bet next 2 dc, ch 2, skip next 5 sts**, dc in next dc, ch 2, working behind last dc made, skip next sc to the right, dc in next dc to the right (crossed dc made); rep from * around, ending last rep at **, sl st in 3rd ch of beg ch to join.

Rnd 4: Sl st in next ch-2 space, ch 1, *sc in ch-2 space, ch 3, skip next ch-2 space, (bobble, ch 2, bobble, ch 3, bobble, ch 2, bobble) in next ch-2 space, ch 3, skip next ch-2 space; rep from * around, sl st in first sc to join.

Rnd 5: Ch 1, *sc in sc, 3 sc in next ch-3 loop, sc in next bobble, 2 sc in next ch-2 space, sc in next bobble, 3 sc in next ch-3 loop, sc in next bobble, 2 sc in next ch-2 space, sc in next bobble, 3 sc in next ch-3 loop; rep from * around, sl st first sc to join. Fasten off.

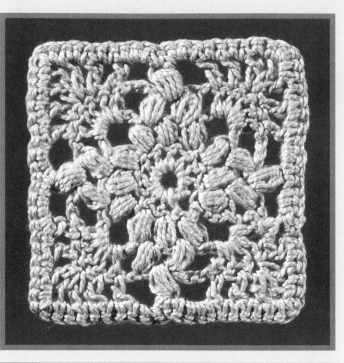

84

3-looped bobble: *(Yo, insert hook in next st, yo, draw yarn through st and up to level of work) 3 times in same st, yo, draw yarn through 7 loops on hook.*

4-looped bobble: *(Yo, insert hook in next st, yo, draw yarn through st and up to level of work) 4 times in same st, yo, draw yarn through 9 loops on hook.*

Ch 6 and sl st in first ch to form a ring.

Rnd 1: Ch 3 (counts as dc), 11 dc in ring, sl st in 3rd ch of beg ch to join.

Rnd 2: Ch 3, 3-looped bobble in same st, *ch 1, 4-looped bobble in next dc, ch 1, 4-looped bobble in next dc, ch 5**, 4-looped bobble in next dc; rep from * around, ending last rep at **, sl st in first bobble to join.

Rnd 3: Sl st in next ch-1 space, ch 3, 3-looped bobble in same ch-1 space, *ch 1, 4-looped bobble in next ch-1 space, ch 2, 5 dc in next ch-5 loop, ch 2**, 4-looped bobble in next ch-1 space; rep from * around, ending last rep at **, sl st in first bobble to join.

Rnd 4: Sl st in next ch-1 space, ch 3, 3-looped bobble in same ch-1 space, *ch 3, skip next ch-2 space, (dc, ch 1) in each of next 2 dc, (dc, ch 1, dc, ch 1, dc) in next dc, (ch 1, dc) in each of next 2 dc, ch 3**, 4-looped bobble in next ch-1 space; rep from * around, ending last rep at **, sl st in first bobble to join.

Rnd 5: Ch 1, *sc in bobble, 3 sc in next ch-3 loop, (sc in next dc, sc in next ch-1 space) 3 times, 3 sc in next dc, (sc in next ch-1 space, sc in next dc) 3 times, 3 sc in next ch-3 loop; rep from * around, sl st in first sc to join. Fasten off.

85

Bobble: (Yo, insert hook in next space, yo, draw yarn through space and up to level of work) 4 times in same space, yo, draw yarn through 9 loops on hook.

Ch 6 and sl st in first ch to form a ring.

Rnd 1: Ch 3 (counts as dc), 2 dc in ring, ch 3, (3 dc, ch 3) 3 times in ring, sl st in 3rd ch of beg ch to join.

Rnd 2: Ch 3 (counts as dc), dc in each of next 2 dc, *ch 1, (bobble, ch 4, bobble) in next ch-4 loop, ch 1**, dc in each of next 3 dc; rep from * around, ending last rep at **, sl st in 3rd ch of beg ch to join.

Rnd 3: Ch 3 (counts as dc), dc in each of next 2 dc, *skip next ch-1 space, dc in next bobble, ch 1, (bobble, ch 5, bobble) in next ch-4 loop, ch 1, dc in next bobble, skip next ch-1 space**, dc in each of next 3 dc; rep from * around, ending last rep at **, sl st in 3rd ch of beg ch to join.

Rnd 4: Ch 3 (counts as dc), dc in each of next 3 dc, *skip next ch-1 space, dc in next bobble, ch 1, (bobble, ch 5, bobble) in next ch-5 loop, ch 1, dc in next bobble, skip next ch-1 space**, dc in each of next 5 dc; rep from * around, ending last rep at **, dc in next dc, sl st in 3rd ch of beg ch to join.

Rnd 5: Ch 3 (counts as dc), dc in each of next 4 dc, *skip next ch-1 space, dc in next bobble, ch 1, (bobble, ch 5, bobble) in next ch-5 loop, ch 1, dc in next bobble, skip next ch-1 space**, dc in each of next 7 dc; rep from * around, ending last rep at **, dc in each of next 2 dc, sl st in 3rd ch of beg ch to join. Fasten off.

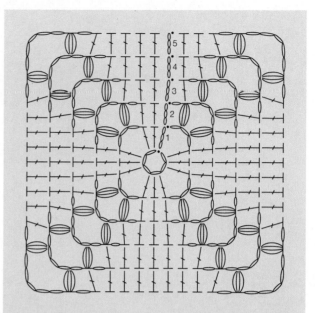

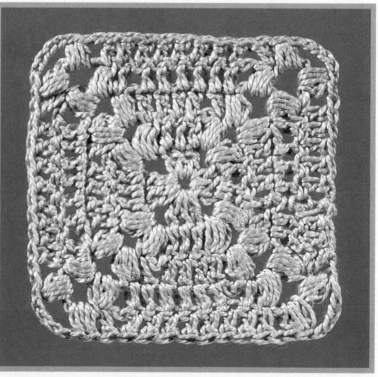

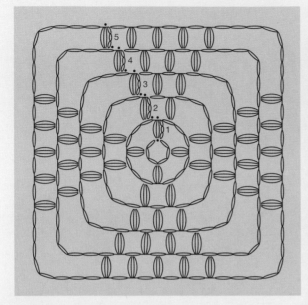

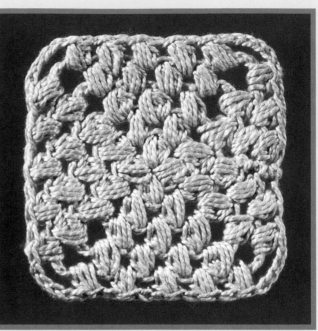

86 **3-looped bobble:** *(Yo, insert hook in next space, yo, draw yarn through space and up to level of work) 3 times in same space, yo, draw yarn through 7 loops on hook.*

4-looped bobble: *(Yo, insert hook in next space, yo, draw yarn through space and up to level of work) 4 times in same space, yo, draw yarn through 9 loops on hook.*

Ch 6 and sl st in first ch to form a ring.

Rnd 1: Ch 3 (counts as dc), 3-looped bobble in ring, ch 3, (4-looped bobble, ch 3) 3 times in ring, sl st in first bobble to join.

Rnd 2: Sl st in next ch-3 loop, ch 3, (3-looped bobble, ch 4, 4-looped bobble) in same ch-4 loop, ch 1, (4-looped bobble, ch 4, 4-looped bobble, ch 1) in each ch-4 loop around, sl st in first bobble to join.

Rnd 3: Sl st in next ch-3 loop, ch 3, (3-looped bobble, ch 6, 4-looped bobble) in same ch-4 loop, *ch 1, 4-looped bobble in next ch-1 space, ch 1**, (4-looped bobble, ch 6, 4-looped bobble) in next ch-4 loop; rep from * around, ending last rep at **, sl st in first bobble to join.

Rnd 4: Sl st in next ch-3 loop, ch 3, (3-looped bobble, ch 7, 4-looped bobble) in same ch-6 loop, *(ch 1, 4-looped bobble) in each of next 2 ch-1 spaces, ch 1**, (4-looped bobble, ch 7, 4-looped bobble) in next ch-6 loop; rep from * around, ending last rep at **, sl st in first bobble to join.

Rnd 5: Sl st in next ch-3 loop, ch 3, (3-looped bobble, ch 8, 4-looped bobble) in same ch-7 loop, *(ch 1, 4-looped bobble) in each of next 3 ch-1 spaces, ch 1**, (4-looped bobble, ch 8, 4-looped bobble) in next ch-7 loop; rep from * around, ending last rep at **, sl st in first bobble to join. Fasten off.

.7.
Puff Stitches

87

3-dc puff st: *(Yo, insert hook in next space, yo, draw yarn through space, draw yarn through 2 loops on hook) 3 times in same space, yo, draw yarn through 4 loops on hook.*

4-dc puff st: *(Yo, insert hook in next space, yo, draw yarn through space, draw yarn through 2 loops on hook) 4 times in same space, yo, draw yarn through 5 loops on hook.*

Ch 6 and sl st in first ch to form a ring.

Rnd 1: Ch 5 (counts as dc, ch 2), (dc, ch 2) 7 times in ring, sl st in 3rd ch of beg ch to join.

Rnd 2: Sl st in next ch-2 space, ch 3 (counts as dc), 3-dc puff st in same ch-2 space, ch 5, (4-dc puff st, ch 5) in each ch-2 space around, sl st in first puff st to join.

Rnd 3: Ch 1, *sc in puff st, ch 2, working over next ch-5 loop, dc in next corresponding dc 2 rnds below, ch 2; rep from * around, sl st in first sc to join.

Rnd 4: Sl st in next ch-2 space, ch 1, (sc, ch 3) in each ch-2 space around, sl st in first sc to join.

Rnd 5: Sl st in next ch-3 loop, ch 3 (counts as dc), (dc, ch 2, 2 dc) in same ch-3 loop, *ch 2, (sc, ch 3) in each of next 2 ch-3 loops, sc in next ch-3 loop, ch 2**, (2 dc, ch 2, 2 dc) in next ch-3 loop; rep from * around, ending last rep at **, sl st in 3rd ch of beg ch to join. Fasten off.

88

2-dc puff st: (Yo, insert hook in next space, yo, draw yarn through space, draw yarn through 2 loops on hook) twice in same space, yo, draw yarn through 3 loops on hook.

3-dc puff st: (Yo, insert hook in next space, yo, draw yarn through space, draw yarn through 2 loops on hook) 3 times in same space, yo, draw yarn through 4 loops on hook.

Ch 6 and sl st in first ch to form a ring.

Rnd 1: Ch 3 (counts as dc), 2-dc puff st in ring, ch 3, (3-dc puff st, ch 3) 7 times in ring, sl st in first puff st to join.

Rnd 2: Sl st in next ch-3 loop, ch 1, (sc, ch 5) in each ch-3 loop around, sl st in first sc to join.

Rnd 3: Sl st to center of next ch-5 loop, ch 3 (counts as dc), (2-dc puff st, ch 3, 3-dc puff st) in same ch-5 loop, *ch 5, sc in next ch-5 loop, ch 5**, (3-dc puff st, ch 3, 3-dc puff st) in next ch-5 loop; rep from * around, ending last rep at **, sl st in first puff st to join.

Rnd 4: Sl st to next ch-3 loop, ch 1, *(sc, ch 5, sc) in ch-3 loop, ch 5, (sc, ch 5) in each of next 2 ch-5 loops; rep from * around, sl st in first sc to join. Fasten off.

89

3-dc puff st: *(Yo, insert hook in next space, yo, draw yarn through space, draw yarn through 2 loops on hook) 3 times in same space, yo, draw yarn through 4 loops on hook.*

4-dc puff st: (Yo, insert hook in next space, yo, draw yarn through space, draw yarn through 2 loops on hook) 4 times in same space, yo, draw yarn through 5 loops on hook.

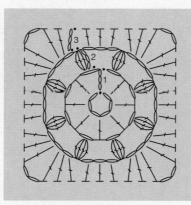

Ch 6 and sl st in first ch to form a ring.

Rnd 1: Ch 4 (counts as dc, ch 1), (dc, ch 1) 7 times in ring, sl st in 3rd ch of beg ch to join.

Rnd 2: Sl st in next ch-1 space, ch 3 (counts as dc), 3-dc puff st in same ch-1 space, ch 3, (4-dc puff st, ch 3) in each ch-1 space around, sl st in first puff st to join.

Rnd 3: Sl st in next ch-3 loop, ch 3 (counts as dc), (2 dc, ch 2, 3 dc) in same ch-3 loop, *3 dc in next ch-3 loop**, (3 dc, ch 2, 3 dc) in next ch-3 loop; rep from * around, ending last rep at **, sl st in 3rd ch of beg ch to join. Fasten off.

90

2-tr puff st: (Yo [twice], insert hook in next st, yo, draw yarn through st, [draw yarn through 2 loops on hook] twice) twice in same st, yo, draw yarn through 3 loops on hook.

3-tr puff st: (Yo [twice], insert hook in next st, yo, draw yarn through st, [draw yarn through 2 loops on hook] twice) 3 times in same st, yo, draw yarn through 4 loops on hook.

Ch 6 and sl st in first ch to form a ring.

Rnd 1: Ch 1, 8 sc in ring, sl st in first sc to join.

Rnd 2: Ch 4 (counts as tr), 2-tr puff st in first sc, ch 4, (3-tr puff st, ch 4) in each sc around, sl st in 4th ch of beg ch to join.

Rnd 3: Ch 1, *sc in puff st, ch 3, skip next ch-4 loop, sc in next puff st, ch 5, skip next ch-4 loop; rep from * around, sl st in first sc to join.

Rnd 4: Sl st in next ch-3 loop, ch 1, *3 sc in ch-3 loop, 7 sc in next ch-5 loop; rep from * around, sl st in first sc to join. Fasten off.

91

2-dc puff st: *(Yo, insert hook in next st, yo, draw yarn through st, draw yarn through 2 loops on hook) twice in same st, yo, draw yarn through 3 loops on hook.*

3-dc puff st: *(Yo, insert hook in next st, yo, draw yarn through st, draw yarn through 2 loops on hook) 3 times in same st, yo, draw yarn through 4 loops on hook.*

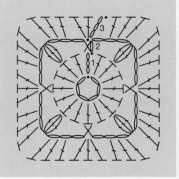

Ch 6 and sl st in first ch to form a ring.

Rnd 1: Ch 1, 8 sc in ring, sl st in first sc to join.

Rnd 2: Ch 1, (sc, ch 1) in each sc around, sl st in first sc to join.

Rnd 3: Ch 3 (counts as dc), 2-dc puff st in same sc, ch 2, *3-dc puff st in next ch-1 space, ch 2**, 3-dc puff st in next sc, ch 2; rep from * around, ending last rep at **, sl st in first puff st to join.

Rnd 4: Ch 1, (sc, ch 3) in each of first 2 puff sts, *(sc, ch 6, sc) in next puff st, ch 3**, (sc, ch 3) in each of next 3 puff sts; rep from * around, ending last rep at **, sc in next puff st, ch 3, sl st in first sc to join. Fasten off.

92

Puff st: *(Yo, insert hook in next st, yo, draw yarn through st, draw yarn through 2 loops on hook) 3 times in same st, yo, draw yarn through 4 loops on hook.*

Ch 6 and sl st in first ch to form a ring.

Rnd 1: Ch 3 (counts as dc), 15 dc in ring, sl st in 3rd ch of beg ch to join.

Rnd 2: Ch 1, *sc in dc, ch 3, skip next dc, puff st in next dc, ch 3, skip next dc; rep from * around, sl st in first sc to join.

Rnd 3: Ch 3 (counts as dc), 2 dc in same sc, *3 dc in each of next 2 ch-3 loops**, 3 dc in next sc; rep from * around, ending last rep at **, sl st in 3rd ch of beg ch to join. Fasten off.

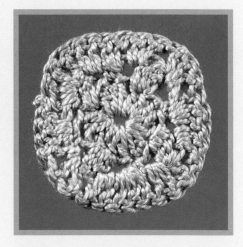

93

Puff st: (Yo, insert hook in next space, yo, draw yarn through space, draw yarn through 2 loops on hook) twice in same space, yo, draw yarn through 3 loops on hook.

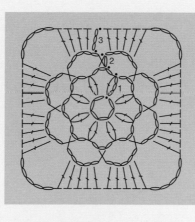

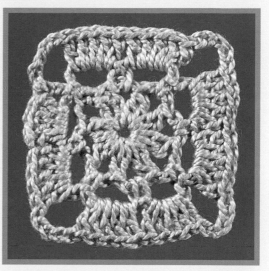

Ch 6 and sl st in first ch to form a ring.

Rnd 1: Ch 3 (counts as dc), dc in ring, ch 3, (puff st, ch 3) 7 times in ring, sl st in 3rd ch of beg ch to join.

Rnd 2: Sl st in next ch-3 loop, ch 1, (sc, ch 5) in each ch-3 loop around, sl st in first sc to join.

Rnd 3: Sl st in next ch-5 loop, ch 3 (counts as dc), 4 dc in same ch-5 loop, *ch 5, 5 dc in next ch-5 loop**, 5 dc in next ch-5 loop; rep from * around, ending last rep at **, sl st in 3rd ch of beg ch to join. Fasten off.

94

3-dc puff st: (Yo, insert hook in next space, yo, draw yarn through space, draw yarn through 2 loops on hook) 3 times in same space, yo, draw yarn through 4 loops on hook.

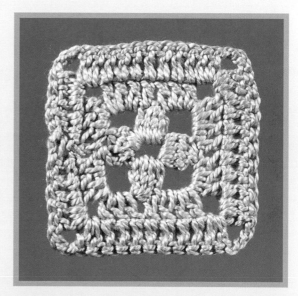

4-dc puff st: (Yo, insert hook in next space, yo, draw yarn through space, draw yarn through 2 loops on hook) 4 times in same space, yo, draw yarn through 5 loops on hook.

Ch 6 and sl st in first ch to form a ring.

Rnd 1: Ch 3 (counts as dc), 3-dc puff st in ring, ch 6, (4-dc puff st, ch 6) 3 times in ring, sl st in first puff st to join.

Rnd 2: Ch 3 (counts as dc), *(3 dc, ch 4, 3 dc) in next ch-6 loop**, dc in next puff st; rep from * around, ending last rep at **, sl st in first sc to join.

Rnd 3: Ch 3 (counts as dc), dc in each of next 3 dc, *(2 dc, ch 4, 2 dc) in next ch-4 loop**, dc in each of next 7 dc; rep from * around, ending last rep at **, dc in each of next 3 dc, sl st in 3rd ch of beg ch to join. Fasten off.

G

95

2-tr puff st:
(Yo [twice], insert hook in next st, yo, draw yarn through st, [draw yarn through 2 loops on hook] twice) twice in same st, yo, draw yarn through 3 loops on hook.

Rnd 1: (Ch 4, 2-tr puff st in 4th ch from hook) 4 times, sl st in ch at base of first puff st to join.

Rnd 2: Ch 1, *sc bet 2 puff sts, ch 11, skip next ch-4 loop; rep from * around, sl st in first sc to join.

Rnd 3: Ch 3 (counts as dc), *(6 dc, ch 3, 6 dc) in next ch-11 loop**, dc in next sc; rep from * around, ending last rep at **, sl st in 3rd ch of beg ch to join. Fasten off.

96

2-dc puff st: *(Yo, insert hook in next space, yo, draw yarn through space, draw yarn through 2 loops on hook) twice in same space, yo, draw yarn through 3 loops on hook.*

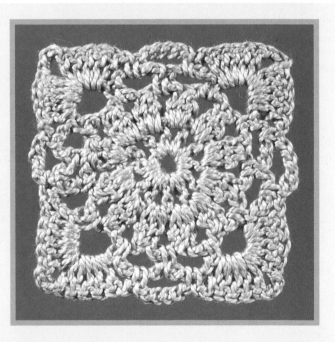

3-dc puff st: *(Yo, insert hook in next space, yo, draw yarn through space, draw yarn through 2 loops on hook) 3 times in same space, yo, draw yarn through 4 loops on hook.*

Ch 6 and sl st in first ch to form a ring.

Rnd 1: Ch 4 (counts as dc, ch 1), (dc, ch 1) 11 times in ring, sl st in 3rd ch of beg ch to join.

Rnd 2: Sl st in next ch-1 space, ch 3 (counts as dc), 2-dc puff st in same ch-1 space, ch 3, (3-dc puff st, ch 3) in each ch-1 space around, sl st in first puff st to join.

Rnd 3: Sl st in next ch-3 loop, ch 1, (sc, ch 5) in each ch-3 loop around, sl st in first sc to join.

Rnd 4: Sl st to the center of next ch-5 loop, ch 1, *sc in ch-5 loop, ch 1, (5 dc, ch 3, 5 dc) in next ch-5 loop, ch 1, sc in next ch-5 loop, ch 5; rep from * around, sl st in first sc to join. Fasten off.

97

2-dc puff st: *(Yo, insert hook in next space, yo, draw yarn through space, draw yarn through 2 loops on hook) twice in same space, yo, draw yarn through 3 loops on hook.*

3-dc puff st: *(Yo, insert hook in next space, yo, draw yarn through space, draw yarn through 2 loops on hook) 3 times in same space, yo, draw yarn through 4 loops on hook.*

Ch 6 and sl st in first ch to form a ring.

Rnd 1: Ch 3 (counts as dc), 2-dc puff st in ring, ch 2, (3-dc puff st, ch 2) 7 times in ring, sl st in first puff st to join.

Rnd 2: Sl st in next ch-2 space, ch 3 (counts as dc), 2 dc in same ch-2 space, *ch 2, (3-dc puff st, ch 3, 3-dc puff st) in next ch-2 space, ch 2**, 3 dc in next ch-2 space; rep from * around, ending last rep at **, sl st in 3rd ch of beg ch to join.

Rnd 3: Ch 3 (counts as dc), dc in each of next 2 dc, *2 dc in next ch-2 space, ch 2, (3-dc puff st, ch 3, 3-dc puff st) in next ch-3 loop, ch 2, 2 dc in next ch-2 space**, dc in each of next 3 dc; rep from * around, ending last rep at **, sl st in 3rd ch of beg ch to join.

Rnd 4: Ch 3 (counts as dc), dc in each of next 4 dc, *2 dc in next ch-2 space, ch 2, (3-dc puff st, ch 3, 3-dc puff st) in next ch-3 loop, ch 2, 2 dc in next ch-2 space**, dc in each of next 7 dc; rep from * around, ending last rep at **, dc in each of next 2 dc, sl st in 3rd ch of beg ch to join.

Rnd 5: Ch 3 (counts as dc), dc in each of next 6 dc, *2 dc in next ch-2 space, ch 2, (3-dc puff st, ch 3, 3-dc puff st) in next ch-3 loop, ch 2, 2 dc in next ch-2 space**, dc in each of next 9 dc; rep from * around, ending last rep at **, dc in each of next 4 dc, sl st in 3rd ch of beg ch to join. Fasten off.

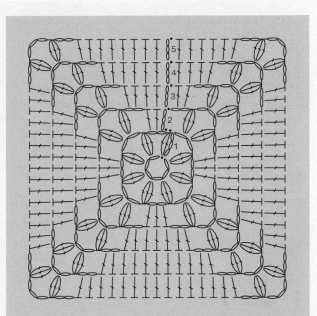

98

2-dc puff st: (Yo, insert hook in next space, yo, draw yarn through space, draw yarn through 2 loops on hook) twice in same space, yo, draw yarn through 3 loops on hook.

3-dc puff st: (Yo, insert hook in next space, yo, draw yarn through space, draw yarn through 2 loops on hook) 3 times in same space, yo, draw yarn through 4 loops on hook.

Ch 6 and sl st in first ch to form a ring.

Rnd 1: Ch 3 (counts as dc), 2-dc puff st in ring, ch 1, 3-dc puff st in ring, ch 5, *3-dc puff st in ring, ch 1, 3-dc puff st in ring, ch 5; rep from * twice, sl st in first puff st to join.

Rnd 2: Sl st in next ch-1 space, ch 3 (counts as dc), 2 dc in same ch-1 space, *ch 1, (3-dc puff st, ch 5, 3-dc puff st) in next ch-5 loop, ch 1**, 3 dc in next ch-1 space; rep from * around, ending last rep at **, sl st in 3rd ch of beg ch to join.

Rnd 3: Ch 3 (counts as dc), dc in each of next 2 dc, *dc in next ch-1 space, ch 2, (3-dc puff st, ch 5, 3-dc puff st) in next ch-5 loop, ch 2, dc in next ch-1 space**, dc in each of next 3 dc; rep from * around, ending last rep at **, sl st in 3rd ch of beg ch to join.

Rnd 4: Ch 3 (counts as dc), dc in each of next 3 dc, *dc in next ch-2 space, ch 2, (3-dc puff st, ch 6, 3-dc puff st) in next ch-5 loop, ch 2, dc in next ch-2 space**, dc in each of next 5 dc; rep from * around, ending last rep at **, dc in next dc, sl st in 3rd ch of beg ch to join.

Rnd 5: Ch 3 (counts as dc), dc in each of next 4 dc, *dc in next ch-2 space, ch 2, (3-dc puff st, ch 6, 3-dc puff st) in next ch-6 loop, ch 2, dc in next ch-2 space**, dc in each of next 7 dc; rep from * around, ending last rep at **, dc in each of next 2 dc, sl st in 3rd ch of beg ch to join. Fasten off.

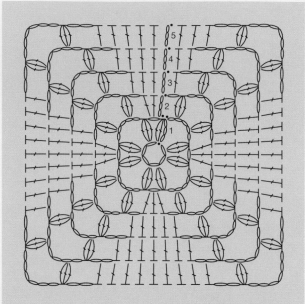

99

2-dc puff st: (Yo, insert hook in next space, yo, draw yarn through space, draw yarn through 2 loops on hook) twice in same space, yo, draw yarn through 3 loops on hook.

3-dc puff st: (Yo, insert hook in next space, yo, draw yarn through space, draw yarn through 2 loops on hook) 3 times in same space, yo, draw yarn through 4 loops on hook.

Ch 6 and sl st in first ch to form a ring.

Rnd 1: Ch 1, 12 sc in ring, sl st in first sc to join.

Rnd 2: Ch 3 (counts as dc), dc in next sc, ch 3, *dc in each of next 2 sc, ch 3; rep from * around, sl st in 3rd ch of beg ch to join.

Rnd 3: Sl st to next ch-3 loop, ch 3 (counts as dc), (2-dc puff st, ch 4, 3-dc puff st) in same ch-3 loop, ch 4, *(3-dc puff st, ch 4, 3-dc puff st) in next ch-3 loop, ch 4; rep from * around, sl st in first puff st to join.

Rnd 4: Sl st in next ch-4 loop, ch 1, (2 sc, ch 3, 2 sc) in each ch-4 loop around, sl st in first sc to join. Fasten off.

100

Ch 6 and sl st in first ch to form a ring.

Rnd 1: Ch 3 (counts as dc), 15 dc in ring, sl st in 3rd ch of beg ch to join.

Rnd 2: Ch 3 (counts as dc), 3-dc cluster, working first half-closed dc in same st as beg ch, work next 2 half-closed dc in next dc, yo, complete cluster, ch 5, *4-dc cluster, working first 2 half-closed dc in next dc, work next 2 half-closed dc in next dc, yo, complete cluster, ch 5; rep from * around, sl st in first cluster to join.

Rnd 3: Sl st in next ch-5 loop, ch 3 (counts as dc), (2 dc, ch 2, 3 dc) in same loop, (3 dc, ch 2, 3 dc) in each ch-5 loop around, sl st in 3rd ch of beg ch to join. Fasten off.

101

3-tr puff st: *(Yo [twice], insert hook in next space, yo, draw yarn through space, [yo, draw yarn through 2 loops on hook] twice) 3 times in same space, yo, draw yarn through 4 loops on hook.*

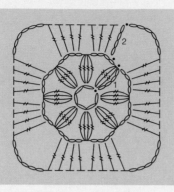

4-tr puff st: *(Yo [twice], insert hook in next space, yo, draw yarn through space, [yo, draw yarn through 2 loops on hook] twice) 4 times in same space, yo, draw yarn through 5 loops on hook.*

Ch 6 and sl st in first ch to form a ring.

Rnd 1: Ch 4 (counts as tr), 3-tr puff st in ring, ch 4, (4-tr puff st, ch 4) 7 times in ring, sl st in first puff st to join.

Rnd 2: Sl st in next ch-4 loop, ch 4 (counts as tr), 3 tr in same loop, *4 tr in next ch-4 loop, ch 6**, 4 tr in next ch-4 loop; rep from * around, ending last rep at **, sl st in 4th ch of beg ch to join. Fasten off.

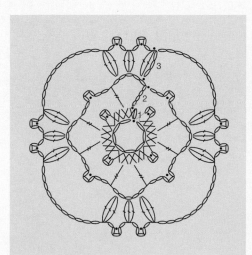

102

Picot: Ch 3, sl st in 3rd ch from hook.

2-dc puff st: (Yo, insert hook in next space, yo, draw yarn through space, draw yarn through 2 loops on hook) twice in same space, yo, draw yarn through 3 loops on hook.

3-dc puff st: (Yo, insert hook in next space, yo, draw yarn through space, draw yarn through 2 loops on hook) 3 times in same space, yo, draw yarn through 4 loops on hook.

Ch 8 and sl st in first ch to form a ring.

Rnd 1: Ch 1, (4 sc, picot, sc) 4 times in ring, sl st in first sc to join.

Rnd 2: Ch 9 (counts as tr, ch 5), tr in next sc, *ch 2, picot, ch 2**, tr in next sc, ch 5, tr in next sc; rep from * around, ending last rep at **, sl st in 4th ch of beg ch to join.

Rnd 3: Sl st to next ch-5 loop, ch 3 (counts as dc), (2-dc puff st, ch 1, picot, ch 1, 3-dc puff st, ch 1, picot, ch 1, 3-dc puff st) in same ch-5 loop, ch 11, *(3-dc puff st, ch 1, picot, ch 1, 3-dc puff st, ch 1, picot, ch 1, 3-dc puff st) in next ch-5 loop, ch 11; rep from * around, sl st in first puff st to join. Fasten off.

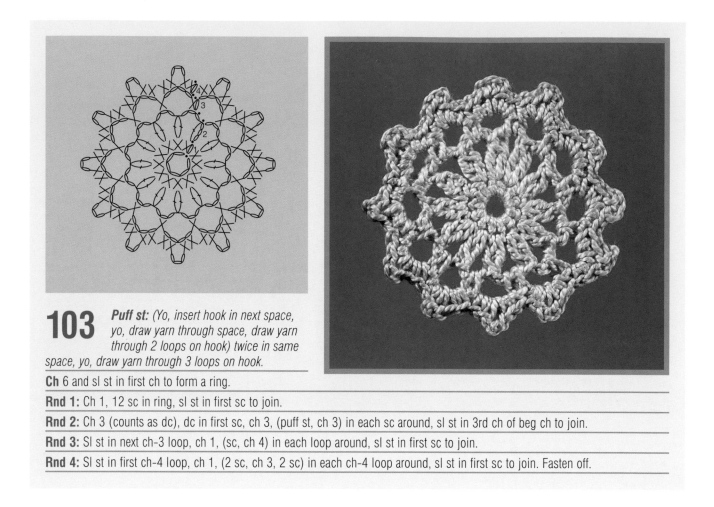

103 *Puff st: (Yo, insert hook in next space, yo, draw yarn through space, draw yarn through 2 loops on hook) twice in same space, yo, draw yarn through 3 loops on hook.*

Ch 6 and sl st in first ch to form a ring.

Rnd 1: Ch 1, 12 sc in ring, sl st in first sc to join.

Rnd 2: Ch 3 (counts as dc), dc in first sc, ch 3, (puff st, ch 3) in each sc around, sl st in 3rd ch of beg ch to join.

Rnd 3: Sl st in next ch-3 loop, ch 1, (sc, ch 4) in each loop around, sl st in first sc to join.

Rnd 4: Sl st in first ch-4 loop, ch 1, (2 sc, ch 3, 2 sc) in each ch-4 loop around, sl st in first sc to join. Fasten off.

104

3-tr puff st: (Yo [twice], insert hook in next space, yo, draw yarn through space, [yo, draw yarn through 2 loops on hook] twice) 3 times in same space, yo, draw yarn through 4 loops on hook.

2-dc puff st: (Yo, insert hook in next space, yo, draw yarn through space, draw yarn through 2 loops on hook) twice in same space, yo, draw yarn through 3 loops on hook.

3-dc puff st: (Yo, insert hook in next space, yo, draw yarn through space, draw yarn through 2 loops on hook) 3 times in same space, yo, draw yarn through 4 loops on hook.

Ch 6 and sl st in first ch to form a ring.

Rnd 1: Ch 4 (counts as dc, ch 1), (dc, ch 1) 7 times in ring, sl st in 3rd ch of beg ch to join.

Rnd 2: Ch 5 (counts as dc, ch 2), *dc in next ch-1 space, ch 2**, dc in next dc, ch 2; rep from * around, ending last rep at **, sl st in 3rd ch of beg ch to join.

Rnd 3: Ch 3 (counts as dc), 2 dc in next ch-2 space, *dc in next dc, 2 dc in next ch-2 space; rep from * around, sl st in 3rd ch of beg ch to join.

Rnd 4: Ch 6 (counts as dc, ch 3), skip next 2 dc, *dc in next dc, ch 3, skip next 2 dc; rep from * around, sl st in 3rd ch of beg ch to join.

Rnd 5: Sl st in next ch-3 loop, ch 3 (counts as dc), 2 dc in same loop, *ch 1, 3 dc in next ch-3 loop, ch 1, 3 dc in next ch-3 loop, ch 2, (3-tr puff st, ch 3, 3-tr puff st, ch 3, 3-tr puff st) in next ch-3 loop, ch 2**, 3 dc in next ch-3 loop; rep from * around, ending last rep at **, sl st in 3rd ch of beg ch to join.

Rnd 6: Sl st to next ch-1 space, ch 3 (counts as dc), 2-dc puff st in same space, *ch 3, (3-dc puff st, ch 3) in each of next 2 spaces, (3-tr puff st, ch 3, 3-tr puff st, ch 3) in each of next 2 ch-3 loops, 3-dc puff st in next ch-3 loop, ch 3**, 3-dc puff st in next ch-3 loop; rep from * around, ending last rep at **, sl st in first puff st to join. Fasten off.

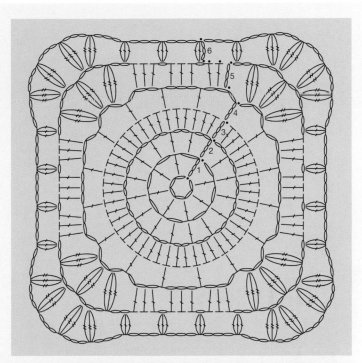

105

2-dc puff st: (Yo, insert hook in next space, yo, draw yarn through space, draw yarn through 2 loops on hook) twice in same space, yo, draw yarn through 3 loops on hook.

3-tr puff st: (Yo [twice], insert hook in next st, yo, draw yarn through st, [yo, draw yarn through 2 loops on hook] twice) 3 times in same st, yo, draw yarn through 4 loops on hook.

4-tr puff st: (Yo [twice], insert hook in next st, yo, draw yarn through st, [yo, draw yarn through 2 loops on hook] twice) 4 times in same st, yo, draw yarn through 5 loops on hook.

Picot: Ch 4, sl st in 4th ch from hook.

Ch 6 and sl st in first ch to form a ring.

Rnd 1: Ch 3 (counts as dc), dc in ring, ch 3, (2-dc puff st, ch 3) 9 times in ring, sl st in 3rd ch of beg ch to join.

Rnd 2: Ch 4 (counts as tr), 3-tr puff st in first dc, ch 5, *(4-tr puff st, ch 5) in each puff st around, sl st in first puff st to join.

Rnd 3: Sl st in next ch-5 loop, ch 1, (3 sc, picot, 3 sc) in each ch-5 loop around, sl st in first sc to join. Fasten off.

106 *2-dc puff st:* (Yo, insert hook in next space, yo, draw yarn through space, draw yarn through 2 loops on hook) twice in same space, yo, draw yarn through 3 loops on hook.

3-dc puff st: (Yo, insert hook in next space, yo, draw yarn through space, draw yarn through 2 loops on hook) 3 times in same space, yo, draw yarn through 4 loops on hook.

Ch 6 and sl st in first ch to form a ring.

Rnd 1: Ch 3 (counts as dc), 2-dc puff st in ring, ch 3, (3-dc puff st, ch 3) 7 times in ring, sl st in first puff st to join.

Rnd 2: Sl st in next ch-3 loop, ch 1, (sc, ch 5) in each ch-3 loop around, sl st in first sc to join.

Rnd 3: Sl st in next ch-5 loop, ch 1, 5 sc in each ch-5 loop around, sl st in first sc to join.

Rnd 4: Sl st in each of next 2 sc, ch 1, *sc in sc, ch 7, skip next 4 sc; rep from * around sl st in first sc to join.

Rnd 5: Sl st in next ch-7 loop, ch 1, (4 sc, ch 3, 4 sc) in each ch-7 loop around, sl st in first sc to join. Fasten off.

107 *2-dc puff st: (Yo, insert hook in next space, yo, draw yarn through space, draw yarn through 2 loops on hook) twice in same space, yo, draw yarn through 3 loops on hook.*

3-dc puff st: (Yo, insert hook in next space, yo, draw yarn through space, draw yarn through 2 loops on hook) 3 times in same space, yo, draw yarn through 4 loops on hook.

Ch 6 and sl st in first ch to form a ring.

Rnd 1: Ch 3 (counts as dc), 15 dc in ring, sl st in 3rd ch of beg ch to join.

Rnd 2: Ch 5 (counts as dc, ch 2), skip first st, (dc, ch 2) in each dc around, sl st in 3rd ch of beg ch to join.

Rnd 3: Sl st in next ch-2 space, ch 3 (counts as dc), 2-dc puff st in first ch-2 space, ch 5, (3-dc puff st, ch 5) in each ch-2 space around, sl st in first puff st to join.

Rnd 4: Sl st to center of first ch-5 loop, ch 1, (sc, ch 5) in each ch-5 loop around sl st in first sc to join. Fasten off.

108

3-tr puff st: (Yo [twice], insert hook in next space, yo, draw yarn through space, [yo, draw yarn through 2 loops on hook] twice) 3 times in same space, yo, draw yarn through 4 loops on hook.

4-tr puff st: (Yo [twice], insert hook in next space, yo, draw yarn through space, [yo, draw yarn through 2 loops on hook] twice) 4 times in same space, yo, draw yarn through 5 loops on hook.

Ch 10 and sl st in first ch to form a ring.

Rnd 1: Ch 4 (counts as tr), 27 tr in ring, sl st in 4th ch of beg ch to join.

Rnd 2: Ch 1, sc in first st, ch 5, skip next tr, *sc in next tr, ch 5, skip next tr; rep from * around, sl st in first sc to join.

Rnd 3: Sl st to center of first ch-5 loop, ch 4 (counts as tr), 3-tr puff st in first ch-5 loop, ch 7, (4-tr puff st, ch 7) in each ch-5 loop around, sl st in first puff st to join. Fasten off.

109

3-dc puff st: (Yo, insert hook in next space, yo, draw yarn through space, draw yarn through 2 loops on hook) 3 times in same space, yo, draw yarn through 4 loops on hook.

4-dc puff st: (Yo, insert hook in next space, yo, draw yarn through space, draw yarn through 2 loops on hook) 4 times in same space, yo, draw yarn through 4 loops on hook.

Ch 10 and sl st in first ch to form a ring.

Rnd 1: Ch 4 (counts as tr), tr in ring, ch 2, (2 tr, ch 2) 11 times in ring, sl st in 4th ch of beg ch to join.

Rnd 2: Sl st to next ch-2 space, ch 3 (counts as dc), 3-dc puff st in first ch-2 space, ch 8, (4-dc puff st, ch 8) in each ch-2 space around, sl st in first puff st to join.

Rnd 3: Sl st to center of first ch-8 loop, ch 1, (sc, ch 7) in each ch-8 loop around, sl st in first sc to join. Fasten off.

110 *2-tr puff st: (Yo [twice], insert hook in next space, yo, draw yarn through space, [yo, draw yarn through 2 loops on hook] twice) twice in same space, yo, draw yarn through 3 loops on hook.*

3-dc puff st: (Yo, insert hook in next space, yo, draw yarn through space, draw yarn through 2 loops on hook) 3 times in same space, yo, draw yarn through 4 loops on hook.

4-dc puff st: (Yo, insert hook in next space, yo, draw yarn through space, draw yarn through 2 loops on hook) 4 times in same space, yo, draw yarn through 4 loops on hook.

Ch 9 and sl st in first ch to form a ring.

Rnd 1: Ch 4 (counts as tr), tr in ring, ch 2, (2-tr puff st, ch 2) 11 times in ring, sl st in 4th ch of beg ch to join.

Rnd 2: Sl st in next ch-2 space, ch 3 (counts as dc), 3-dc puff st in first ch-2 space, ch 5, (4-dc puff st, ch 5) in each ch-2 space around, sl st in first puff st to join.

Rnd 3: Sl st to center of first ch-5 loop, ch 1, (sc, ch 7) in each ch-5 loop around, sl st in first sc to join. Fasten off.

111

2-tr puff st: *(Yo [twice], insert hook in next space, yo, draw yarn through space, [yo, draw yarn through 2 loops on hook] twice) twice in same space, yo, draw yarn through 3 loops on hook.*

3-tr puff st: *(Yo [twice], insert hook in next space, yo, draw yarn through space, [yo, draw yarn through 2 loops on hook] twice) 3 times in same space, yo, draw yarn through 4 loops on hook.*

Ch 10 and sl st in first ch to form a ring.

Rnd 1: Ch 4 (counts as tr), 2-tr puff st in ring, ch 6, (3-tr puff st, ch 6) 7 times in ring, sl st in first puff st to join.

Rnd 2: Sl st to center of first ch-6 loop, ch 4 (counts as tr), (2-tr puff st, ch 5, 3-tr puff st) in first ch-6 loop, *ch 6, (sc, ch 5, 3-tr puff st) in next ch-6 loop, ch 6**, (3-tr puff st, ch 5, 3-tr puff st) in next ch-6 loop; rep from * around, ending last rep at **, sl st in first puff st to join. Fasten off.

112

Ch 8 and sl st in first ch to form a ring.

Rnd 1: Ch 3 (counts as dc), 19 dc in ring, sl st in 3rd ch of beg ch to join.

Rnd 2: Ch 4 (counts as dc, ch 1), skip next dc, *dc bet last skipped and next dc, ch 1, skip next dc; rep from * around, ending with (dc, ch 1) in space bet last dc and beg ch, sl st in 3rd ch of beg ch to join.

Rnd 3: Ch 3 (counts as dc), skip next ch-1 space, dc in next dc, ch 5, *work 2-dc cluster, working first half-closed dc in same dc holding last dc, skip next ch-1 space, work 2nd half-closed dc in next dc, yo, complete cluster, ch 5; rep from * around, sl st in 3rd ch of beg ch to join.

Rnd 4: Sl st to center of first ch-5 loop, ch 1, (sc, ch 5) in each ch-5 loop around, sl st in first sc to join. Fasten off.

113

2-tr puff st: (Yo [twice], insert hook in next space, yo, draw yarn through space, [yo, draw yarn through 2 loops on hook] twice) twice in same space, yo, draw yarn through 3 loops on hook.

3-tr puff st: (Yo [twice], insert hook in next space, yo, draw yarn through space, [yo, draw yarn through 2 loops on hook] twice) 3 times in same space, yo, draw yarn through 4 loops on hook.

5-tr puff st: (Yo [twice], insert hook in next space, yo, draw yarn through space, [yo, draw yarn through 2 loops on hook] twice) 5 times in same space, yo, draw yarn through 6 loops on hook.

Ch 8 and sl st in first ch to form a ring.

Rnd 1: Ch 6 (counts as dc, ch 3), (dc, ch 3) 7 times in ring, sl st in 3rd ch of beg ch to join.

Rnd 2: Sl st in first ch-3 loop, ch 4 (counts as tr), (2-tr puff st, ch 5, 3-tr puff st) in first ch-3 loop, ch 5, (3-tr puff st, ch 5, 3-tr puff st, ch 5) in each ch-3 loop around, sl st in first puff st to join.

Rnd 3: Sl st in next ch-5 loop, ch 1, (sc, ch 4, 5-tr puff st) in first ch-5 loop, *ch 5, 5-tr puff st in next ch-5 loop, ch 5**, (sc, ch 4, 5-tr puff st) in next ch-5 loop; rep from * around, ending last rep at **, sl st in first sc to join. Fasten off.

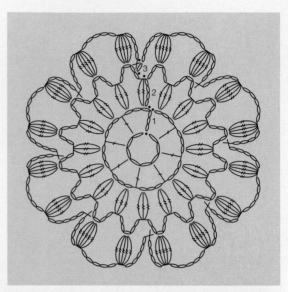

114

3-tr puff st: *(Yo [twice], insert hook in next space, yo, draw yarn through space, [yo, draw yarn through 2 loops on hook] twice) 3 times in same space, yo, draw yarn through 4 loops on hook.*

4-tr puff st: *(Yo [twice], insert hook in next space, yo, draw yarn through space, [yo, draw yarn through 2 loops on hook] twice) 4 times in same space, yo, draw yarn through 5 loops on hook.*

Ch 6 and sl st in first ch to form a ring.

Rnd 1: Ch 3 (counts as dc), 13 dc in ring, sl st in 3rd ch of beg ch to join.

Rnd 2: Ch 10 (counts as dtr, ch 5), skip first st, (dtr, ch 5) in each dc around, sl st in 5th ch of beg ch to join.

Rnd 3: Sl st to center of next ch-5 loop, ch 4 (counts as tr), 3-tr puff st in first ch-5 loop, ch 5, (4-tr puff st, ch 5) in each ch-5 loop around, sl st in first puff st to join.

Rnd 4: Sl st to center of first ch-5 loop, ch 3 (counts as dc), 2 dc in first ch-5 loop, ch 5, (3 dc, ch 5) in each ch-5 loop around, sl st in 3rd ch of beg ch to join. Fasten off.

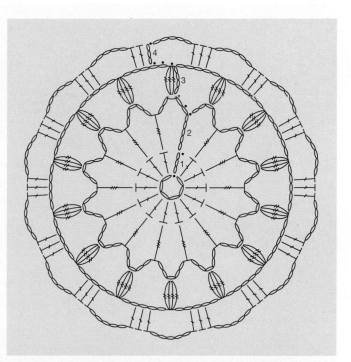

115

2-dc puff st: *(Yo, insert hook in next st or space, yo, draw yarn through st or space, draw yarn through 2 loops on hook) twice in same st or space, yo, draw yarn through 3 loops on hook.*

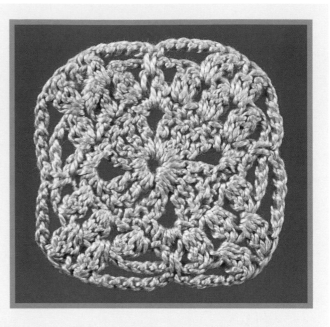

3-dc puff st: *(Yo, insert hook in next st or space, yo, draw yarn through st or space, draw yarn through 2 loops on hook) 3 times in same st or space, yo, draw yarn through 4 loops on hook.*

Ch 6 and sl st in first ch to form a ring.

Rnd 1: Ch 4 (counts as tr), 3 tr in ring, ch 2, (4 tr, ch 2) 3 times in ring, sl st in 4th ch of beg ch to join.

Rnd 2: Ch 1, sc in first 4 sts, *(2 sc, ch 2, 2 sc) in next ch-2 space**, sc in each of next 4 tr; rep from * around, ending last rep at **, sl st in first sc to join.

Rnd 3: Ch 3 (counts as dc), 2-dc puff st in first sc, *(ch 1, skip next sc, 3-dc puff st in next sc) twice, ch 7, skip next (sc, ch 2, 2 sc)**, 3-dc puff st in next sc; rep from * around, ending last rep at **, sl st in first puff st to join.

Rnd 4: Sl st in next ch-1 space, ch 3 (counts as dc), 2-dc puff st in first ch-1 space, *ch1, 3-dc puff st in next ch-1 space, ch 6, sc in next ch-7 loop, ch 6**, 3-dc puff st in next ch-1 space; rep from * around, ending last rep at **, sl st in first puff st to join. Fasten off.

116

2-dc puff st: (Yo, insert hook in next st or space, yo, draw yarn through st or space, draw yarn through 2 loops on hook) twice in same st or space, yo, draw yarn through 3 loops on hook.

Ch 6 and sl st in first ch to form a ring.

Rnd 1: Ch 1, 12 sc in ring, sl st in first sc to join.

Rnd 2: Ch 3 (counts as dc), dc in first sc, ch 3, (2-dc puff st, ch 3) in each dc around, sl st in 3rd ch of beg ch to join.

Rnd 3: Sl st in first ch-3 loop, ch 1, (sc, ch 4) in each ch-3 loop around, sl st in first sc to join.

Rnd 4: Sl st in next ch-4 loop, ch 1, (2 sc, ch 3, 2 sc) in each ch-4 loop around, sl st in first sc to join.

Rnd 5: Sl st in next sc, sl st in next ch-3 loop, ch 3 (counts as dc), (dc, ch 4, 2-dc puff st) in first ch-3 loop, (2-dc puff st, ch 3, 2-dc puff st) in each ch-3 loop around, sl st in 3rd ch of beg ch to join.

Rnd 6: Sl st in next ch-4 loop, ch 1 (2 sc, ch 3, 2 sc) in each ch-4 loop around, sl st in first sc to join. Fasten off.

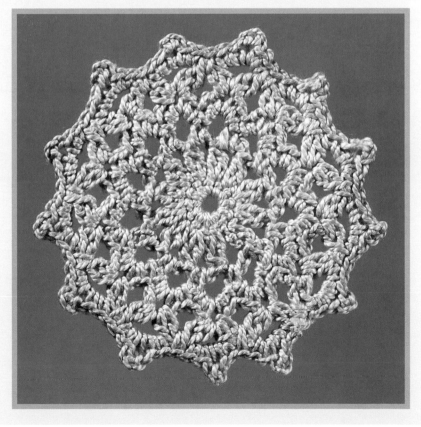

.8.
Popcorn Stitches

117 ***Beginning popcorn (beg pop):*** Ch 3 (counts as dc), 4 dc in same space, drop loop from hook, insert hook from front to back in 3rd ch of beg ch, place dropped loop on hook, draw loop through st.

Popcorn (pop): 5 dc in same space, drop loop from hook, insert hook from front to back in first dc of 5-dc group, place dropped loop on hook, draw loop through st.

Picot: Ch 3, sl st in 3rd ch from hook.

Ch 6 and sl st in first ch to form a ring.

Rnd 1: Beg pop in ring, ch 3, (pop, ch 3) 7 times in ring, sl st in first pop to join.

Rnd 2: Sl st in first ch-3 loop, ch 3 (counts as dc), dc in first ch-3 loop, *(3 dc, ch 3, 3 dc) in next ch-3 loop**, 2 dc in next ch-3 loop; rep from * around, ending last rep at **, sl st in 3rd ch of beg ch to join.

Rnd 3: Ch 1, sc in first 5 sts, *(hdc, 2 dc, picot, 2 dc, hdc) in next ch-3 loop**, sc in each of next 8 dc; rep from * around, ending last rep at **, sc in each of next 3 dc, sl st in 3rd ch of beg ch to join. Fasten off.

118 *Popcorn (pop):* 4 dc in same st, drop loop from hook, insert hook from front to back in first dc of 4-dc group, place dropped loop on hook, draw loop through st.

Ch 6 and sl st in first ch to form a ring.

Rnd 1: Ch 5 (counts as dc, ch 2), (dc, ch 2) 7 times in ring, sl st in 3rd ch of beg ch to join.

Rnd 2: Ch 3 (counts as dc), 2 dc in first st, ch 2, skip next ch-2 space, *3 dc in next dc, ch 2, skip next ch-2 space; rep from * around, sl st in 3rd ch of beg ch to join.

Rnd 3: Ch 3 (counts as dc), dc in first st, *dc in next dc, 2 dc in next dc, ch 2, skip next ch-2 space**, 2 dc in next dc; rep from * around, ending last rep at **, sl st in 3rd ch of beg ch to join.

Rnd 4: Ch 1, *sc in dc, ch 4, skip next dc, pop in next dc, ch 4, skip next dc, sc in next dc, ch 5, skip next ch-2 space; rep from * around, sl st in first sc to join. Fasten off.

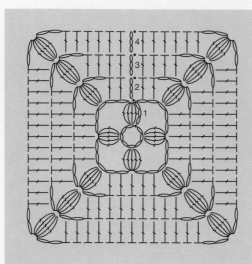

119

Beginning popcorn (beg pop): Ch 3 (counts as dc), 4 dc in same space, drop loop from hook, insert hook from front to back in 3rd ch of beg ch, place dropped loop on hook, draw loop through st.

Popcorn (pop): 5 dc in same space, drop loop from hook, insert hook from front to back in first dc of 5-dc group, place dropped loop on hook, draw loop through st.

Ch 8 and sl st in first ch to form a ring.

Rnd 1: Beg pop in ring, ch 5, (pop, ch 5) 3 times in ring, sl st in first pop to join.

Rnd 2: Ch 3 (counts as dc), *(2 dc, ch 2, pop, ch 2, 2 dc) in next ch-5 loop**, dc in next pop; rep from * around, ending last rep at **, sl st in 3rd ch of beg ch to join.

Rnd 3: Ch 3 (counts as dc), dc in each of next 2 dc, *2 dc in next ch-2 space, ch 2, pop in next pop, ch 2, 2 dc in next ch-2 space**, dc in each of next 5 dc; rep from * around, ending last rep at **, dc in each of next 2 dc, sl st in 3rd ch of beg ch to join.

Rnd 4: Ch 3 (counts as dc), dc in each of next 4 dc, *2 dc in next ch-2 space, ch 2, pop in next pop, ch 2, 2 dc in next ch-2 space**, dc in each of next 9 dc; rep from * around, ending last rep at **, dc in each of next 4 dc, sl st in 3rd ch of beg ch to join. Fasten off.

120

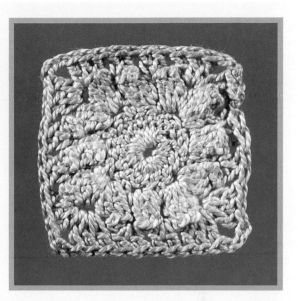

Beginning popcorn (beg pop):
Ch 3 (counts as dc), 3 dc in same space, drop loop from hook, insert hook from front to back in 3rd ch of beg ch, place dropped loop on hook, draw loop through st.

Popcorn (pop): 4 dc in same space, drop loop from hook, insert hook from front to back in first dc of 4-dc group, place dropped loop on hook, draw loop through st.

Ch 6 and sl st in first ch to form a ring.

Rnd 1: Ch 3 (counts as dc), 15 dc in ring, sl st in 3rd ch of beg ch to join.

Rnd 2: Ch 1, sc in first st, ch 3, skip next dc, *sc in next dc, ch 3, skip next dc; rep from * around, sl st in first sc to join.

Rnd 3: Sl st in next ch-3 loop, beg pop in same ch-3 loop, *ch 1, (pop, ch 3, pop) in next ch-3 loop, ch 1**, pop in next ch-3 loop; rep from * around, ending last rep at **, sl st in first pop to join.

Rnd 4: Sl st in next ch-1 space, ch 3 (counts as dc), dc in same ch-1 space, *ch 1, (3 dc, ch 3, 3 dc) in next ch-3 loop, ch 1, 2 dc in next ch-1 space, ch 1**, 2 dc in next ch-1 space; rep from * around, ending last rep at **, sl st in 3rd ch of beg ch to join. Fasten off.

121

Beginning popcorn (beg pop):
Ch 3 (counts as dc), 4 dc in same st, drop loop from hook, insert hook from front to back in 3rd ch of beg ch, place dropped loop on hook, draw loop through st.

Popcorn (pop): 5 dc in same st, drop loop from hook, insert hook from front to back in first dc of 5-dc group, place dropped loop on hook, draw loop through st.

Ch 12 and sl st in first ch to form a ring.

Rnd 1: Ch 3 (counts as dc), 4 dc in ring, ch 2, (5 dc, ch 2) 3 times in ring, sl st in 3rd ch of beg ch to join.

Rnd 2: Ch 3 (counts as dc), dc in each of next 4 dc, *(dc, ch 3, dc) in next ch-3 loop**, dc in each of next 5 dc; rep from * around, ending last rep at **, sl st in 3rd ch of beg ch to join.

Rnd 3: Ch 3 (counts as dc), *pop in next dc, dc in next dc, pop in next dc, dc in each of next 2 dc, (dc, ch 3, dc) in next ch-3 loop**, dc in each of next 2 dc; rep from * around, ending last rep at **, dc in next dc, sl st in 3rd ch of beg ch to join.

Rnd 4: Ch 3 (counts as dc), dc in each of next 6 sts, *(dc, ch 4, dc) in next ch-3 loop**, dc in each of next 9 dc; rep from * around, ending last rep at **, dc in each of next 2 dc, sl st in 3rd ch of beg ch to join.

Rnd 5: Beg pop in first st, *(dc in next dc, pop in next dc) twice, dc in each of next 3 dc, (dc, ch 4, dc) in next ch-4 loop, dc in each of next 3 dc**, pop in next dc; rep from * around, ending last rep at **, sl st in first pop to join.

Rnd 6: Ch 3 (counts as dc), dc in each of next 8 sts, *(dc, ch 5, dc) in next ch-4 loop**, dc in each of next 13 sts; rep from * around, ending last rep at **, dc in each of next 4 dc, sl st in 3rd ch of beg ch to join. Fasten off.

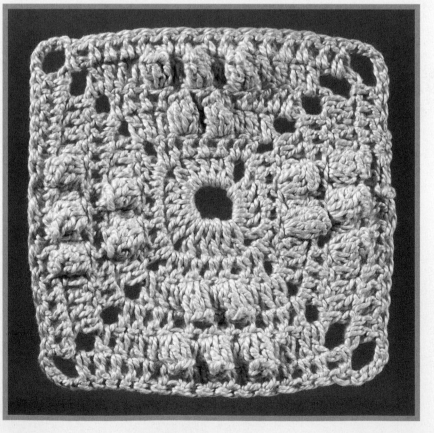

122

Beginning popcorn (beg pop): Ch 3 (counts as dc), 4 dc in same space, drop loop from hook, insert hook from front to back in 3rd ch of beg ch, place dropped loop on hook, draw loop through st.

Popcorn (pop): 5 dc in same space, drop loop from hook, insert hook from front to back in first dc of 5-dc group, place dropped loop on hook, draw loop through st.

Ch 10 and sl st in first ch to form a ring.

Rnd 1: Beg pop in ring, ch 1, *pop in ring, ch 4**, pop in ring, ch 1; rep from * twice, rep from * to ** once, sl st in first pop to join.

Rnd 2: Ch 5 (counts as dc, ch 2), skip next ch-1 space, *dc in next pop, ch 2, (pop, ch 4, pop) in next ch-4 loop, ch 2**, dc in next pop, ch 2; rep from * around, ending last rep at **, sl st in 3rd ch of beg ch to join.

Rnd 3: Ch 5 (counts as dc, ch 2), skip next ch-2 space, *dc in next dc, ch 2, skip next ch-2 space, dc in next pop, ch 2, (pop, ch 4, pop) in next ch-4 loop, ch 2, dc in next pop, ch 2, skip next ch-2 space**, dc in next dc, ch 2; rep from * around, ending last rep at **, sl st in 3rd ch of beg ch to join.

Rnd 4: Ch 5 (counts as dc, ch 2), skip next ch-2 space, *(dc in next dc, ch 2, skip next ch-2 space) twice, dc in next pop, ch 2, (pop, ch 4, pop) in next ch-4 loop, ch 2, dc in next pop, ch 2, skip next ch-2 space, dc in next dc, ch 2, skip next ch-2 space**, dc in next dc, ch 2, skip next ch-2 space; rep from * around, ending last rep at **, sl st in 3rd ch of beg ch to join.

Rnd 5: Ch 5 (counts as dc, ch 2), skip next ch-2 space, *(dc in next dc, ch 2, skip next ch-2 space) 3 times, dc in next pop, ch 2, (pop, ch 4, pop) in next ch-4 loop, ch 2, dc in next pop, ch 2, skip next ch-2 space, (dc in next dc, ch 2, skip next ch-2 space) twice**, dc in next dc, ch 2, skip next ch-2 space; rep from * around, ending last rep at **, sl st in 3rd ch of beg ch to join. Fasten off.

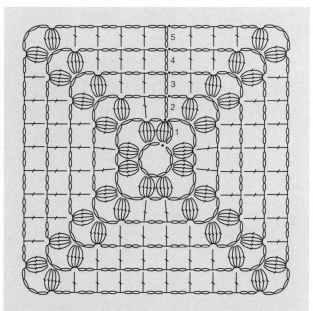

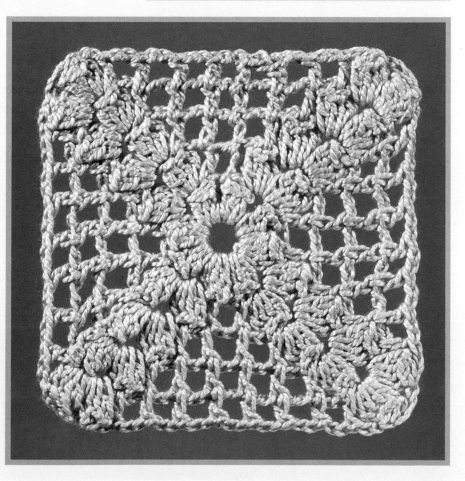

123

Beginning popcorn (beg pop): *Ch 3 (counts as dc), 3 dc in same st, drop loop from hook, insert hook from front to back in 3rd ch of beg ch, place dropped loop on hook, draw loop through st.*

Popcorn (pop): *4 dc in same st, drop loop from hook, insert hook from front to back in first dc of 4-dc group, place dropped loop on hook, draw loop through st.*

Ch 8 and sl st in first ch to form a ring.

Rnd 1: Ch 4 (counts as dc, ch 1), (dc, ch 1) 15 times in ring, sl st in 3rd ch of beg ch to join.

Rnd 2: Sl st in next ch-1 space, beg pop in first ch-1 space, ch 1, (pop, ch 1) in each ch-1 space around, sl st in first pop to join.

Rnd 3: Sl st in next ch-1 space, ch 3 (counts as dc), (dc, ch 3, 2 dc) in first ch-1 space, *ch 3, (sc, ch 3) in each of next 3 ch-1 spaces**, (2 dc, ch 3, 2 dc) in next ch-1 space; rep from * around, ending last rep at **, sl st in 3rd ch of beg ch to join.

Rnd 4: Sl st to next ch-3 loop, ch 3 (counts as dc), (3 dc, ch 2, 4 dc) in first ch-3 loop, *ch 2, skip next ch-3 loop, (4 dc, ch 2) in each of next 2 ch-3 loops, skip next ch-3 loop**, (4 dc, ch 2, 4 dc) in next ch-3 loop; rep from * around, ending last rep at **, sl st in 3rd ch of beg ch to join.

Rnd 5: Sl st to next ch-2 space, ch 3 (counts as dc), (2 dc, ch 2, 3 dc) in first ch-2 space, *(3 dc, ch 2) in each of next 3 ch-2 spaces** (3 dc, ch 2, 3 dc) in next ch-2 space; rep from * around, ending last rep at **, sl st in 3rd ch of beg ch to join.

Rnd 6: Sl st to next ch-2 space, ch 3 (counts as dc), (2 dc, ch 2, 3 dc) in first ch-2 space, *3 dc in each of next 4 ch-2 spaces** (3 dc, ch 2, 3 dc) in next ch-2 space; rep from * around, ending last rep at **, sl st in 3rd ch of beg ch to join. Fasten off.

124

Beginning popcorn (beg pop): *Ch 3 (counts as dc), 4 dc in same space, drop loop from hook, insert hook from front to back in 3rd ch of beg ch, place dropped loop on hook, draw loop through st.*

Popcorn (pop): *5 dc in same space, drop loop from hook, insert hook from front to back in first dc of 5-dc group, place dropped loop on hook, draw loop through st.*

Ch 6 and sl st in first ch to form a ring.

Rnd 1: Ch 3 (counts as dc), 15 dc in ring, sl st in 3rd ch of beg ch to join.

Rnd 2: Ch 5 (counts as dc, ch 2), (dc, ch 2) in each dc around, sl st in 3rd ch of beg ch to join.

Rnd 3: Sl st in first ch-2 space, beg pop in first ch-2 space, *ch 7, (pop, ch 5) in each of next 3 ch-2 spaces**, pop in next ch-2 space; rep from * around, ending last rep at **, sl st in first pop to join.

Rnd 4: Sl st to center of next ch-7 loop, ch 3 (counts as dc), (3 dc, ch 3, 4 dc) in first ch-7 loop, *ch 2, dc in next ch-5 loop, ch 2, (dc, ch 2, dc) in next ch-5 loop, ch 2, dc in next ch-5 loop, ch 2**, (4 dc, ch 3, 4 dc) in next ch-7 loop; rep from * around, ending last rep at **, sl st in 3rd ch of beg ch to join.

Rnd 5: Ch 3 (counts as dc), *dc in each of next 3 dc, (3 dc, ch 3, 3 dc) in next ch-3 loop, dc in each of next 4 dc, (ch 2, dc) in each of next 5 dc; rep from * around, omitting last dc, sl st in 3rd ch of beg ch to join.

Rnd 6: Ch 5 (counts as dc, ch 2), skip next 2 dc, *dc in each of next 4 dc, (3 dc, ch 3, 3 dc) in next ch-3 loop, dc in each of next 4 dc, ch 2, skip next 2 dc, (dc, ch 2) in each of next 5 dc**, dc in next dc, ch 2, skip next 2 dc; rep from * around, ending last rep at **, sl st in 3rd ch of beg ch to join. Fasten off.

.9.
Post Stitches

125

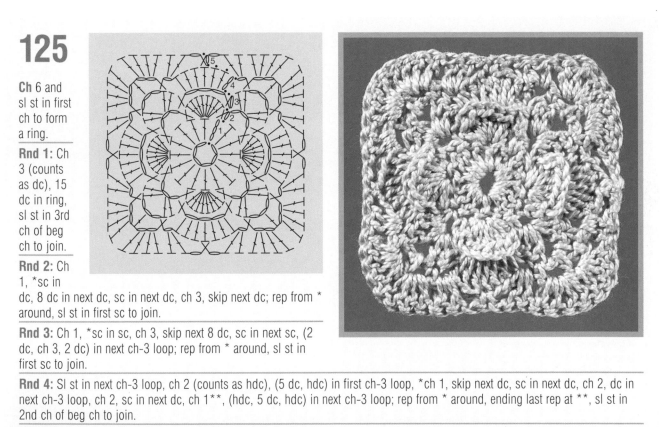

Ch 6 and sl st in first ch to form a ring.

Rnd 1: Ch 3 (counts as dc), 15 dc in ring, sl st in 3rd ch of beg ch to join.

Rnd 2: Ch 1, *sc in dc, 8 dc in next dc, sc in next dc, ch 3, skip next dc; rep from * around, sl st in first sc to join.

Rnd 3: Ch 1, *sc in sc, ch 3, skip next 8 dc, sc in next sc, (2 dc, ch 3, 2 dc) in next ch-3 loop; rep from * around, sl st in first sc to join.

Rnd 4: Sl st in next ch-3 loop, ch 2 (counts as hdc), (5 dc, hdc) in first ch-3 loop, *ch 1, skip next dc, sc in next dc, ch 2, dc in next ch-3 loop, ch 2, sc in next dc, ch 1**, (hdc, 5 dc, hdc) in next ch-3 loop; rep from * around, ending last rep at **, sl st in 2nd ch of beg ch to join.

Rnd 5: Sl st in each of next 3 dc, ch 1, *sc in dc, ch 1, 2 dc in next ch-1 space, 4 dc in each of next 2 ch-2 spaces, 2 dc in next ch-1 space; ch 1; rep from * around, sl st in first sc to join. Fasten off.

126

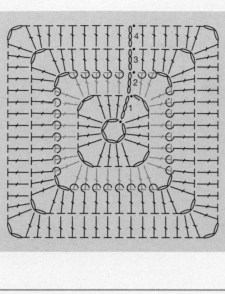

Front post double crochet (FPdc): *Yo, insert hook from front to back to front again around the post of next st, yo, draw yarn through st, (yo, draw yarn through 2 loops on hook) twice.*

Ch 6 and sl st in first ch to form a ring.

Rnd 1: Ch 3 (counts as dc), 3 dc in ring, ch 2, (4 dc, ch 2) 3 times in ring, sl st in 3rd ch of beg ch to join.

Rnd 2: Ch 3 (counts as dc), dc in each of next 3 dc, *(2 dc, ch 2, dc) in next ch-2 space**, dc in each of next 4 dc; rep from * around, ending last rep at **, sl st in 3rd ch of beg ch to join.

Rnd 3: Ch 3 (counts as dc), *FPdc in each of next 5 dc, (2 dc, ch 2, 2 dc) in next ch-2 space, FPdc in each of next 3 dc; rep from * around, omitting last FPdc, sl st in 3rd ch of beg ch to join.

Rnd 4: Ch 3 (counts as dc), dc in each of next 7 dc, *(2 dc, ch 2, 2 dc) in next ch-2 space, dc in each of next 5 dc; rep from * around, omitting last dc, sl st in 3rd ch of beg ch to join. Fasten off.

127

Picot: *Ch 3, sl st in 3rd ch from hook.*

Front post treble crochet (FPtr): *Yo (twice), insert hook from front to back to front again around the post of next st, yo, draw yarn through st, (yo, draw yarn through 2 loops on hook) 3 times.*

Ch 6 and sl st in first ch to form a ring.

Rnd 1: Ch 5 (counts as dc, ch 2), (dc, ch 2) 7 times in ring, sl st in 3rd ch of beg ch to join.

Rnd 2: Ch 3 (counts as dc), *(2 dc, picot, dc) in next ch 2 space**, dc in next dc; rep from * around, ending last rep at **, sl st in 3rd ch of beg ch to join.

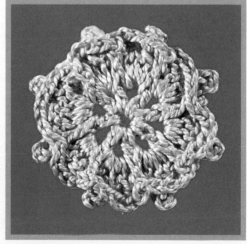

Rnd 3: Ch 1, *sc in dc, FPtr around the post of next corresponding dc 2 rnds below, ch 5, skip next (2 dc, picot, dc) in current row; rep from * around, sl st in first sc to join. Fasten off.

128

3-dc puff st: *(Yo, insert hook in next space, yo, draw yarn through space, draw yarn through 2 loops on hook) 3 times in same space, yo, draw yarn through 4 loops on hook.*

4-dc puff st: *(Yo, insert hook in next space, yo, draw yarn through space, draw yarn through 2 loops on hook) 4 times in same space, yo, draw yarn through 4 loops on hook.*

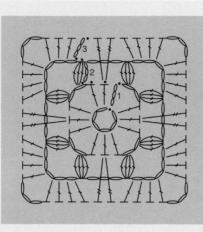

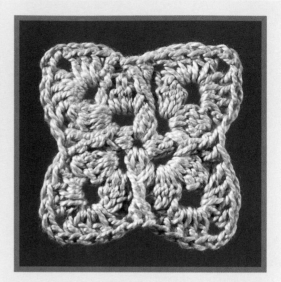

Ch 6 and sl st in first ch to form a ring.

Rnd 1: Ch 3 (counts as dc), 2 dc in ring, ch 2, (3 dc, ch 2) 3 times in ring, sl st in 3rd ch of beg ch to join.

Rnd 2: Sl st to next ch-2 space, ch 3 (counts as dc), (3-dc puff st, ch 5, 4-dc puff st) in first ch-2 space, ch 3, *(4-dc puff st, ch 5, 4-dc puff st) in next ch-2 space, ch 3; rep from * around, sl st in 3rd ch of beg ch to join.

Rnd 3: Sl st in next ch-5 loop, ch 3 (counts as dc), (3 dc, ch 3, 4 dc) in first ch-5 loop, *working over next ch-3 loop, work 2 tr in center dc 2 rnds below**, (4 dc, ch 3, 4 dc) in next ch-5 loop; rep from * around, ending last rep at **, sl st in 3rd ch of beg ch to join. Fasten off.

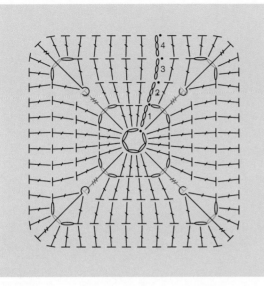

129 *Front post treble crochet (FPtr):* Yo (twice), insert hook from front to back to front again around the post of next st, yo, draw yarn through st, (yo, draw yarn through 2 loops on hook) 3 times.

Ch 6 and sl st in first ch to form a ring.

Rnd 1: Ch 3 (counts as dc), 3 dc in ring, ch 3, (4 dc, ch 3) 3 times in ring, sl st in 3rd ch of beg ch to join.

Rnd 2: Ch 3 (counts as dc), *dc in each of next 3 dc, dc in next ch-3 loop, working over ch-3 loop, dtr in center ring, dc in same ch-3 loop in Rnd 1**, dc in next dc; rep from * around, ending last rep at **, sl st in 3rd ch of beg ch to join.

Rnd 3: Ch 3 (counts as dc), *dc in each of next 4 dc, (dc, ch 3, dc) in next dtr, dc in each of next 2 dc; rep from * around, omitting last dc, sl st in 3rd ch of beg ch to join.

Rnd 4: Ch 3 (counts as dc), *dc in each of next 5 dc, 2 dc in next ch-3 loop, working over ch-3 loop, FPtr in corresponding dtr 2 rnds below, 2 dc in same ch-3 loop in Rnd 3**, dc in each of next 3 dc; rep from * around, omitting last dc, sl st in 3rd ch of beg ch to join. Fasten off.

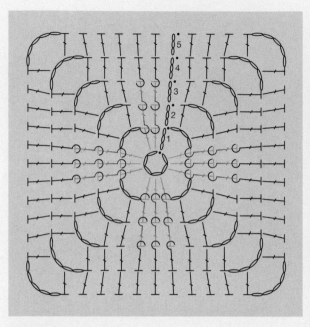

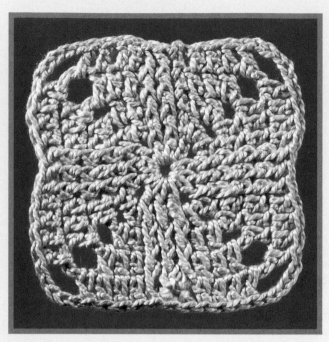

130 ***Front post double crochet (FPdc):*** *Yo, insert hook from front to back to front again around the post of next st, yo, draw yarn through st, (yo, draw yarn through 2 loops on hook) twice.*

Ch 6 and sl st in first ch to form a ring.

Rnd 1: Ch 3 (counts as dc), 2 dc in ring, ch 3, (3 dc, ch 3) 3 times in ring, sl st in 3rd ch of beg ch to join.

Rnd 2: Ch 3 (counts as dc), FPdc in each of next 2 dc, *(dc, ch 4, dc) in next ch-3 loop**, FPdc in each of next 3 dc; rep from * around, ending last rep at **, sl st in 3rd ch of beg ch to join.

Rnd 3: Ch 3 (counts as dc), FPdc in each of next 2 dc, *dc in next dc, (dc, ch 4, dc) in next ch-4 loop, dc in next dc**, FPdc in each of next 3 dc; rep from * around, ending last rep at **, sl st in 3rd ch of beg ch to join.

Rnd 4: Ch 3 (counts as dc), FPdc in each of next 2 dc, *dc in each of next 2 dc, (dc, ch 5, dc) in next ch-4 loop, dc in each of next 2 dc**, FPdc in each of next 3 dc; rep from * around, ending last rep at **, sl st in 3rd ch of beg ch to join.

Rnd 5: Ch 3 (counts as dc), *dc in each of next 5 dc, (dc, ch 5, dc) in next ch-5 loop, dc in each of next 4 dc; rep from * around, omitting last dc, sl st in 3rd ch of beg ch to join. Fasten off.

131

Front post double crochet (FPdc): *Yo, insert hook from front to back to front again around the post of next st, yo, draw yarn through st, (yo, draw yarn through 2 loops on hook) twice.*

Ch 6 and sl st in first ch to form a ring.

Rnd 1: Ch 3 (counts as dc), 2 dc in ring, ch 3, (3 dc, ch 3) 3 times in ring, sl st in 3rd ch of beg ch to join.

Rnd 2: Ch 3 (counts as dc), *FPdc around the post of next dc, 2 dc in next dc, ch 4, skip next ch-3 loop**, 2 dc in next dc; rep from * around, ending last rep at **, sl st in 3rd ch of beg ch to join.

Rnd 3: Ch 3 (counts as dc), *FPdc around the post of next dc, dc in next dc, 2 dc in next dc, ch 4, skip next ch-4 loop, 2 dc in next dc**, dc in next dc; rep from * around, ending last rep at **, sl st in 3rd ch of beg ch to join.

Rnd 4: Ch 3 (counts as dc), *FPdc around the post of next dc, dc in each of next 2 dc, 2 dc in next dc, ch 5, skip next ch-4 loop, 2 dc in next dc**, dc in each of next 2 dc; rep from * around, ending last rep at **, dc in next dc, sl st in 3rd ch of beg ch to join.

Rnd 5: Ch 3 (counts as dc), *FPdc around the post of next dc, dc in each of next 3 dc, 2 dc in next dc, ch 5, skip next ch-5 loop, 2 dc in next dc**, dc in each of next 3 dc; rep from * around, ending last rep at **, dc in each of next 2 dc, sl st in 3rd ch of beg ch to join. Fasten off.

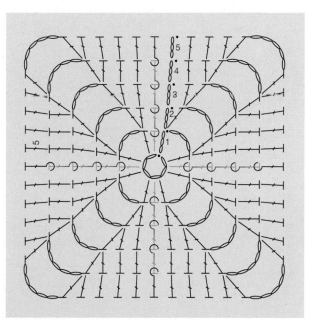

132

Front post double crochet (FPdc): *Yo, insert hook from front to back to front again around the post of next st, yo, draw yarn through st, (yo, draw yarn through 2 loops on hook) twice.*

Ch 6 and sl st in first ch to form a ring.

Rnd 1: Ch 5 (counts as dc, ch 2), (dc, ch 2) 7 times in ring, sl st in 3rd ch of beg ch to join.

Rnd 2: Sl st in next ch-2 space, ch 3 (counts as dc), 4 dc in first ch-2 space, ch 1, (5 dc, ch 1) in each ch-2 space around, sl st in 3rd ch of beg ch to join.

Rnd 3: Ch 3 (counts as dc), *2 dc in next dc, FPdc around the post of next dc, 2 dc in next dc, dc in next dc, ch 1, skip next ch-1 space**, dc in next dc; rep from * around, ending last rep at **, sl st in 3rd ch of beg ch to join.

Rnd 4: Ch 1, *sc in dc, hdc in next dc, dc in next dc, FPdc around the post of next dc, dc in next dc, hdc in next dc, sc in next dc, skip next ch-1 space; rep from * around, sl st in first sc to join. Fasten off.

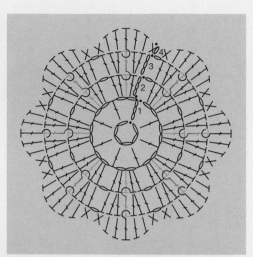

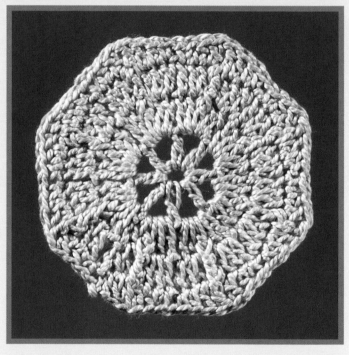

133

Back post double crochet (BPdc): *Yo, insert hook from back to front to back again around the post of next st, yo, draw yarn through st, (yo, draw yarn through 2 loops on hook) twice.*

Beginning popcorn (beg pop): *Ch 3 (counts as dc), 4 dc in same st, drop loop from hook, insert hook from front to back in 3rd ch of beg ch, place dropped loop on hook, draw loop through st.*

Popcorn (pop): *5 dc in same st, drop loop from hook, insert hook from front to back in first dc of 5-dc group, place dropped loop on hook, draw loop through st.*

Ch 6 and sl st in first ch to form a ring.

Rnd 1: Ch 3 (counts as dc), 3 dc in ring, ch 2, (4 dc, ch 2) 3 times in ring, sl st in 3rd ch of beg ch to join.

Rnd 2: Ch 3 (counts as dc), *dc in each of next 3 dc, (2 dc, ch 2, 2 dc) in next ch-2 space**, dc in next dc; rep from * around, ending last rep at **, sl st in 3rd ch of beg ch to join.

Rnd 3: Ch 3 (counts as dc), *BPdc in each of of next 5 dc, (2 dc, ch 2, 2 dc) in next ch-2 space**, BPdc in each of of next 3 dc; rep from * around, ending last rep at **, BPdc in each of of next 2 dc, sl st in 3rd ch of beg ch to join.

Rnd 4: Beg pop in first st, *dc in each of next 2 dc, (pop in next dc, dc in next dc) twice, dc in next dc, (2 dc, ch 2, 2 dc) in next ch-2 space, dc in each of next 2 dc, pop in next dc, dc in next dc**, pop in next dc; rep from * around, ending last rep at **, sl st in 3rd ch of beg ch to join.

Rnd 5: Ch 3 (counts as dc), *dc in each of next 9 sts, (2 dc, ch 2, 2 dc) in next ch-2 space**, dc in each of next 7 sts; rep from * around, ending last rep at **, dc in each of next 6 sts, sl st in 3rd ch of beg ch to join. Fasten off.

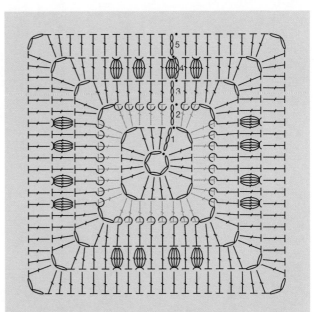

.10.
Shells

134 **Ch** 6 and sl st in first ch to form a ring.

Rnd 1: Ch 3 (counts as dc), 15 dc in ring, sl st in 3rd ch of beg ch to join.

Rnd 2: Ch 1, *sc in dc, skip next dc, 7 dc in next dc, skip next dc; rep from * around, sl st in first sc to join.

Rnd 3: Ch 3 (counts as dc), (dc, ch 3, 2 dc) in first sc, *ch 3, skip next 3 dc, sc in next dc, ch 3, skip next 3 dc**, (2 dc, ch 3, 2 dc) in next sc; rep from * around, ending last rep at **, sl st in 3rd ch of beg ch to join. Fasten off.

135 **Ch** 6 and sl st in first ch to form a ring.

Rnd 1: Ch 4 (counts as dc, ch 1), (dc, ch 1) 7 times in ring, sl st in 3rd ch of beg ch to join.

Rnd 2: Sl st in next ch-1 space, ch 3 (counts as dc), 2 dc in first ch-1 space, ch 1, (3 dc, ch 1) in each ch-1 space around, sl st in 3rd ch of beg ch to join.

Rnd 3: Sl st to next ch-1 space, ch 3 (counts as dc), 2 dc in first ch-1 space, *ch 1, (3 dc, ch 3, 3 dc) in next ch-1 space, ch 1**, 3 dc in next ch-1 space; rep from * around, ending last rep at **, sl st in 3rd ch of beg ch to join. Fasten off.

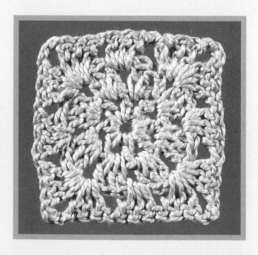

136

Ch 6 and sl st in first ch to form a ring.

Rnd 1: Ch 3 (counts as dc), dc in ring, ch 2, (2 dc, ch 2) 7 times in ring, sl st in 3rd ch of beg ch to join.

Rnd 2: Sl st to next ch-2 space, ch 3 (counts as dc), (dc, ch 2, 2 dc) in first ch-2 space, (2 dc, ch 2, 2 dc) in each ch-2 space around, sl st in 3rd ch of beg ch to join.

Rnd 3: Sl st to next ch-2 space, ch 3 (counts as dc), (2 dc, ch 3, 3 dc) in first ch-2 space, (3 dc, ch 3, 3 dc) in each ch-2 space around, sl st in 3rd ch of beg ch to join.

Rnd 4: Sl st to next ch-3 loop, ch 3 (counts as dc), (3 dc, ch 5, 4 dc) in first ch-3 loop, (4 dc, ch 5, 4 dc) in each ch-3 loop around, sl st in 3rd ch of beg ch to join. Fasten off.

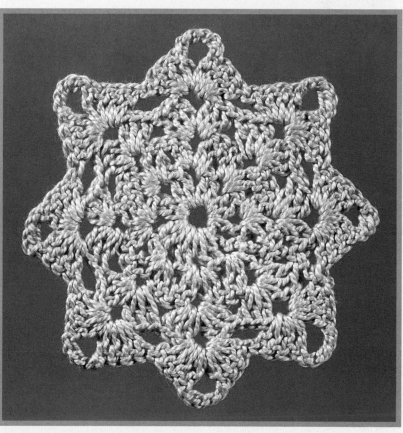

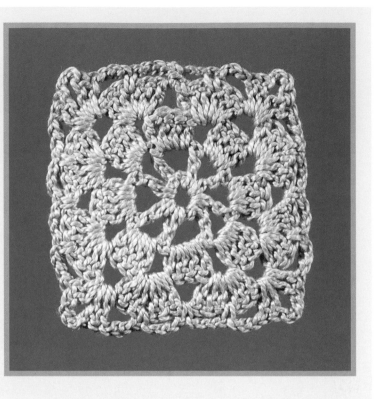

137

Ch 6 and sl st in first ch to form a ring.

Rnd 1: Ch 6 (counts as dc, ch 3), (dc, ch 3) 7 times in ring, sl st in 3rd ch of beg ch to join.

Rnd 2: Sl st in next ch-3 loop, ch 3 (counts as dc), 3 dc in first ch-3 loop, ch 1, (4 dc, ch 1) in each ch-3 loop around, sl st in 3rd ch of beg ch to join.

Rnd 3: Sl st to next ch-1 space, ch 3 (counts as dc), 5 dc in first ch-1 space, ch 1, (6 dc, ch 1) in each ch-1 space around, sl st in 3rd ch of beg ch to join.

Rnd 4: Turn, sl st in next ch-1 space, turn, ch 3 (counts as dc), (dc, ch 3, 2 dc) in first ch-1 space, *ch 3, skip next 3 dc, sc bet last skipped and next dc, ch 3, sc in next ch-1 space, ch 3, skip next 3 dc, sc bet last skipped and next dc, ch 3**, (2 dc, ch 3, 2 dc) in next ch-1 space; rep from * around, ending last rep at **, sl st in 3rd ch of beg ch to join. Fasten off.

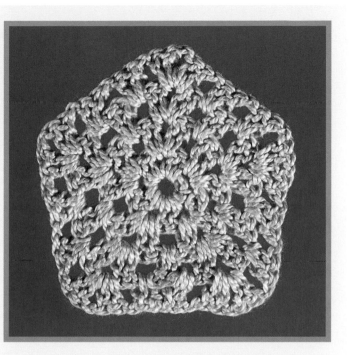

138

Ch 6 and sl st in first ch to form a ring.

Rnd 1: Ch 3 (counts as dc), dc in ring, ch 1 (2 dc, ch 1) 4 times in ring, sl st in 3rd ch of beg ch to join.

Rnd 2: Sl st to next ch-1 space, ch 3 (counts as dc), (dc, ch 1, 2 dc) in first ch-1 space, ch 1, (2 dc, ch 1, 2 dc, ch 1) in each ch-1 space around, sl st in 3rd ch of beg ch to join.

Rnd 3: Sl st to next ch-1 space, ch 3 (counts as dc), (dc, ch 1, 2 dc) in first ch-1 space, *ch 1, 2 dc in next ch-1 space, ch 1**, (2 dc, ch 1, 2 dc) in next ch-1 space; rep from * around, ending last rep at **, sl st in 3rd ch of beg ch to join.

Rnd 4: Sl st to next ch-1 space, ch 3 (counts as dc), (dc, ch 1, 2 dc) in first ch-1 space, *(ch 1, 2 dc) in each of next 2 ch-1 spaces, ch 1**, (2 dc, ch 1, 2 dc) in next ch-1 space; rep from * around, ending last rep at **, sl st in 3rd ch of beg ch to join. Fasten off.

139

Ch 6 and sl st in first ch to form a ring.

Rnd 1: Ch 3 (counts as dc), 15 dc in ring, sl st in 3rd ch of beg ch to join.

Rnd 2: Ch 1, *sc in dc, skip next dc, 5 hdc in next dc, skip next dc; rep from * around, sl st in first sc to join.

Rnd 3: Ch 3 (counts as dc), 6 dc in first sc, *skip next 2 hdc, sc in next hdc, skip next 2 hdc**, 7 dc in next sc; rep from * around, ending last rep at **, sl st in 3rd ch of beg ch to join.

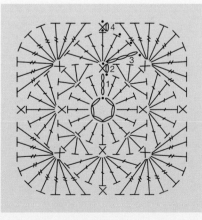

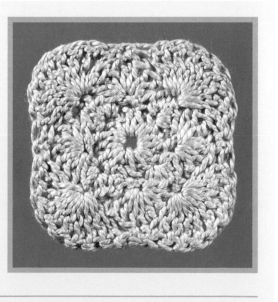

Rnd 4: Sl st in each of next 3 dc, ch 1, *sc in dc, skip next 3 dc, 9 tr in next sc, skip next 3 dc; rep from * around, sl st in first sc to join. Fasten off.

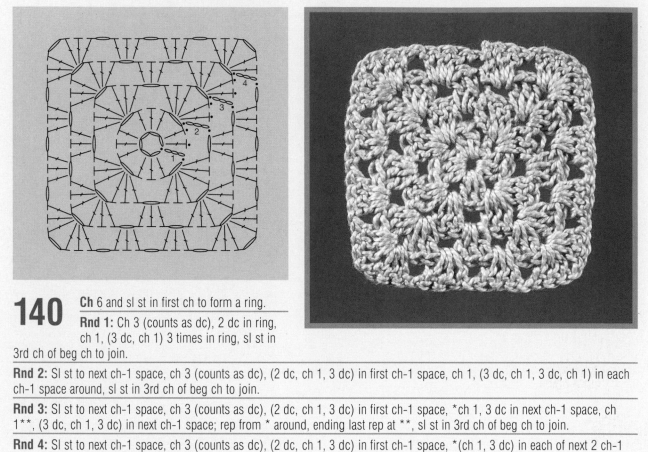

140

Ch 6 and sl st in first ch to form a ring.

Rnd 1: Ch 3 (counts as dc), 2 dc in ring, ch 1, (3 dc, ch 1) 3 times in ring, sl st in 3rd ch of beg ch to join.

Rnd 2: Sl st to next ch-1 space, ch 3 (counts as dc), (2 dc, ch 1, 3 dc) in first ch-1 space, ch 1, (3 dc, ch 1, 3 dc, ch 1) in each ch-1 space around, sl st in 3rd ch of beg ch to join.

Rnd 3: Sl st to next ch-1 space, ch 3 (counts as dc), (2 dc, ch 1, 3 dc) in first ch-1 space, *ch 1, 3 dc in next ch-1 space, ch 1**, (3 dc, ch 1, 3 dc) in next ch-1 space; rep from * around, ending last rep at **, sl st in 3rd ch of beg ch to join.

Rnd 4: Sl st to next ch-1 space, ch 3 (counts as dc), (2 dc, ch 1, 3 dc) in first ch-1 space, *(ch 1, 3 dc) in each of next 2 ch-1 spaces, ch 1**, (3 dc, ch 1, 3 dc) in next ch-1 space; rep from * around, ending last rep at **, sl st in 3rd ch of beg ch to join. Fasten off.

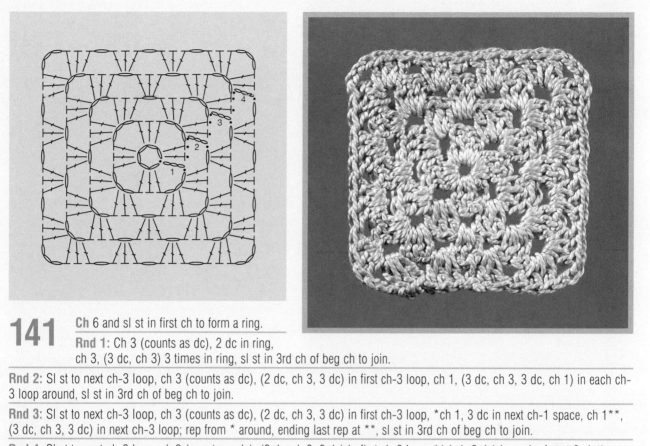

141 Ch 6 and sl st in first ch to form a ring.

Rnd 1: Ch 3 (counts as dc), 2 dc in ring, ch 3, (3 dc, ch 3) 3 times in ring, sl st in 3rd ch of beg ch to join.

Rnd 2: Sl st to next ch-3 loop, ch 3 (counts as dc), (2 dc, ch 3, 3 dc) in first ch-3 loop, ch 1, (3 dc, ch 3, 3 dc, ch 1) in each ch-3 loop around, sl st in 3rd ch of beg ch to join.

Rnd 3: Sl st to next ch-3 loop, ch 3 (counts as dc), (2 dc, ch 3, 3 dc) in first ch-3 loop, *ch 1, 3 dc in next ch-1 space, ch 1**, (3 dc, ch 3, 3 dc) in next ch-3 loop; rep from * around, ending last rep at **, sl st in 3rd ch of beg ch to join.

Rnd 4: Sl st to next ch-3 loop, ch 3 (counts as dc), (2 dc, ch 3, 3 dc) in first ch-3 loop, *(ch 1, 3 dc) in each of next 2 ch-1 spaces, ch 1**, (3 dc, ch 3, 3 dc) in next ch-3 loop; rep from * around, ending last rep at **, sl st in 3rd ch of beg ch to join. Fasten off.

142

Ch 6 and sl st in first ch to form a ring.

Rnd 1: Ch 3 (counts as dc), 2 dc in ring, ch 2, (3 dc, ch 2) 3 times in ring, sl st in 3rd ch of beg ch to join.

Rnd 2: Sl st to next ch-3 loop, ch 3 (counts as dc), (2 dc, ch 2, 3 dc) in first ch-2 space, ch 2, (3 dc, ch 2, 3 dc, ch 2) in each ch-2 space around, sl st in 3rd ch of beg ch to join.

Rnd 3: Ch 3 (counts as dc), *dc in each of next 2 dc, (3 dc, ch 2, 3 dc) in next ch-2 space, dc in each of next 3 dc, 2 dc in next ch-2 space**, dc in next dc; rep from * around, ending last rep at **, sl st in 3rd ch of beg ch to join.

Rnd 4: Sl st in each of next 2 dc, ch 3 (counts as dc), 2 dc in same dc, skip next 3 dc, *(3 dc, ch 2, 3 dc) in next ch-2 space, skip next 3 dc, 3 dc in next dc, skip next 2 dc, 3 dc in next dc, skip next 3 dc**, 3 dc in next dc; rep from * around, ending last rep at **, sl st in 3rd ch of beg ch to join.

Rnd 5: Ch 3 (counts as dc), *dc in each of next 5 dc, (2 dc, ch 2, 2 dc) in next ch-2 space, dc in each of next 10 dc; rep from * around, omitting last dc, sl st in 3rd ch of beg ch to join.

Rnd 6: Ch 1, sc in each st around, working 2 sc in each corner ch-2 space, sl st in first sc to join. Fasten off.

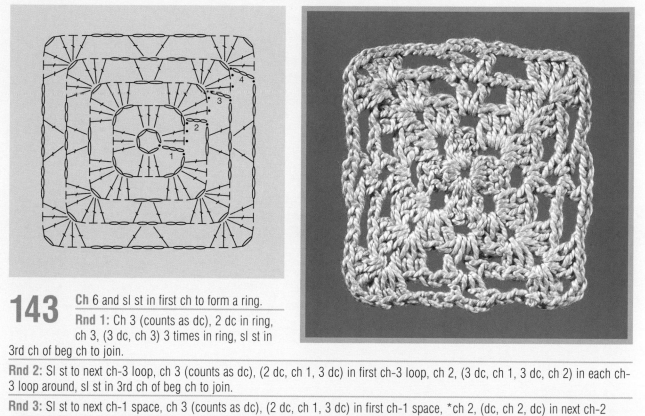

143 Ch 6 and sl st in first ch to form a ring.

Rnd 1: Ch 3 (counts as dc), 2 dc in ring, ch 3, (3 dc, ch 3) 3 times in ring, sl st in 3rd ch of beg ch to join.

Rnd 2: Sl st to next ch-3 loop, ch 3 (counts as dc), (2 dc, ch 1, 3 dc) in first ch-3 loop, ch 2, (3 dc, ch 1, 3 dc, ch 2) in each ch-3 loop around, sl st in 3rd ch of beg ch to join.

Rnd 3: Sl st to next ch-1 space, ch 3 (counts as dc), (2 dc, ch 1, 3 dc) in first ch-1 space, *ch 2, (dc, ch 2, dc) in next ch-2 space, ch 2**, (3 dc, ch 1, 3 dc) in next ch-1 space; rep from * around, ending last rep at **, sl st in 3rd ch of beg ch to join.

Rnd 4: Sl st to next ch-1 space, ch 3 (counts as dc), (2 dc, ch 1, 3 dc) in first ch-1 space, *ch 3, skip next ch-2 space, (dc, ch 3, dc) in next ch-2 space, ch 3, skip next ch-2 space**, (3 dc, ch 1, 3 dc) in next ch-1 space; rep from * around, ending last rep at **, sl st in 3rd ch of beg ch to join. Fasten off.

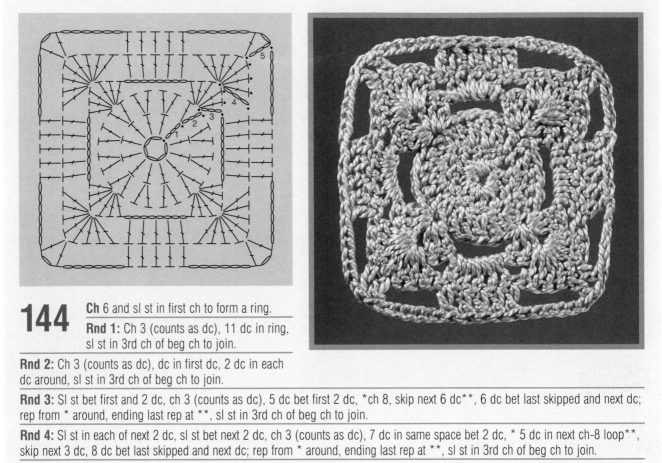

144   Ch 6 and sl st in first ch to form a ring.

Rnd 1: Ch 3 (counts as dc), 11 dc in ring, sl st in 3rd ch of beg ch to join.

Rnd 2: Ch 3 (counts as dc), dc in first dc, 2 dc in each dc around, sl st in 3rd ch of beg ch to join.

Rnd 3: Sl st bet first and 2 dc, ch 3 (counts as dc), 5 dc bet first 2 dc, *ch 8, skip next 6 dc**, 6 dc bet last skipped and next dc; rep from * around, ending last rep at **, sl st in 3rd ch of beg ch to join.

Rnd 4: Sl st in each of next 2 dc, sl st bet next 2 dc, ch 3 (counts as dc), 7 dc in same space bet 2 dc, * 5 dc in next ch-8 loop**, skip next 3 dc, 8 dc bet last skipped and next dc; rep from * around, ending last rep at **, sl st in 3rd ch of beg ch to join.

Rnd 5: Sl st in each of next 3 dc, sl st bet next 2 dc, ch 4 (counts as dc, ch 1), dc in same space bet 2 dc, *ch 6, skip next 4 dc, dc in each of next 5 dc, ch 6, skip next 4 dc**, (dc, ch 1, dc) bet last skipped and next dc; rep from * around, ending last rep at **, sl st in 3rd ch of beg ch to join. Fasten off.

145

Ch 6 and sl st in first ch to form a ring.

Rnd 1: Ch 3 (counts as dc), 2 dc in ring, ch 1, (3 dc, ch 1) 4 times in ring, sl st in 3rd ch of beg ch to join.

Rnd 2: Sl st to next ch-1 space, ch 1, (sc, ch 3, sc, ch 3) in each ch-1 space around, sl st in first sc to join.

Rnd 3: Sl st in next ch-3 loop, ch 3 (counts as dc), (2 dc, ch 1, 3 dc) in first ch-3 loop, *ch 1, 3 dc in next ch-3 loop, ch 1**, (3 dc, ch 1, 3 dc) in next ch-3 loop; rep from * around, ending last rep at **, sl st in 3rd ch of beg ch to join.

Rnd 4: Sl st to next ch-1 space, ch 1, *(sc, ch 3, sc) in ch-1 corner space, (ch 3, sc) in each of next 2 ch-1 spaces, ch 3; rep from * around, sl st in 3rd ch of beg ch to join.

Rnd 5: Sl st in next ch-3 loop, ch 3 (counts as dc), (2 dc, ch 1, 3 dc) in first ch-3 loop, *(ch 1, 3 dc) in each of next 3 ch-3 loops, ch 1**, (3 dc, ch 1, 3 dc) in next ch-3 loop; rep from * around, ending last rep at **, sl st in 3rd ch of beg ch to join.

Rnd 6: Sl st to next ch-1 space, ch 1, *(sc, ch 3, sc) in ch-1 corner space, (ch 3, sc) in each of next 4 ch-1 spaces, ch 3; rep from * around, sl st in 3rd ch of beg ch to join.

Rnd 7: Sl st in next ch-3 loop, ch 3 (counts as dc), (2 dc, ch 1, 3 dc) in first ch-3 loop, *(ch 1, 3 dc) in each of next 5 ch-3 loops, ch 1**, (3 dc, ch 1, 3 dc) in next ch-3 loop; rep from * around, ending last rep at **, sl st in 3rd ch of beg ch to join. Fasten off.

.11.
Picots

146

Picot: Ch 4, sl st in 4th ch from hook.

Ch 12 and sl st in first ch to form a ring.

Rnd 1: Ch 5 (counts as dc, ch 2), *dc in ring, ch 5, dc in ring, ch 2; rep from * twice, dc in ring, ch 5, sl st in 3rd ch of beg ch to join.

Rnd 2: Ch 1, *sc in dc, 2 sc in next ch-2 space, sc in next dc, ch 3, picot, ch 3, skip next ch-5 loop; rep from * around, sl st in first sc to join. Fasten off.

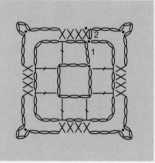

147

Picot: Ch 4, sl st in 4th ch from hook.

Ch 6 and sl st in first ch to form a ring.

Rnd 1: Ch 3 (counts as dc), 15 dc in ring, sl st in 3rd ch of beg ch to join.

Rnd 2: Ch 1, (sc, picot) in each dc around, sl st in 3rd ch of beg ch to join. Fasten off.

148

Picot: Ch 4, sl st in 4th ch from hook.

Ch 8 and sl st in first ch to form a ring.

Rnd 1: Ch 1, 16 sc in ring, sl st in first sc to join.

Rnd 2: Ch 1, *sc in sc, picot, skip next sc; rep from * around, sl st in first sc to join. Fasten off.

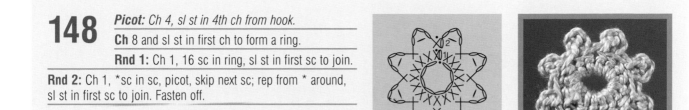

149

Picot: Ch 5, sl st in 5th ch from hook.

Ch 9 and sl st in first ch to form a ring.

Rnd 1: Ch 1, 16 sc in ring, sl st in first sc to join.

Rnd 2: Ch 4 (counts as tr), 2 tr in first sc, *3 tr in next sc, ch 7, skip next 2 sc**, 3 tr in next sc; rep from * around, ending last rep at **, sl st in 4th ch of beg ch to join.

Rnd 3: Ch 1, *sc in tr, dc in next tr, 2 dc in next tr, picot, 2 dc in next tr, dc in next tr, sc in next tr, 8 sc in next ch-7 loop; rep from * around, sl st in first sc to join. Fasten off.

150

Picot: Ch 4, sl st in 4th ch from hook.

Ch 6 and sl st in first ch to form a ring.

Rnd 1: Ch 1, 16 sc in ring, sl st in first sc to join.

Rnd 2: Ch 3 (counts as dc), skip first sc, dc in each sc around, sl st in 3rd ch of beg ch to join.

Rnd 3: Ch 1, (sc, picot) in each dc around, sl st in first sc to join. Fasten off.

151

Picot: Ch 4, sl st in 4th ch from hook.

Ch 6 and sl st in first ch to form a ring.

Rnd 1: Ch 4 (counts as dc, ch 1), (dc, ch 1) 7 times in ring, sl st in 3rd ch of beg ch to join.

Rnd 2: Sl st in next ch-1 space, ch 1, (sc, picot, sc) in first ch-1 space, (ch 1, sc, picot, sc) in each of next 7 ch-1 spaces, sc in first sc to join.

Rnd 3: Ch 8 (counts as dc, ch 5), skip next (sc, picot, sc), (dc, ch 5) in each ch-1 space around, sl st in 3rd ch of beg ch to join.

Rnd 4: Ch 1, *sc in dc, 8 sc in next ch-5 loop; rep from * around, sl st in first sc to join. Fasten off.

152

Ch-3 picot: Ch 3, sl st in 3rd ch from hook.

Ch-4 picot: Ch 4, sl st in 4th ch from hook.

Ch 8 and sl st in first ch to form a ring.

Rnd 1: Ch 3 (counts as dc), 23 dc in ring, sl st in 3rd ch of beg ch to join.

Rnd 2: Ch 4 (counts as dc, ch 1), (dc, ch 1) in each dc around, sl st in 3rd ch of beg ch to join.

Rnd 3: Sl st in first ch-1 space, ch 1, *sc in ch-1 space, ch 2, dc in next ch-1 space, ch-3 picot, sl st in last dc made, ch-4 picot, sl st in last dc made, ch-3 picot, sl st in last dc made, ch 2; rep from * around, sl st in first sc to join. Fasten off.

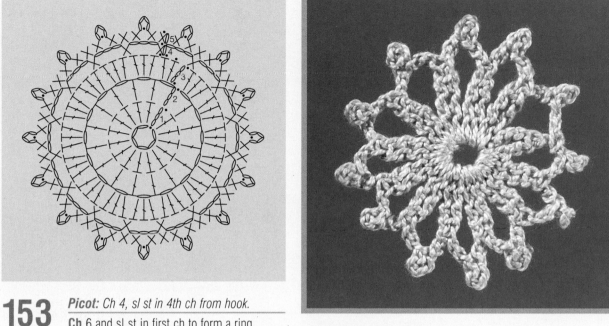

153

Picot: Ch 4, sl st in 4th ch from hook.

Ch 6 and sl st in first ch to form a ring.

Rnd 1: Ch 3 (counts as dc), 15 dc in ring, sl st in 3rd ch of beg ch to join.

Rnd 2: Ch 4 (counts as dc, ch 1), skip first st, (dc, ch 1) in each dc around, sl st in 3rd ch of beg ch to join.

Rnd 3: Sl st in next ch-1 space, ch 3 (counts as dc), 2 dc in first ch-1 space, 3 dc in each ch-1 space around, sl st in 3rd ch of beg ch to join.

Rnd 4: Sl st in each of next 2 dc, sl st bet next 2 dc, ch 1, sc bet same 2 dc, ch 3, *skip next 3 dc, sc bet last skipped and next dc, ch 3; rep from * around, skip next 3 dc, sl st in first sc to join.

Rnd 5: Ch 1, *sc in sc, (sc, picot, sc) in next ch-3 loop; rep from * around, sl st in first sc to join. Fasten off.

154

Picot: Ch 3, sl st in 3rd ch from hook.

Ch 6 and sl st in first ch to form a ring.

Rnd 1: Ch 1, 12 sc in ring, sl st in first sc to join.

Rnd 2: Ch 3 (counts as dc), dc in first sc, ch 3, skip next sc, *puff st in next sc, ch 3, ch 3, skip next sc; rep from * around, sl st in 3rd ch of beg ch to join.

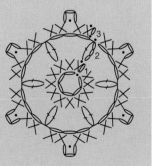

Rnd 3: Sl st in next ch-3 loop, ch 1, (2 sc, picot, 2 sc) in each ch-3 loop around, sl st in first sc to join. Fasten off.

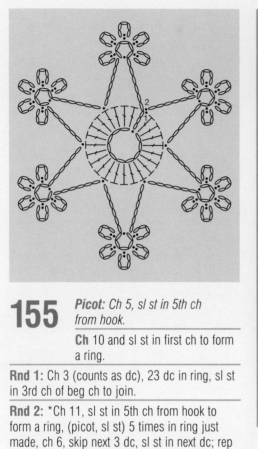

155

Picot: Ch 5, sl st in 5th ch from hook.

Ch 10 and sl st in first ch to form a ring.

Rnd 1: Ch 3 (counts as dc), 23 dc in ring, sl st in 3rd ch of beg ch to join.

Rnd 2: *Ch 11, sl st in 5th ch from hook to form a ring, (picot, sl st) 5 times in ring just made, ch 6, skip next 3 dc, sl st in next dc; rep from * around, ending with last sl st in first sl st to join. Fasten off.

156

Picot: Ch 3, sl st in 3rd ch from hook.

Ch 6 and sl st in first ch to form a ring.

Rnd 1: Ch 3 (counts as dc), 11 dc in ring, sl st in 3rd ch of beg ch to join.

Rnd 2: *Ch 4, picot, ch 3, sl st in next dc; rep from * around, ending with last sl st in first sl st to join. Fasten off.

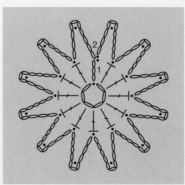

157

Picot: Ch 4, sl st in 4th ch from hook.

Ch 6 and sl st in first ch to form a ring.

Rnd 1: Ch 3 (counts as dc), 2 dc in ring, ch 2, (3 dc, ch 2) 5 times in ring, sl st in 3rd ch of beg ch to join.

Rnd 2: Sl st to next ch-2 space, ch 1, (sc, ch 5) in each ch-2 space around, sl st in first sc to join.

Rnd 3: Sl st in next ch-5 loop, ch 3 (counts as dc), (2 dc, picot, 3 dc) in first ch-5 loop, ch 3, (3 dc, picot, 3 dc, ch 3) in each ch-5 loop around, sl st in 3rd ch of beg ch to join. Fasten off.

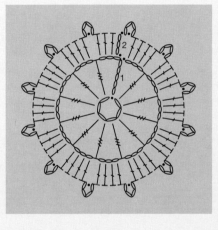

158

Picot: Ch 4, sl st in 4th ch from hook.

Ch 6 and sl st in first ch to form a ring.

Rnd 1: Ch 8 (counts as dtr, ch 3), (dtr, ch 3) 11 times in ring, sl st in 5th ch of beg ch to join.

Rnd 2: Sl st in next ch-3 loop, ch 3 (counts as dc), 3 dc in first ch-3 loop, picot, (4 dc, picot) in each ch-3 loop around, sl st in 3rd ch of beg ch to join. Fasten off.

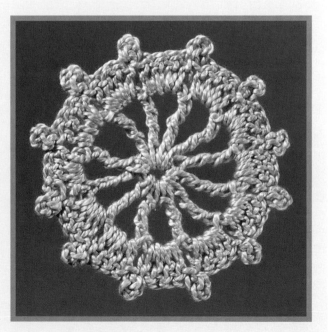

159

2-dc puff st: (Yo, insert hook in next space, yo, draw yarn through space, draw yarn through 2 loops on hook) twice in same space, yo, draw yarn through 3 loops on hook.

3-dc puff st: (Yo, insert hook in next space, yo, draw yarn through space, draw yarn through 2 loops on hook) 3 times in same space, yo, draw yarn through 4 loops on hook.

Picot: Ch 4, sl st in 4th ch from hook.

Ch 6 and sl st in first ch to form a ring.

Rnd 1: Ch 3 (counts as dc), 2-dc puff st in ring, ch 3, (3-dc puff st, ch 3) 7 times in ring, sl st in first puff st to join.

Rnd 2: Sl st in next ch-3 loop, ch 3 (counts as dc), 4 dc in first ch-3 loop, 5 dc in each ch-3 loop around, sl st in 3rd ch of beg ch to join.

Rnd 3: Sl st in each of next 4 dc, picot, *sl st in each of next 5 dc, picot; rep from * around, sl st in first sl st to join. Fasten off.

160

Picot: Ch 3, sl st in 3rd ch from hook.

Ch 6 and sl st in first ch to form a ring.

Rnd 1: *Ch 5, sc in 2nd ch from hook, sc in each of next 3 ch, sl st in ring; rep from * 7 times, ending with last sl st in first sl st to join (8 spokes made).

Rnd 2: Sl st in each of next 5 ch sts, (ch 5, sl st) in tip of each spoke around, ending with last sl st in first sl st to join.

Rnd 3: Sl st in next ch-5 loop, ch 1, *(2 sc, picot, 2 sc, picot, 2 sc, picot, 2 sc) in each ch-5 loop round, sl st in first sc to join. Fasten off.

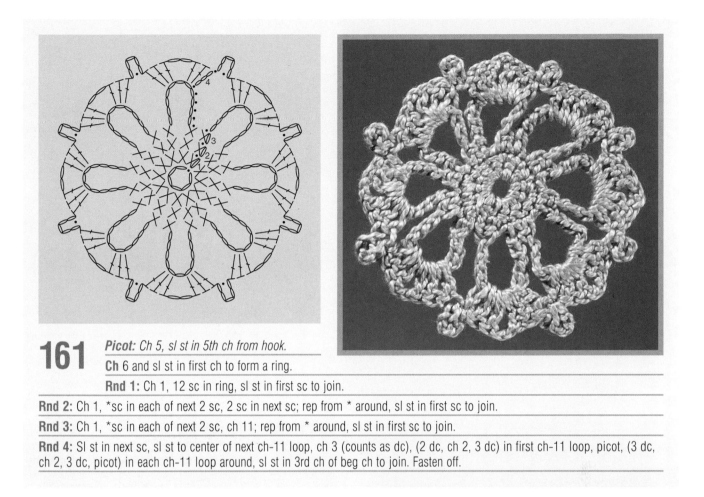

161

Picot: Ch 5, sl st in 5th ch from hook.

Ch 6 and sl st in first ch to form a ring.

Rnd 1: Ch 1, 12 sc in ring, sl st in first sc to join.

Rnd 2: Ch 1, *sc in each of next 2 sc, 2 sc in next sc; rep from * around, sl st in first sc to join.

Rnd 3: Ch 1, *sc in each of next 2 sc, ch 11; rep from * around, sl st in first sc to join.

Rnd 4: Sl st in next sc, sl st to center of next ch-11 loop, ch 3 (counts as dc), (2 dc, ch 2, 3 dc) in first ch-11 loop, picot, (3 dc, ch 2, 3 dc, picot) in each ch-11 loop around, sl st in 3rd ch of beg ch to join. Fasten off.

162

Puff st: (Yo [3 times], insert hook in next space, yo, draw yarn through space, [yo, draw yarn through 2 loops on hook] 3 times) twice in same space, yo, draw yarn through 3 loops on hook.

Picot: Ch 3, sl st in 3rd ch from hook.

Ch 8 and sl st in first ch to form a ring.

Rnd 1: Ch 5 (counts as dtr), dtr in ring, ch 2, picot, ch 2, *puff st in ring, ch 2, picot, ch 2; rep from * 10 times, sl st in 5th ch of beg ch to join. Fasten off.

163

Picot: Ch 3, sl st in 3rd ch from hook.

Ch 8 and sl st in first ch to form a ring.

Rnd 1: Ch 3 (counts as dc), 2 dc in ring, ch 2, picot, ch 2, *3 dc in ring, ch 2, picot, ch 2; rep from * 5 times, sl st in 3rd ch of beg ch to join.

Rnd 2: Sl st in next dc, ch 1, *sc in dc, ch 10, skip next (dc, ch 2, picot, ch 2, dc); rep from * around, sl st in first sc to join. Fasten off.

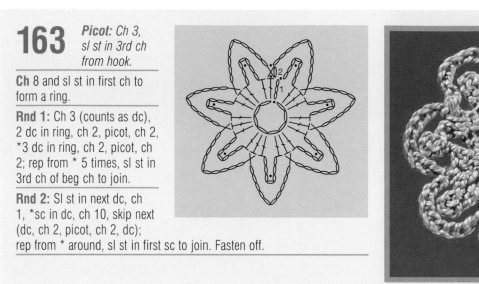

164

Ch-4 picot: Ch 4, sl st in 4th ch from hook.

Ch-5 picot: Ch 5, sl st in 5th ch from hook.

Ch 6 and sl st in first ch to form a ring.

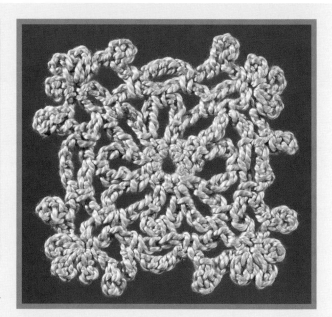

Rnd 1: Ch 1, 8 sc in ring, sl st in first sc to join.

Rnd 2: Ch 1, (sc, ch 8) in each sc around, sl st in first sc to join.

Rnd 3: Sl st to center of next ch-8 loop, ch 1, *sc in ch-8 loop, ch 4, (sc, ch 5, sc) in next ch-8 loop, ch 4; rep from * around, sl st in first sc to join.

Rnd 4: Sl st to center of first ch-4 loop, ch 1, *sc in ch-4 loop, ch 2, ch-4 picot, ch 2, sc in next ch-5 loop, ch-4 picot, sl st in last sc made, ch-5 picot, sl st in last sc made, ch-4 picot, sl st in last sc made, ch 2, ch-4 picot, ch 2, sc in next ch-4 loop, ch 5; rep from * around, sl st in first sc to join. Fasten off.

165

Ch-3 picot: Ch 3, sl st in 3rd ch from hook.

Ch-4 picot: Ch 4, sl st in 4th ch from hook.

Ch-5 picot: Ch 5, sl st in 5th ch from hook.

Ch 6 and sl st in first ch to form a ring.

Rnd 1: Ch 3 (counts as dc), 2 dc in ring, ch 4 picot, (3 dc, ch-4 picot) 7 times in ring, sl st in 3rd ch of beg ch to join.

Rnd 2: Sl st in next dc, ch 8 (counts as dc, ch 5), skip next (dc, picot, dc), *dc in next dc, ch 5, skip next (dc, picot, dc); rep from * around, sl st in 3rd ch of beg ch to join.

Rnd 3: Ch 1, *sc in dc, ch 5, sc in next ch-5 loop, ch 5; rep from * around, sl st in first sc to join.

Rnd 4: Sl st to center of first ch-5 loop, ch 1, *sc in ch-5 loop, ch 2, (dc, ch-3 picot, dc, ch-5 picot, dc, ch-3 picot, dc) in next ch-5 loop, ch 2; rep from * around, sl st in first sc to join. Fasten off.

166

Picot: Ch 4, sl st in 4th ch from hook.

Ch 6 and sl st in first ch to form a ring.

Rnd 1: (Ch 3, dc, ch 3, sl st) 8 times in ring.

Rnd 2: Sl st to top of first ch-3 loop, ch 3 (counts as dc), 2-dc cluster, working first half-closed dc in next dc, work 2nd half-closed dc in next ch-3 loop, yo, complete cluster, ch 6, 3-dc cluster worked across next (ch-3 loop, dc, ch-3 loop), ch 6; rep from * around, sl st in 3rd ch of beg ch to join.

Rnd 3: Ch 1, *sc in next cluster, 6 sc in next ch-6 loop; rep from * around, sl st in first sc to join.

Rnds 4-5: Ch 1, sc in each sc around, sl st in first sc to join.

Rnd 6: Ch 1, sc in first 4 sc, *picot, sc in each of next 7 sc; rep from * 6 times, picot, sc in each of last 3 sc, sl st in first sc to join. Fasten off.

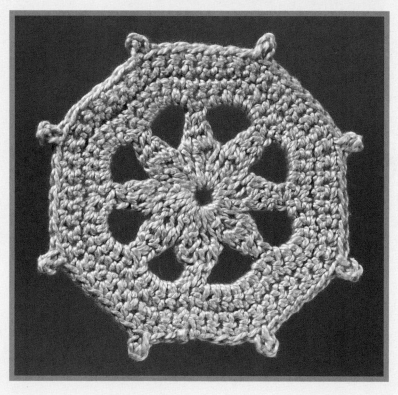

167 ***2-tr puff st:*** *(Yo [twice], insert hook in next st, yo, draw yarn through st, [yo, draw yarn through 2 loops on hook] twice) twice in same st, yo, draw yarn through 3 loops on hook.*

3-tr puff st: *(Yo [twice], insert hook in next st, yo, draw yarn through st, [yo, draw yarn through 2 loops on hook] twice) 3 times in same st, yo, draw yarn through 4 loops on hook.*

Picot: *Ch 3, sl st in 3rd ch from hook.*

Ch 10 and sl st in first ch to form a ring.

Rnd 1: Ch 1, 18 sc in ring, sl st in first sc to join.

Rnd 2: Ch 4 (counts as tr), 2-tr puff st in first sc, ch 10, skip next 2 sc, *3-tr puff st in next sc, ch 10, skip next 2 sc; rep from * around, sl st in first puff st to join.

Rnd 3: Sl st in next ch-10 loop, ch 1, (3 sc, picot, 3 sc, picot, 3 sc, picot, 3 sc) in each ch-10 loop around, sl st in first sc to join. Fasten off.

168

Picot: Ch 4, sl st in 4th ch from hook.

Ch 6 and sl st in first ch to form a ring.

Rnd 1: Ch 1, 12 sc in ring, sl st in first sc to join.

Rnd 2: Ch 6 (counts as dc, ch 3), skip next sc, *dc in next sc, ch 3, skip next sc; rep from * around, sl st in 3rd ch of beg ch to join.

Rnd 3: Sl st in next ch-3 loop, ch 1, (sc, hdc, 3 dc, hdc, sc) in each ch-3 loop around, sl st in first sc to join.

Rnd 4: Sl st in each of next 3 sts, ch 1, *sc in center dc of shell, ch 10, skip next 6 sts; rep from * around, sl st in first sc to join.

Rnd 5: Sl st in next ch-10 loop, ch 1, (5 sc, picot, 5 sc) in each ch-10 loop around, sl st in first sc to join. Fasten off.

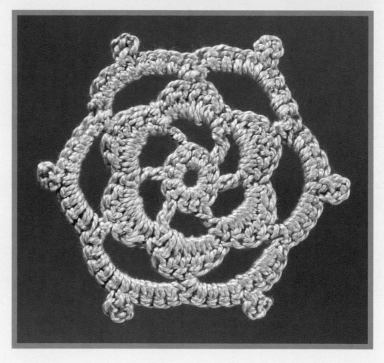

169

Picot: *Ch 3, sl st in 3rd ch from hook.*

Ch 6 and sl st in first ch to form a ring.

Rnd 1: Ch 1, (sc, ch 7) 8 times in ring, sl st in first sc to join.

Rnd 2: Sl st to center of first ch-6 loop, ch 1, (sc, ch 5) in each ch-6 loop around, sl st in first sc to join.

Rnd 3: Ch 1, *sc in sc, ch 3, (dc, ch 3, dc) in next ch-3 loop, ch 3; rep from * around, sl st in first sc to join.

Rnd 4: Ch 1, *sc in sc, ch 3, skip next ch-3 loop, (dc, picot) 5 times in next ch-3 loop, dc in same ch-3 loop, ch 3, skip next ch-3 loop; rep from * around, sl st in first sc to join. Fasten off.

170

Picot: Ch 3, sl st in 3rd ch from hook.

Ch 13 and sl st in first ch to form a ring.

Rnd 1 (RS): Ch 1, 25 sc in ring, sl st in first sc to join.

Rnd 2: Ch 1, *sc in sc, ch 6, skip next 4 sc; rep from * around, sl st in first sc to join.

Rnd 3: Sl st in next ch-6 loop, ch 1, (sc, hdc, dc, 4 tr, dc, hdc, sc) in each ch-6 loop around, sl st in first sc to join.

Rnd 4: Sl st in each of next 2 sts, ch 1, *sc in dc, picot, ch 5, picot, skip next 4 sts; rep from * around, sl st in first sc to join. Fasten off.

Rnd 5: With RS facing, join yarn in center of any ch-5 loop, ch 1, (sc, ch 9) in each ch-5 loop around, sl st in first sc to join.

Rnd 6: Sl st in next ch-9 loop, ch 1, (3 sc, picot, 3 sc, picot, 3 sc, picot, 3 sc) in each ch-9 loop around, sl st in first sc to join. Fasten off.

171

Picot: Ch 3, sl st in 3rd ch from hook.

Ch 12 and sl st in first ch to form a ring.

Rnd 1: Ch 4 (counts as tr), 4 tr in ring, ch 2, (5 tr, ch 2) 5 times in ring, sl st in 4th ch of beg ch to join.

Rnd 2: Sl st to next ch-2 space, ch 1, (2 sc, ch 9) in each ch-2 space around, sl st in first sc to join.

Rnd 3: Sl st to next ch-9 loop, ch 1, 13 sc in each ch-9 loop around, sl st in first sc to join.

Rnd 4: Sl st in each of next 3 sc, ch 1, *sc in each of next 7 sc, ch 9, skip next 6 sc; rep from * around, sl st in first sc to join.

Rnd 5: Ch 1, *sc in each of next 7 sc, (sc, picot, [2 sc, picot] 4 times, sc) in next ch-9 loop; rep from * around, sl st in first sc to join. Fasten off.

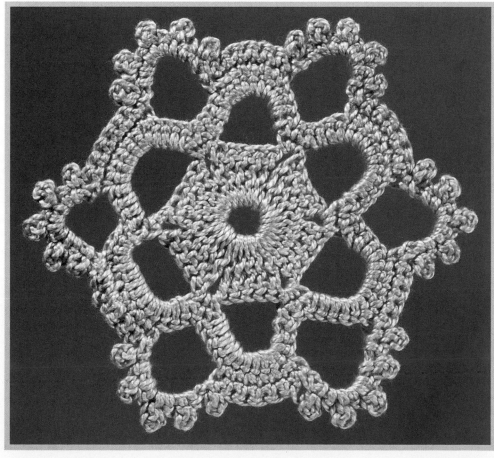

172

Picot: Ch 3, sl st in 3rd ch from hook.

Ch 14 and sl st in first ch to form a ring.

Rnd 1: Ch 1, 18 sc in ring, sl st in first sc to join.

Rnd 2: Ch 1, *sc in sc, ch 18, skip next 5 sc; rep from * around, sl st in first sc to join.

Rnd 3: Sl st in next ch-18 loop, ch 1, 18 sc in each ch-18 loop around, sl st in first sc to join.

Rnd 4: Ch 1, *sc in sc, ch 3, skip next sc; rep from * around, sl st in first sc to join.

Rnd 5: Sl st to center of next ch-3 loop, ch 1, (sc, ch 4) in each ch-3 loop around, sl st in first sc to join.

Rnd 6: Sl st in next ch-4 loop, ch 1, 4 sc in each ch-4 loop around, sl st in first sc to join.

Rnd 7: Ch 1, *sc in each of next 4 sc, picot; rep from * around, sl st in first sc to join. Fasten off.

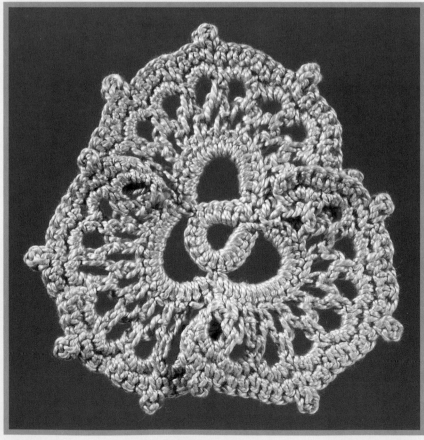

.12.
Mixed Stitches

173

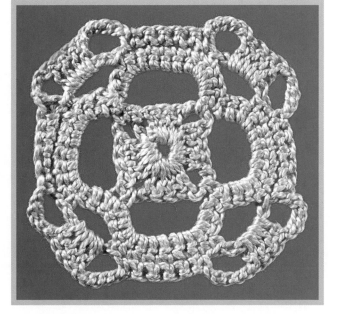

Ch 6 and sl st in first ch to form a ring.

Rnd 1: Ch 3 (counts as dc), 3 dc in ring, (ch 3, 4 dc) 3 times in ring, ch 1, hdc in 3rd ch of beg ch to join.

Rnd 2: (Ch 10, sl st) in each ch-3 loop around, ending with last sl st in hdc at end of Rnd 1 to join.

Rnd 3: Ch 1, *sc in sl st, 12 sc in next ch-11 loop; rep from * around, sl st in first sc to join.

Rnd 4: Sl st in each of next 3 sc, ch 1, *sc in each of next 8 sc, ch 5, skip next 5 sc; rep from * around, sl st in first sc to join.

Rnd 5: Sl st in next sc, ch 1, *sc in each of next 6 sc, ch 5, 4 dc in next ch-5 loop, ch 5, skip next sc; rep from * around, sl st in first sc to join. Fasten off.

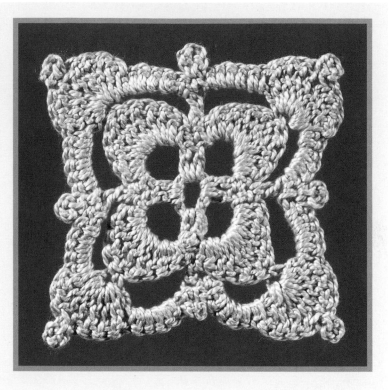

174

Picot: Ch 4, sl st in 4th ch from hook.

Ch 8 and sl st in first ch to form a ring.

Rnd 1: Ch 3 (counts as dc), dc in ring, ch 6, (2 dc, ch 6) 3 times in ring, sl st in 3rd ch of beg ch to join.

Rnd 2: Ch 1, *sc in each of next 2 dc, (sc, hdc, 2 dc, 3 tr, 2 dc, hdc, sc) in next ch-6 loop; rep from * around, sl st in first sc to join.

Rnd 3: Sl st bet first 2 sc, ch 9 (counts as dc, ch 6), *skip next 6 sts, sc in next tr, ch 6, skip next 6 sts**, dc bet last skipped and next sc; rep from * around, ending last rep at **, sl st in 3rd ch of beg ch to join.

Rnd 4: Sl st in next ch-6 loop, ch 1, *6 sc in ch-6 loop, (4 dc, picot, 4 dc) in next sc, 6 sc in next ch-6 loop, picot; rep from * around, sl st in first sc to join. Fasten off.

175

Picot: Ch 4, sl st in 4th ch from hook.

Ch 8 and sl st in first ch to form a ring.

Rnd 1: Ch 1, 12 sc in ring, sl st in first sc to join.

Rnd 2: Ch 7 (counts as tr, ch 3), tr in first sc, ch 5, skip next 2 sc, *(tr, ch 3, tr) in next sc, ch 5, skip next 2 sc; rep from * around, sl st in 4th ch of beg ch to join.

Rnd 3: Sl st to next ch-5 loop, ch 3 (counts as dc), (4 dc, picot, 4 dc, picot, 5 dc) in first ch-5 loop, (5 dc, picot, 4 dc, picot, 5 dc) in each ch-5 loop around, sl st in 3rd ch of beg ch to join. Fasten off.

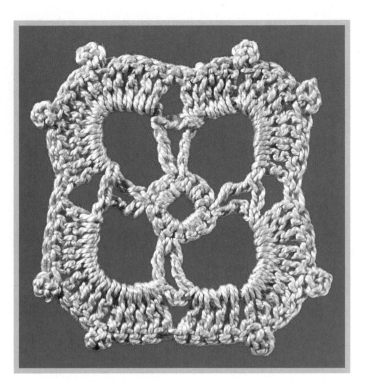

176

Ch 6 and sl st in first ch to form a ring.

Rnd 1: Ch 3 (counts as dc), 15 dc in ring, sl st in 3rd ch of beg ch to join.

Rnd 2: Ch 3 (counts as dc), dc in next dc, ch 2, *dc in each of next 2 dc, ch 2; rep from * around, sl st in 3rd ch of beg ch to join.

Rnd 3: Sl st in next dc, ch 3 (counts as dc), *2 dc in next ch-2 space, dc in next dc, ch 3**, dc in next dc; rep from * around, ending last rep at **, sl st in 3rd ch of beg ch to join.

Rnd 4: Ch 2 (counts as hdc), *hdc in each of next 3 dc, 4 hdc in next ch-3 loop**, hdc in next dc; rep from * around, ending last rep at **, sl st in 2nd ch of beg ch to join. Fasten off.

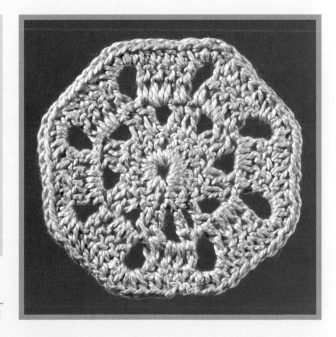

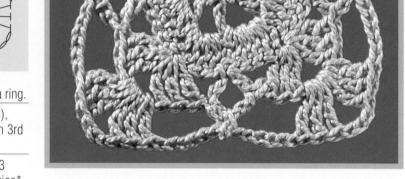

177

Ch 6 and sl st in first ch to form a ring.

Rnd 1: Ch 6 (counts as dc, ch 3),
(dc, ch 3) 5 times in ring, sl st in 3rd
ch of beg ch to join.

Rnd 2: Ch 3 (counts as dc), *5 dc in next ch-3
loop, (dc in next dc, 4 dc in next ch-3 loop) twice*,
dc in next dc; rep from * to * once, sl st in 3rd ch of beg ch to join.

Rnd 3: Ch 8 (counts as dc, ch 5), dc in first st, *skip next 3 dc, (3 tr, ch 3, 3 tr) in next dc, skip next 3 dc**, (dc, ch 5, dc) in next dc; rep from * around, ending last rep at **, sl st in 3rd ch of beg ch to join.

Rnd 4: Sl st to center of next ch-5 loop, ch 1, *sc in ch-5 loop, ch 6, (3 tr, ch 3, 3 tr) in next ch-3 loop, ch 6; rep from * around, sl st in first sc to join. Fasten off.

178

Ch 10 and sl st in first ch to form a ring.

Rnd 1: Ch 4 (counts as tr), 6 tr in ring, ch 4, (7 tr, ch 4) 3 times in ring, sl st in 4th ch of beg ch to join.

Rnd 2: Ch 1, *sc in each of next 7 tr, 3 sc in next ch-3 loop; rep from * around, sl st in first sc to join.

Rnd 3: Sl st in next sc, ch 5 (counts as dc, ch 2), (skip next sc, dc in next sc, ch 2) 3 times, *(dc, ch 2, dc) in next sc, ch 2, dc in next sc**, (ch 2, skip next sc, dc in next sc) 4 times; rep from * around, ending last rep at **, ch 2, sl st in 3rd ch of beg ch to join.

Rnd 4: Sl st in next ch-2 space, ch 1, (sc, ch 5) in each ch-2 space around, sl st in first sc to join.

Rnd 5: Sl st to center of first ch-5 loop, ch 1, (sc, ch 5) in each ch-5 loop around, sl st in first sc to join. Fasten off.

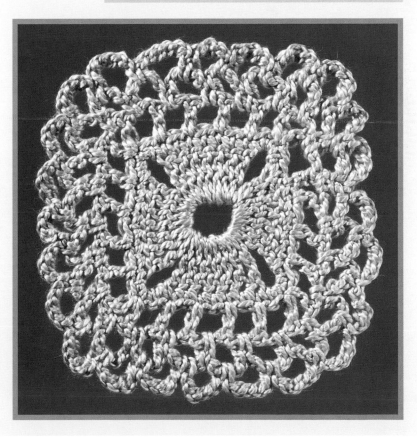

179

Picot: Ch 4, sl st in 4th ch from hook.

Ch 8 and sl st in first ch to form a ring.

Rnd 1: Ch 6 (counts as dc, ch 3), (dc, ch 3) 7 times in ring, sl st in 3rd ch of beg ch to join.

Rnd 2: Sl st in next ch-3 loop, ch 1, (sc, hdc, 3 dc, hdc, sc) in each ch-3 loop around, sl st in first sc to join.

Rnd 3: Sl st in each of next 3 sts, ch 1, *sc in center dc of shell, ch 2, skip next 3 sts, (dc, ch 3, dc) bet last skipped and next sc, ch 2, skip next 3 sts, sc in next dc, ch 6, skip next 6 sts; rep from * around, sl st in first sc to join.

Rnd 4: Sl st to next ch-3 loop, ch 1, *sc in ch-3 loop, ch 4, skip next ch-2 space, (3 dc, ch 3, 3 dc) in next ch-6 loop, ch 4, skip next ch-2 space; rep from * around, sl st in first sc to join.

Rnd 5: Ch 1, *sc in sc, picot, ch 4, skip next ch-4 loop, dc in each of next 3 dc, ch 2, picot, ch 2, skip next ch-3 loop dc in each of next 3 dc, ch 4, skip next ch-4 loop; rep from * around, sl st in first sc to join. Fasten off.

180

Ch 10 and sl st in first ch to form a ring.

Rnd 1: Ch 1, 24 sc in ring, sl st in first sc to join.

Rnd 2: Ch 1, *sc in sc, ch 8, skip next 5 sc; rep from * around, sl st in first sc to join.

Rnd 3: Ch 1, *sc in sc, 9 sc in next ch-8 loop; rep from * around, sl st in first sc to join.

Rnd 4: Ch 1, *sc in each of next 5 sc, (sc, ch 1, sc) in next sc, sc in each of next 4 sc; rep from * around, sl st in first sc to join.

Rnd 5: Sl st in next sc, ch 4 (counts as dc, ch 1), skip next sc, *dc in next sc, ch 1, skip next 2 sc, (dc, ch 3, dc) in next ch-1 space, ch 1, skip next 2 sc, (dc in next sc, ch 1, skip next sc) 3 times; rep from * around, omitting last (dc, ch 1), sl st in first sc to join.

Rnd 6: Ch 1, *(sc in dc, sc in next ch-1 space) twice, sc in next dc, (sc, ch 1, sc) in next ch-3 loop, (sc in next dc, sc in next ch-1 space) 3 times; rep from * around, sl st in first sc to join.

Rnd 7: Sl st in next sc, ch 4 (counts as dc, ch 1), skip next sc, *dc in next sc, ch 1, skip next sc, dc in next sc, ch 1, (dc, ch 2, dc) in next ch-1 space, ch 1, dc in next sc, ch 1, (skip next sc, dc in next sc, ch 1) 4 times; around, omitting last (dc, ch 1), sl st in 3rd ch of beg ch to join.

Rnd 8: Ch 1, *(sc in dc, sc in next ch-1 space) 3 times, sc in next dc, (sc, ch 1, sc) in next ch-2 space, (sc in next dc, sc in next ch-1 space) 5 times; rep from * around, sl st in first sc to join. Fasten off.

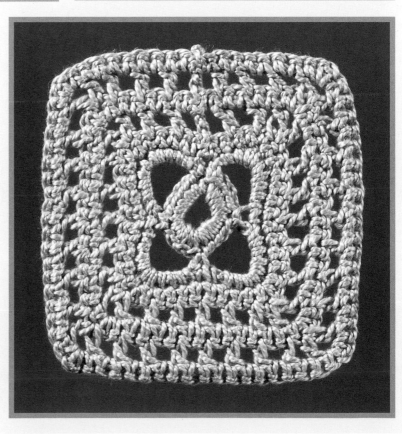

181

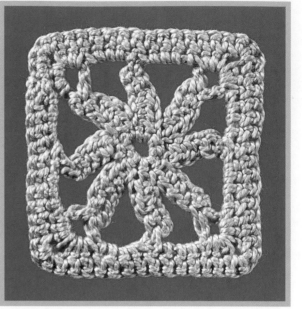

Ch 6 and sl st in first ch to form a ring.

Rnd 1 (RS): Ch 1, *sc in ring, ch 5, sc in 2nd ch from hook, sc in next ch, hdc in each of next 2 ch; rep from * 7 times, sl st in first sc to join (8 petals made). Fasten off.

Rnd 2: With RS facing, join yarn in the tip of any petal, *ch 4, (dc, ch 2, dc) in tip of next petal, ch 4, sl st in tip of next petal; rep from * around, ending with last sl st in first sl st to join.

Rnd 3: Ch 1, *sc in sl st, 4 sc in next ch-4 loop, sc in next dc, 3 sc in next ch-2 space, sc in next dc, 4 sc in next ch-4 loop; rep from * around, sl st in first sc to join.

Rnd 4: Ch 1, sc in each of next 7 sc, (sc, ch 1, sc) in next sc, sc in each of next 6 sc; rep from * around, sl st in first sc to join. Fasten off.

182

Center Square:

Ch 20.

Row 1 (RS): Dc in 8th ch from hook, *ch 2, skip next 2 ch, dc in next ch; rep from * 3 times, turn.

Row 2: Ch 5 (counts as dc, ch 2), skip next ch-2 space, (dc, ch 2) in each of next 4 dc, dc in 5th ch of turning ch, turn.

Rows 3-5: Ch 5 (counts as dc, ch 2), skip next ch-2 space, (dc, ch 2) in each of next 4 dc, dc in 3rd ch of turning ch, turn. Fasten off.

Border:

Rnd 1: With RS facing, join yarn in upper right-hand corner loop, ch 3 (counts as dc), 9 dc in corner loop, *2 dc in each of next 3 ch-2 spaces, 10 dc in next corner loop, working across side edge of Center Square, 2 dc in each of next 3 row-end sts*, 10 dc in next corner loop; rep from * to * once, sl st in 3rd ch of beg ch to join.

Rnd 2: Ch 3, skip next 3 dc, sl st in each of next 2 dc, ch 3, skip next 3 dc, sl st in next dc, ch 7, skip next 6 dc, sl st in next dc; rep from * around, ending with last sl st in first sl st to join.

Rnd 3: *Turn*, sl st in next ch-7 loop, *turn*, ch 7 (counts as tr, ch 3), *skip next ch-3 loop, sl st bet next 2 sl sts, ch 3, skip next ch-3 loop, (tr, ch 1) 11 times in next ch-7 loop**, tr in same ch-7 loop; rep from * around, ending last rep at **, sl st in 4th ch of beg ch to join. Fasten off.

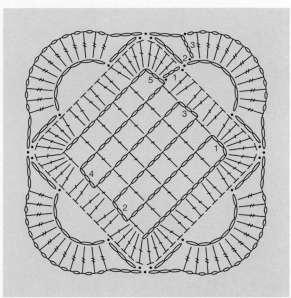

183 **2-dc puff st:** *(Yo, insert hook in next st, yo, draw yarn through st, draw yarn through 2 loops on hook) twice in same st, yo, draw yarn through 3 loops on hook.*

3-tr puff st: *(Yo [twice], insert hook in next st, yo, draw yarn through st, [yo, draw yarn through 2 loops on hook] twice) 3 times in same st, yo, draw yarn through 4 loops on hook.*

Ch 6 and sl st in first ch to form a ring.

Rnd 1: Ch 5 (counts as dc, ch 2), (dc, ch 2) 7 times in ring, sl st in 3rd ch of beg ch to join.

Rnd 2: Ch 7 (counts as dc, ch 4), 2-dc puff st in 5th ch from hook, skip next ch-2 space, *dc in next dc, ch 4, 2-dc puff st in last dc made, skip next ch-2 space; rep from * around, sl st in 3rd ch of beg ch to join.

Rnd 3: Ch 1, *sc in dc, ch 3, skip next ch-4 loop, (3-tr puff st, ch 4, 3-tr puff st, ch 4, 3-tr puff st) in next dc, ch 3; rep from * around, sl st in first sc to join.

Rnd 4: Sl st in next ch-3 loop, ch 1, *4 sc in ch-3 loop, 4 sc in next ch-4 loop, ch 2, 4 sc in next ch-4 loop, 4 sc in next ch-3 loop; rep from * around, sl st in first sc to join.

Rnd 5: Ch 4 (counts as tr), *tr in each of next 2 sc, dc in each of next 5 sc, (2 dc, ch 2, 2 dc) in next ch-2 space, dc in each of next 5 sc, tr in each of next 4 sc; rep from * around, omitting last tr, sl st in 4th ch of beg ch to join. Fasten off.

184

2-dc puff st: *(Yo, insert hook in next space, yo, draw yarn through space, draw yarn through 2 loops on hook) twice in same space, yo, draw yarn through 3 loops on hook.*

3-dc puff st: *(Yo, insert hook in next space, yo, draw yarn through space, draw yarn through 2 loops on hook) 3 times in same space, yo, draw yarn through 4 loops on hook.*

Picot: *Ch 4, sl st in 4th ch from hook.*

Ch 8 and sl st in first ch to form a ring.

Rnd 1: Ch 3 (counts as dc), 2-dc puff st in ring, *ch 1, 3-dc puff st in ring, ch 3, 3-dc puff st in ring; rep from * twice, ch 1, 3-dc puff st in ring, ch 3, sl st in 3rd ch of beg ch to join.

Rnd 2: Sl st in next ch-1 space, ch 3 (counts as dc), (dc, ch 2, 2 dc) in first ch-1 space, *ch 2, (2-dc puff st, ch 3, 2-dc puff st) in next ch-3 loop, ch 2**, (2 dc, ch 2, 2 dc) in next ch-2 space; rep from * around, ending last rep at **, sl st in 3rd ch of beg ch to join.

Rnd 3: Sl st in next ch-2 space, ch 3 (counts as dc), (dc, ch 2, 2 dc) in first ch-2 space, *ch 4, skip next ch-2 space, (2-dc puff st, ch 3, 2-dc puff st) in next ch-3 loop, ch 4, skip next ch-2 space**, (2 dc, ch 2, 2 dc) in next ch-2 space; rep from * around, ending last rep at **, sl st in 3rd ch of beg ch to join.

Rnd 4: Sl st in next ch-2 space, ch 3 (counts as dc), (dc, picot, 2 dc) in first ch-2 space, *ch 5, skip next ch-4 loop, (2-dc puff st, ch 5, 2-dc puff st) in next ch-3 loop, ch 5, skip next ch-4 loop**, (2 dc, picot, 2 dc) in next ch-2 space; rep from * around, ending last rep at **, sl st in 3rd ch of beg ch to join. Fasten off.

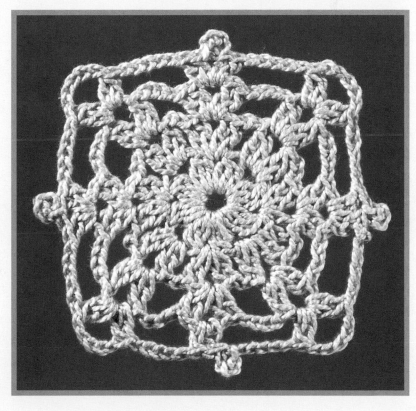

185

Ch 6 and sl st in first ch to form a ring.

Rnd 1: Ch 8 (counts as dc, ch 5), (dc, ch 5) 4 times in ring, sl st in 3rd ch of beg ch to join.

Rnd 2: Ch 1, *sc in dc, 9 sc in next ch-5 loop; rep from * around, sl st in first sc to join.

Rnd 3: Ch 1, *sc in sc, ch 9, skip next 9 sc; rep from * around, sl st in first sc to join.

Rnd 4: Ch 1, *sc in sc, 16 sc in next ch-9 loop; rep from * around, sl st in first sc to join.

Rnd 5: Ch 1, *sc in sc, ch 12, skip next 16 sc; rep from * around, sl st in first sc to join.

Rnd 6: Ch 1, *sc in sc, 20 sc in next ch-12 loop; rep from * around, sl st in first sc to join. Fasten off.

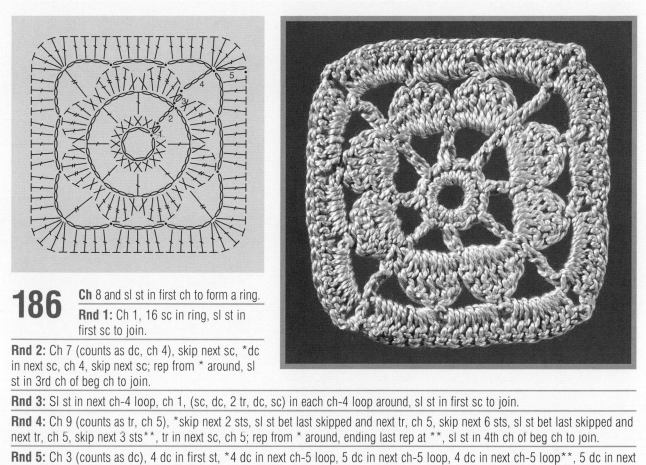

186

Ch 8 and sl st in first ch to form a ring.

Rnd 1: Ch 1, 16 sc in ring, sl st in first sc to join.

Rnd 2: Ch 7 (counts as dc, ch 4), skip next sc, *dc in next sc, ch 4, skip next sc; rep from * around, sl st in 3rd ch of beg ch to join.

Rnd 3: Sl st in next ch-4 loop, ch 1, (sc, dc, 2 tr, dc, sc) in each ch-4 loop around, sl st in first sc to join.

Rnd 4: Ch 9 (counts as tr, ch 5), *skip next 2 sts, sl st bet last skipped and next tr, ch 5, skip next 6 sts, sl st bet last skipped and next tr, ch 5, skip next 3 sts**, tr in next sc, ch 5; rep from * around, ending last rep at **, sl st in 4th ch of beg ch to join.

Rnd 5: Ch 3 (counts as dc), 4 dc in first st, *4 dc in next ch-5 loop, 5 dc in next ch-5 loop, 4 dc in next ch-5 loop**, 5 dc in next tr; rep from * around, sl st in 3rd ch of beg ch to join. Fasten off.

187

Ch 6 and sl st in first ch to form a ring.

Rnd 1: Ch 3 (counts as dc), 2 dc in ring, ch 4, (3 dc, ch 4) 5 times in ring, sl st in 3rd ch of beg ch to join.

Rnd 2: Ch 4 (counts as tr), 2 tr bet first 2 tr, *tr in next tr, 2 tr bet same tr and next tr, tr in next tr, ch 4, skip next ch-4 loop**, tr in next tr, 2 tr bet same tr and next tr; rep from * around, ending last rep at **, sl st in 4th ch of beg ch to join.

Rnd 3: Ch 4 (counts as tr), tr bet first 2 tr, *tr bet next 2 tr, tr in next tr, ch 4, skip next tr, tr in next tr, tr bet same tr and next tr, tr bet next 2 tr, tr in next tr, ch 5, skip next ch-4 loop**, tr in next tr, tr bet same tr and next tr; rep from * around, ending last rep at **, sl st in 4th ch of beg ch to join. Fasten off.

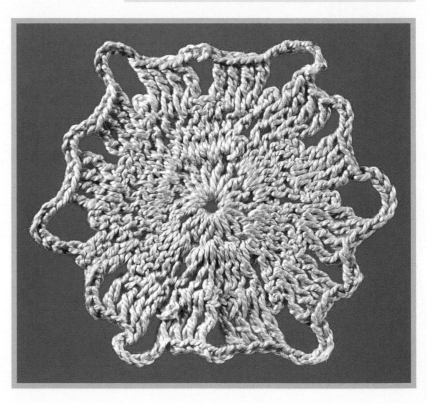

188

Ch 9 and sl st in first ch to form a ring.

Rnd 1: Ch 6 (counts as dc, ch 3), (dc, ch 3) 9 times in ring, sl st in 3rd ch of beg ch to join.

Rnd 2: Sl st in next ch-3 loop, ch 3 (counts as dc), 3 dc in first ch-3 loop, ch 2, (4 dc, ch 2) in each ch-3 loop around, sl st in 3rd ch of beg ch to join.

Rnd 3: Sl st to next ch-2 space, ch 3 (counts as dc), 4 dc in first ch-2 space, ch 3, (5 dc, ch 3) in each ch-2 space around, sl st in 3rd ch of beg ch to join.

Rnd 4: Sl st to next ch-3 loop, ch 1, (sc, ch 9) in each ch-3 loop around, sl st in first sc to join.

Rnd 5: Sl st in next ch-9 loop, ch 1, 11 sc in each ch-9 loop around, sl st in first sc to join.

Rnd 6: Ch 1, sc in each sc around, sl st in first sc to join. Fasten off.

189

2-dc puff st: (Yo, insert hook in next space, yo, draw yarn through space, draw yarn through 2 loops on hook) twice in same space, yo, draw yarn through 3 loops on hook.

3-dc puff st: (Yo, insert hook in next st or space, yo, draw yarn through st or space, draw yarn through 2 loops on hook) 3 times in same st or space, yo, draw yarn through 4 loops on hook.

Picot: Ch 4, sl st in 4th ch from hook.

Ch 6 and sl st in first ch to form a ring.

Rnd 1: Ch 1, 12 sc in ring, sl st in first sc to join.

Rnd 2: Ch 1, *sc in sc, ch 3, skip next 2 sc; rep from * around, sl st in first sc to join.

Rnd 3: Ch 1, *sc in sc, (hdc, 3 dc, hdc) in next ch-3 loop; rep from * around, sl st in first sc to join.

Rnd 4: Sl st in each of next 3 sts, ch 1, *sc in dc, ch 5, skip next 5 sts; rep from * around, sl st in first sc to join.

Rnd 5: Sl st in next ch-5 loop, ch 1, (sc, hdc, 5 dc, hdc, sc) in each ch-5 loop around, sl st in first sc to join.

Rnd 6: Sl st in each of next 4 sts, ch 1, *sc in dc, ch 4, skip next 4 sts, working over last rnd, 3-dc puff st in next corresponding sc 2 rnds below, ch 4, skip next 4 sts; rep from * around, sl st in first sc to join.

Rnd 7: Sl st in next ch-4 loop, ch 3 (counts as dc), (2-dc puff st, ch 2, 3-dc puff st) in first ch-4 loop, ch 3, *sc in next puff st, ch 3, (3-dc puff st, ch 2, 3-dc puff st) in next ch-4 loop, ch 2**, (3-dc puff st, ch 2, 3-dc puff st) in next ch-4 loop, ch 3; rep from * around, ending last rep at **, sl st in first puff st to join.

Rnd 8: Ch 1, *sc in puff st, (sc, picot, sc) in next ch-2 space, sc in next puff st, ch 3, skip next ch-3 loop, tr in next sc, picot, ch 3, skip next ch-3 loop, sc in next puff st, (sc, picot, sc) in next ch-2 space, sc in next puff st, (sc, picot, sc) in next ch-2 space; rep from * around, sl st in first sc to join. Fasten off.

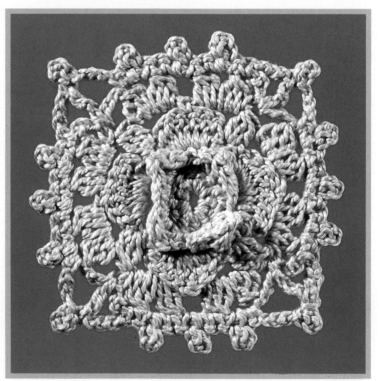

190

Puff st: (Yo, insert hook in next space, yo, draw yarn through space, draw yarn through 2 loops on hook) twice in same space, yo, draw yarn through 3 loops on hook.

Ch 6 and sl st in first ch to form a ring.

Rnd 1: Ch 3 (counts as dc), dc in ring, ch 2, (puff st, ch 2) 11 times in ring, sl st in 3rd ch of beg ch to join.

Rnd 2: Sl st in next ch-2 space, ch 1, *(sc, ch 9, sc) in ch-2 space, ch 5, sc in next ch-2 space, ch 5; rep from * around, sl st in first sc to join.

Rnd 3: Sl st in next ch-9 loop, ch 3 (counts as dc), (6 dc, ch 3, 7 dc) in first ch-9 loop, *sc in next ch-5 loop, ch 5, sc in next ch-5 loop**, (7 dc, ch 3, 7 dc) in next ch-9 loop; rep from * around, ending last rep at **, sl st in 3rd ch of beg ch to join.

Rnd 4: Sl st to next ch-3 loop, ch 1, *sc in ch-3 loop, ch 4, 3 tr in next ch-5 loop, ch 4; rep from * around, sl st in first sc to join. Fasten off.

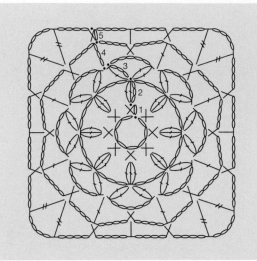

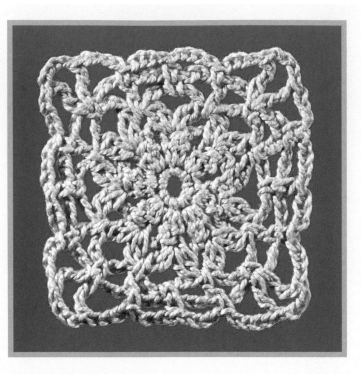

191

2-dc puff st: (Yo, insert hook in next st, yo, draw yarn through st, draw yarn through 2 loops on hook) twice in same st, yo, draw yarn through 3 loops on hook.

3-dc puff st: (Yo, insert hook in next st, yo, draw yarn through st, draw yarn through 2 loops on hook) 3 times in same st, yo, draw yarn through 4 loops on hook.

Ch 8 and sl st in first ch to form a ring.

Rnd 1: Ch 1, 8 sc in ring, sl st in first sc to join.

Rnd 2: Ch 3 (counts as dc), 2-dc puff st in first sc, ch 3, (3-dc puff st, ch 3) in each sc around, sl st in first puff st to join.

Rnd 3: Ch 3 (counts as dc), dc in first puff st, (2-dc puff st, ch 5, 2-dc puff st) in each of next 7 puff sts, 2-dc puff st in first puff st already holding beg ch and dc, ch 5, sl st in 3rd ch of beg ch to join.

Rnd 4: Sl st bet first dc and next puff st, ch 7 (counts as dc, ch 4), *sc in next ch-5 loop, ch 4**, dc bet next 2 puff sts, ch 4; rep from * around, ending last rep at **, sl st in first sc to join.

Rnd 5: Ch 1, *sc in dc, ch 4, skip next ch-4 loop, (tr, ch 4, tr) in next sc, ch 4, skip next ch-4 loop, sc in next dc, ch 4, skip next ch-4 loop, hdc in next sc, ch 4; rep from * around, sl st in first sc to join. Fasten off.

192

4-tr puff st: *(Yo [twice], insert hook in next st, yo, draw yarn through st, [yo, draw yarn through 2 loops on hook] twice) 4 times in same st, yo, draw yarn through 5 loops on hook.*

5-tr puff st: *(Yo [twice], insert hook in next st, yo, draw yarn through st, [yo, draw yarn through 2 loops on hook] twice) 5 times in same st, yo, draw yarn through 6 loops on hook.*

Ch 8 and sl st in first ch to form a ring.

Rnd 1: Ch 1, 12 sc in ring, sl st in first sc to join.

Rnd 2: Ch 4 (counts as tr), 4-tr puff st in first sc, ch 3, (5-tr puff st, ch 3) in each sc around, sl st in 4th ch of beg ch to join.

Rnd 3: Sl st in next ch-3 loop, ch 1, (sc, ch 5) in each ch-3 loop around, sl st in first sc to join.

Rnd 4: Sl st in next ch-5 loop, ch 5 (counts as dtr), 6 dtr in first ch-5 loop, *5 tr in each of next 2 ch-5 loop**, 7 dtr in next ch-5 loop; rep from * around, ending last rep at **, sl st in 5th ch of beg ch to join.

Rnd 5: Ch 1, sc in each st around, sl st in first sc to join. Fasten off.

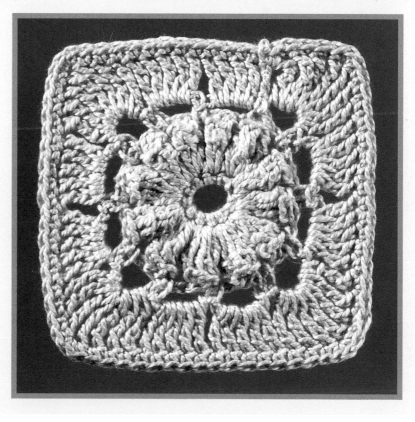

193
2-dc puff st: (Yo, insert hook in next
space, yo, draw yarn through space, draw
yarn through 2 loops on hook) twice in
same space, yo, draw yarn through 3 loops on hook.

3-dc puff st: (Yo, insert hook in next space, yo, draw yarn through space, draw yarn through 2 loops on hook) 3 times in same
space, yo, draw yarn through 4 loops on hook.

Ch 6 and sl st in first ch to form a ring.

Rnd 1: Ch 1, 8 sc in ring, sl st in first sc to join.

Rnd 2: Ch 3 (counts as dc), dc in next sc, ch 1, *2-dc cluster, working first half-closed dc in same sc as last dc made, work 2nd
half-closed dc in next sc, yo, complete cluster, ch 1; rep from * around, ending with last half-closed dc of last cluster in first sc, sl
st in 3rd ch of beg ch to join.

Rnd 3: Sl st in next ch-1 space, ch 3 (counts as dc), 2-dc puff st in first ch-1 space, ch 5, (3-dc puff st, ch 5) in each ch-1 space
around, sl st in first puff st to join.

Rnd 4: Ch 1, (sc, ch 6) in each puff st around, sl st in first sc to join.

Rnd 5: Ch 1, (sc, ch 7) in each sc around, sl st in first sc to join.

Rnd 6: Ch 1, (sc, ch 8) in each sc around, sl st in first sc to join.

Rnd 7: Ch 1, (sc, ch 9) in each sc around, sl st in first sc to join. Fasten off.

194

2-dc puff st: *(Yo, insert hook in next space, yo, draw yarn through space, draw yarn through 2 loops on hook) twice in same space, yo, draw yarn through 3 loops on hook.*

3-dc puff st: *(Yo, insert hook in next space, yo, draw yarn through space, draw yarn through 2 loops on hook) 3 times in same space, yo, draw yarn through 4 loops on hook.*

Ch 6 and sl st in first ch to form a ring.

Rnd 1: Ch 1, 8 sc in ring, sl st in first sc to join.

Rnd 2: Ch 3 (counts as dc), dc in next sc, ch 1, *2-dc cluster, working first half-closed dc in same sc as last dc made, work 2nd half-closed dc in next sc, yo, complete cluster, ch 1; rep from * around, ending with last half-closed dc of last cluster in first sc, sl st in 3rd ch of beg ch to join.

Rnd 3: Sl st in next ch-1 space, ch 3 (counts as dc), 2-dc puff st in first ch-1 space, ch 5, (3-dc puff st, ch 5) in each ch-1 space around, sl st in puff st to join.

Rnd 4: Ch 1, (sc, ch 6) in each puff st around, sl st in first sc to join.

Rnd 5: Ch 1, (sc, ch 7) in each sc around, sl st in first sc to join.

Rnd 6: Ch 1, (sc, ch 8) in each sc around, sl st in first sc to join.

Rnd 7: Ch 1, (sc, ch 9) in each sc around, sl st in first sc to join.

Rnd 8: Ch 1, *sc in sc, (2 sc, ch 5, 2 sc) in next ch-9 loop; rep from * around, sl st in first sc to join.

Rnd 9: Turn, sl st in each of next 2 sc, turn, ch 4 (counts as tr), 4-tr cluster worked across next 4 sc, *ch 9, dc in next ch-5 loop, ch 9**, 5-tr cluster worked across next 5 sc; rep from * around, ending last rep at **, sl st in 4th ch of beg ch to join. Fasten off.

195

Picot: Ch 4, sl st in 4th ch from hook.

Ch 6 and sl st in first ch to form a ring.

Rnd 1: Ch 3 (counts as dc), 11 dc in ring, sl st in 3rd ch of beg ch to join.

Rnd 2: Sl st bet first 2 sts, ch 4 (counts as tr), tr bet first 2 sts, ch 1, *2 tr bet next 2 dc, ch 1; rep from * around, sl st in 4th ch of beg ch to join.

Rnd 3: Sl st to next ch-1 space, ch 1, *sc in ch-1 space, ch 6, sc in next ch-1 space, ch 9, sc in next ch-1 space, ch 6; rep from * around, sl st in first sc to join.

Rnd 4: Sl st in next ch-6 loop, ch 1, *(5 sc, picot, 5 sc) in ch-5 loop, 17 dc in next ch-9 loop, (5 sc, picot, 5 sc) in next ch-5 loop; rep from * around, sl st in first sc to join. Fasten off.

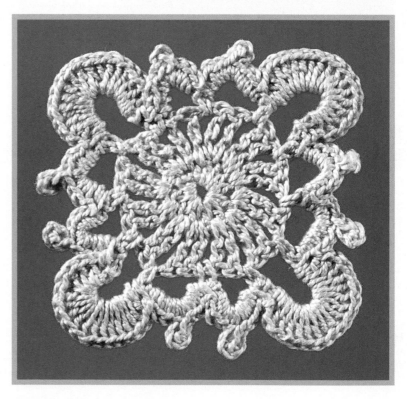

196

Ch 6 and sl st in first ch to form a ring.

Rnd 1: Ch 1, 16 sc in ring, sl st in first sc to join.

Rnd 2: Ch 8 (counts as tr, ch 4), skip next sc, *tr in next sc, ch 4, skip next sc; rep from * around, sl st in 4th ch of beg ch to join.

Rnd 3: Ch 1, 6 sc in each ch-4 loop around, sl st in first sc to join.

Rnd 4: Ch 1, sc in first sc, ch 11, skip next 4 sc, *sc bet last skipped and next sc, ch 11, skip next 5 sc; rep from * around, sl st in first sc to join.

Rnd 5: Ch 1, 13 sc in each ch-11 loop around, sl st in first sc to join.

Rnd 6: Ch 1, sc in sc, ch 5, skip next 5 sc, * sc in next sc, ch 5, skip next 6 sc **, sc bet last skipped and next sc, ch 5, skip next 6 sc; rep from * around, ending last repeat at **, sl st in first sc to join.

Rnd 7: Ch 1, 6 sc in each ch-5 loop around, sl st in first sc to join. Fasten off.

.13.
Triangle Blocks

197

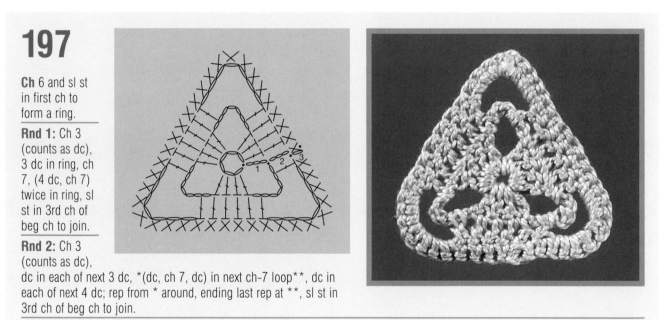

Ch 6 and sl st in first ch to form a ring.

Rnd 1: Ch 3 (counts as dc), 3 dc in ring, ch 7, (4 dc, ch 7) twice in ring, sl st in 3rd ch of beg ch to join.

Rnd 2: Ch 3 (counts as dc), dc in each of next 3 dc, *(dc, ch 7, dc) in next ch-7 loop**, dc in each of next 4 dc; rep from * around, ending last rep at **, sl st in 3rd ch of beg ch to join.

Rnd 3: Ch 1, *sc in each of next 5 dc, 7 sc in next ch-7 loop, sc in next dc; rep from * around, sl st in first sc to join. Fasten off.

198

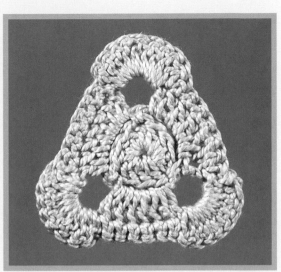

Ch 6 and sl st in first ch to form a ring.

Rnd 1: Ch 3 (counts as dc), 14 dc in ring, sl st in 3rd ch of beg ch to join.

Rnd 2: Ch 1, *sc in dc, ch 6, skip next 4 dc; rep from * around, sl st in first sc to join.

Rnd 3: Sl st in next ch-6 loop, ch 3 (counts as dc), 6 dc in first ch-6 loop, ch 4, (7 dc, ch 4) in each of next 2 ch-6 loops, sl st in 3rd ch of beg ch to join.

Rnd 4: Ch 1, *sc in each of next 7 dc, 9 dc in next ch-4 loop; rep from * around, sl st in first sc to join. Fasten off.

199

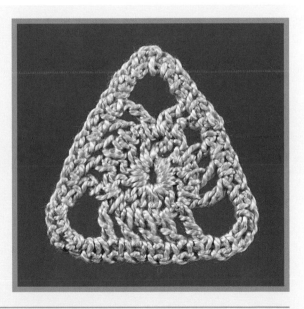

Ch 6 and sl st in first ch to form a ring.

Rnd 1: Ch 4 (counts as dc, ch 1), (dc, ch 1) 11 times in ring, sl st in 3rd ch of beg ch to join.

Rnd 2: Sl st in next ch-1 space, ch 4 (counts as dc, ch 1), *(tr, ch 7, tr) in next ch-1 space, ch 1, (dc, ch 1) in each of next 3 loops; rep from * around, omitting last (dc, ch 1), sl st in 3rd ch of beg ch to join.

Rnd 3: Sl st in next ch-1 space, ch 1, sc in first ch-1 space, ch 1, *(sc, ch 1, sc, ch 3, sc, ch 1, sc) in next ch-7 loop, ch 1, (sc, ch 1) in each of next 4 ch-1 spaces; rep from * around, omitting last (sc, ch 1), sl st in first sc to join. Fasten off.

200

Ch 6 and sl st in first ch to form a ring.

Rnd 1: Ch 3 (counts as dc), dc in ring, ch 2, (2 dc, ch 2) 5 times in ring, sl st in 3rd ch of beg ch to join.

Rnd 2: Ch 4 (counts as dc, ch 1), dc bet first 2 sts, ch 1, dc in next dc, sc in next ch-2 space, *dc in next dc, ch 1, dc bet same dc and next dc, ch 1, dc in next dc, sc in next ch-2 space; rep from * around, sl st in 3rd ch of beg ch to join.

Rnd 3: Ch 1, *sc in next ch-1 space, ch 1, skip next ch-1 space, sc in next dc, (2 tr, ch 5, 2 tr) in next sc, sc in next dc, ch 1, skip next dc, sc in next ch-1 space, ch 1, skip next dc, hdc in next sc, ch 1; rep from * around, sl st in first sc to join. Fasten off.

201

2-dc puff st: *(Yo, insert hook in next st, yo, draw yarn through st, draw yarn through 2 loops on hook) twice in same st, yo, draw yarn through 3 loops on hook.*

3-dc puff st: *(Yo, insert hook in next st, yo, draw yarn through st, draw yarn through 2 loops on hook) 3 times in same st, yo, draw yarn through 4 loops on hook.*

Ch 6 and sl st in first ch to form a ring.

Rnd 1: Ch 10 (counts as dc, ch 7), *dc in ring, ch 3, dc in ring, ch 7; rep from * once, dc in ring, ch 3, sl st in 3rd ch of beg ch to join.

Rnd 2: Sl st in next ch-7 loop, ch 3 (counts as dc), (3 dc, ch 7, 4 dc) in same ch-7 loop, *3 dc in next ch-3 loop**, (4 dc, ch 7, 4 dc) in next ch-7 loop; rep from * around, ending last rep at **, sl st in 3rd ch of beg ch to join.

Rnd 3: Ch 3 (counts as dc), 2-dc puff st in same st, *ch 3, (4 dc, ch 7, 4 dc) in next ch-7 loop, ch 3, skip next 3 dc, 3-dc puff st in next dc, ch 3, skip next dc, sc in next dc, ch 3, skip next dc**, 3-dc puff st in next dc; rep from * around, ending last rep at **, sl st in first puff st to join. Fasten off.

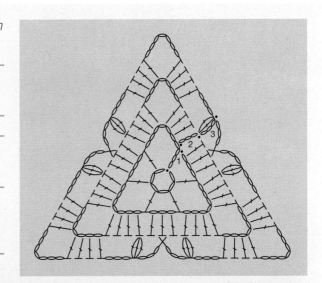

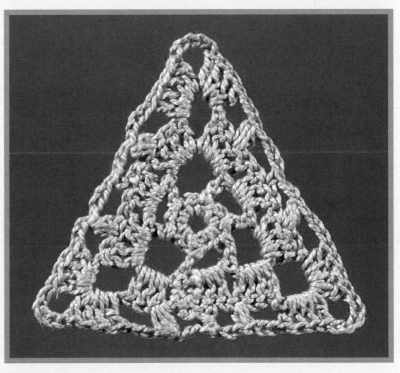

202

Ch 6 and sl st in first ch to form a ring.

Rnd 1: Ch 3 (counts as dc), 3 dc in ring, ch 4, (4 dc, ch 4) twice in ring, sl st in 3rd ch of beg ch to join.

Rnd 2: Ch 3 (counts as dc), dc in each of next 3 dc, *(dc, ch 5, dc) in next ch-4 loop**, dc in each of next 4 dc; rep from * around, ending last rep at **, sl st in 3rd ch of beg ch to join.

Rnd 3: Ch 3 (counts as dc), dc in each of next 4 dc, *(dc, ch 6, dc) in next ch-5 loop**, dc in each of next 6 dc; rep from * around, ending last rep at **, dc in next dc, sl st in 3rd ch of beg ch to join.

Rnd 4: Ch 3 (counts as dc), dc in each of next 5 dc, *(dc, ch 7, dc) in next ch-6 loop**, dc in each of next 8 dc; rep from * around, ending last rep at **, dc in each of next 2 dc, sl st in 3rd ch of beg ch to join.

Rnd 5: Ch 1, *sc in each of next 7 dc, (4 sc, ch 2, 4 sc) in next ch-7 loop**, sc in each of next 10 dc; rep from * around, ending last rep at **, sc in each of next 3 dc, sl st in first sc to join. Fasten off.

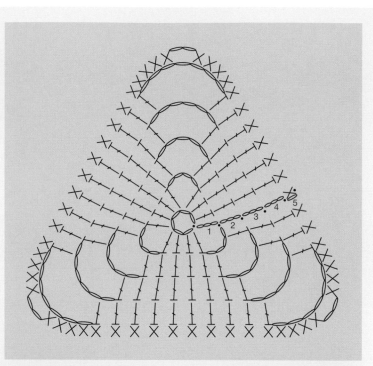

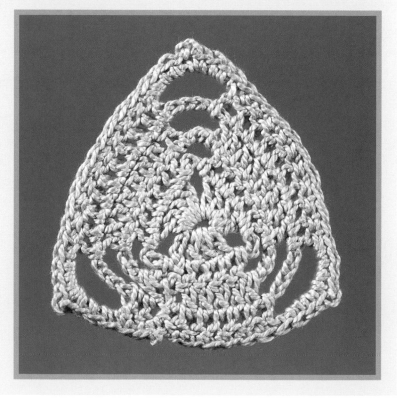

203

2-dc puff st: *(Yo, insert hook in next space, yo, draw yarn through space, draw yarn through 2 loops on hook) twice in same space, yo, draw yarn through 3 loops on hook.*

4-tr puff st: *(Yo [twice], insert hook in next space, yo, draw yarn through space, [yo, draw yarn through 2 loops on hook] twice) 4 times in same space, yo, draw yarn through 5 loops on hook.*

Ch 6 and sl st in first ch to form a ring.

Rnd 1: Ch 3 (counts as dc), dc in ring, ch 2, (2-dc puff st, ch 2) 11 times in ring, sl st in 3rd ch of beg ch to join.

Rnd 2: Sl st in next ch-2 space, ch 1, *sc in ch-1 space, ch 5, 4-tr puff st in next ch-2 space, ch 5; rep from * around, sl st in first sc to join.

Rnd 3: Ch 6 (counts as dc, ch 3), *skip next ch-5 loop, (3 tr, ch 3, 2 tr, ch 3, 3 tr) in next puff st, ch 3, skip next ch-5 loop, dc in next sc, ch 3, skip next ch-5 loop, sc in next puff st, ch 3, skip next ch-5 loop**, dc in next sc; rep from * around, ending last rep at **, sl st in 3rd ch of beg ch to join. Fasten off.

.14.
Circles

204   Ch 8 and sl st in first ch to form a ring.

Rnd 1: Ch 3 (counts as dc), 19 dc in ring, sl st in 3rd ch of beg ch to join. Fasten off.

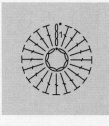

205   Ch 4 and sl st in first ch to form a ring.

Rnd 1: Ch 4 (counts as dc, ch 1), (dc, ch 1) 7 times in ring, sl st in 3rd ch of beg ch to join.

Rnd 2: Sl st in next ch-1 space, ch 3 (counts as dc), 2 dc in first ch-1 space, ch 1, (3 dc, ch 1) in each ch-1 space around, sl st in 3rd ch of beg ch to join. Fasten off.

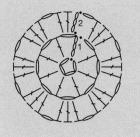

206

2-dc puff st: *(Yo, insert hook in next space, yo, draw yarn through space, draw yarn through 2 loops on hook) twice in same space, yo, draw yarn through 3 loops on hook.*

3-dc puff st: *(Yo, insert hook in next space, yo, draw yarn through space, draw yarn through 2 loops on hook) 3 times in same space, yo, draw yarn through 4 loops on hook.*

Ch 6 and sl st in first ch to form a ring.

Rnd 1: Ch 5 (counts as dc, ch 2), (dc, ch 2) 7 times in ring, sl st in 3rd ch of beg ch to join.

Rnd 2: Sl st in next ch-2 space, ch 3 (counts as dc), 2-dc puff st in first ch-2 space, ch 3, (3-dc puff st, ch 3) in each ch-2 space around, sl st in first puff st to join. Fasten off.

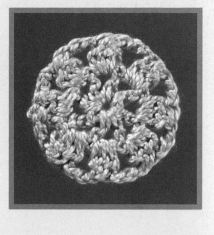

207

2-dc puff st: *(Yo, insert hook in next space, yo, draw yarn through space, draw yarn through 2 loops on hook) twice in same space, yo, draw yarn through 3 loops on hook.*

3-dc puff st: *(Yo, insert hook in next space, yo, draw yarn through space, draw yarn through 2 loops on hook) 3 times in same space, yo, draw yarn through 4 loops on hook.*

Ch 6 and sl st in first ch to form a ring.

Rnd 1: Ch 3 (counts as dc), dc in ring, ch 1, (2 dc, ch 1) 4 times in ring, sl st in 3rd ch of beg ch to join.

Rnd 2: Sl st to next ch-1 space, ch 3 (counts as dc), 2-dc puff st in first ch-1 space, ch 4, (3-dc puff st, ch 4) in each ch-1 space around, sl st in first puff st to join.

Rnd 3: Ch 1, *sc in puff st, 5 sc in next ch-4 loop; rep from * around, sl st in first sc to join. Fasten off.

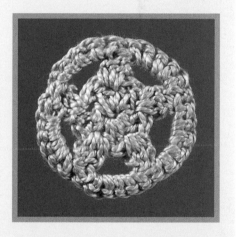

208

Ch 6 and sl st in first ch to form a ring.

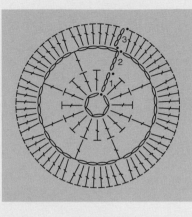

Rnd 1: Ch 3 (counts as dc), 15 dc in ring, sl st in 3rd ch of beg ch to join.

Rnd 2: Ch 7 (counts as dc, ch 4), skip next dc, *dc in next dc, ch 4, skip next dc; rep from * around, sl st in 3rd ch of beg ch to join.

Rnd 3: Sl st in next ch-4 loop, ch 3, 7 dc in first ch-4 loop, 8 dc in each ch-4 loop around, sl st in 3rd ch of beg ch to join. Fasten off.

209

2-dc puff st: *(Yo, insert hook in next space, yo, draw yarn through space, draw yarn through 2 loops on hook) twice in same space, yo, draw yarn through 3 loops on hook.*

Ch 6 and sl st in first ch to form a ring.

Rnd 1: Ch 1, 16 sc in ring, sl st in first sc to join.

Rnd 2: Ch 4 (counts as dc, ch 1), (dc, ch 1) in each sc around, sl st in 3rd ch of beg ch to join.

Rnd 3: Sl st in next ch-1 space, ch 1, 2 sc in each ch-1 space around, sl st in first sc to join.

Rnd 4: Sl st bet first and 2nd sc, ch 3 (counts as dc), dc bet first and 2nd sc, *(ch 4, skip next 3 sc, 2-dc puff st bet last skipped and next sc) 4 times, ch 4, skip next 4 sc**, 2-dc puff st bet last skipped and next sc; rep from * to ** once, sl st in 3rd ch of beg ch to join. Fasten off.

210

2-dc puff st: (Yo, insert hook in next st, yo, draw yarn through st, draw yarn through 2 loops on hook) twice in same st, yo, draw yarn through 3 loops on hook.

3-dc puff st: (Yo, insert hook in next st, yo, draw yarn through st, draw yarn through 2 loops on hook) 3 times in same st, yo, draw yarn through 4 loops on hook.

Beginning popcorn (beg pop): *Ch 3 (counts as dc), 3 dc in same st, drop loop from hook, insert hook from front to back in 3rd ch of beg ch, place dropped loop on hook, draw loop through st.*

Popcorn (pop): *4 dc in same st, drop loop from hook, insert hook from front to back in first dc of 4-dc group, place dropped loop on hook, draw loop through st.*

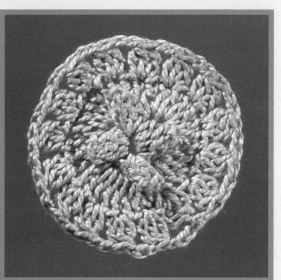

Ch 6 and sl st in first ch to form a ring.

Rnd 1: Beg pop in ring, ch 3, (pop, ch 3) 3 times in ring, sl st in first pop to join.

Rnd 2: Ch 3 (counts as dc), *7 dc in next ch-3 loop**, dc in next pop; rep from * around, ending last rep at **, sl st in 3rd ch of beg ch to join.

Rnd 3: Sl st in next dc, ch 3 (counts as dc), 2-dc puff st in same dc, ch 2, skip next dc, *3-dc puff st in next dc, ch 2, skip next dc; rep from * around, sl st in first puff st to join. Fasten off.

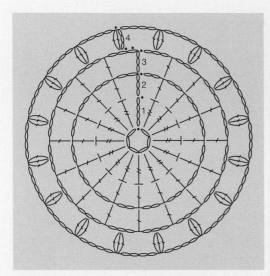

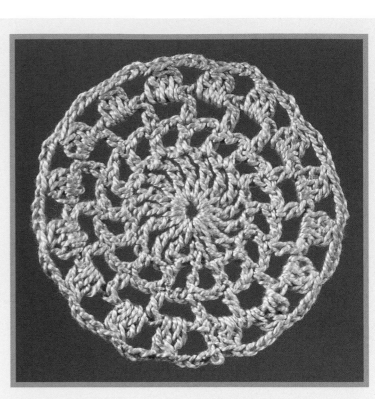

211

2-dc puff st: (Yo, insert hook in next space, yo, draw yarn through space, draw yarn through 2 loops on hook) twice in same space, yo, draw yarn through 3 loops on hook.

3-dc puff st: (Yo, insert hook in next space, yo, draw yarn through space, draw yarn through 2 loops on hook) 3 times in same space, yo, draw yarn through 4 loops on hook.

Ch 6 and sl st in first ch to form a ring.

Rnd 1: Ch 4 (counts as tr), 15 tr in ring, sl st in 4th ch of beg ch to join.

Rnd 2: Ch 5 (counts as dc, ch 2), (dc, ch 2) in each tr around, sl st in 4th ch of beg ch to join.

Rnd 3: Ch 6 (counts as dc, ch 3), skip next ch-2 space, (dc, ch 3) in each dc around, sl st in 3rd ch of beg ch to join.

Rnd 4: Sl st to center of next ch-3 loop, ch 3 (counts as dc), 2-dc puff st in first ch-3 loop, ch 4, (3-dc puff st, ch 4) in each ch-3 loop around, sl st in first puff st to join. Fasten off.

212

Ch 6 and sl st in first ch to form a ring.

Rnd 1: Ch 6 (counts as dc, ch 3), (dc, ch 3) 5 times in ring, sl st in 3rd ch of beg ch to join.

Rnd 2: Sl st in next ch-3 loop, ch 4 (counts as dc, ch 1), (dc, ch 1) 3 times in first ch-3 loop, (dc, ch 1) 4 times in each ch-3 loop around, sl st in 3rd ch of beg ch to join.

Rnd 3: Sl st in next ch-1 space, ch 10 (counts as dc, ch 7), skip next ch-1 space, *dc in next ch-1 space, ch 7, skip next ch-1 space; rep from * around, sl st in 3rd ch of beg ch to join.

Rnd 4: Sl st to center of next ch-7 loop, ch 1, sc in ch-7 loop, *ch 1, tr in next ch-7 loop, ch 3, working behind last tr made, tr in last ch-7 loop (crossed tr made), ch 1**, sc in next ch-7 loop already holding first tr of last crossed tr; rep from * around, ending last rep at **, sl st in first sc to join. Fasten off.

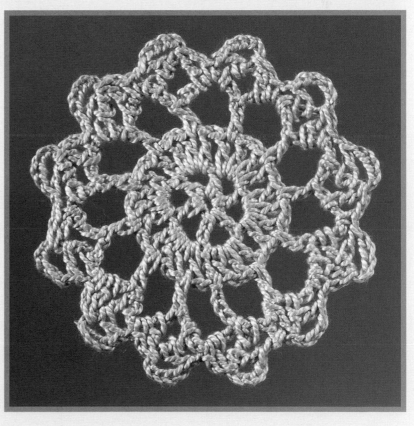

213

Ch 6 and sl st in first ch to form a ring.

Rnd 1: Ch 1, 12 sc in ring, sl st in first sc to join.

Rnd 2: Ch 5 (counts as dc, ch 2), (dc, ch 2) in each sc around, sl st in 3rd ch of beg ch to join.

Rnd 3: Ch 1, *sc in dc, skip next ch-2 space, 6 dc in next dc, skip next ch-2 space; rep from * around, sl st in first sc to join.

Rnd 4: Sl st in each of next 2 dc, ch 1, *sc in dc, ch 6, skip next 2 dc, sc in next dc, ch 6, skip next 3 sts; rep from * around, sl st in first sc to join.

Rnd 5: Ch 1, *sc in sc, 7 sc in next ch-6 loop; rep from * around, sl st in first sc to join. Fasten off.

214

Picot: *Ch 4, sl st in 4th ch from hook.*

Ch 6 and sl st in first ch to form a ring.

Rnd 1: Ch 3 (counts as dc), 15 dc in ring, sl st in 3rd ch of beg ch to join.

Rnd 2: Ch 5 (counts as dc, ch 2), (dc, ch 2) in each dc around, sl st in 3rd ch of beg ch to join.

Rnd 3: Ch 6 (counts as dc, ch 3), (dc, ch 3) in each dc around, sl st in 3rd ch of beg ch to join.

Rnd 4: Ch 7 (counts as dc, ch 4), (dc, ch 4) in each dc around, sl st in 3rd ch of beg ch to join.

Rnd 5: Sl st in next ch-4 loop, ch 3 (counts as dc), 4 dc in first ch-4 loop, picot, (5 dc, picot) in each ch-4 loop around, sl st in 3rd ch of beg ch to join. Fasten off.

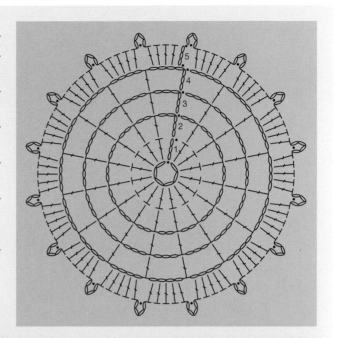

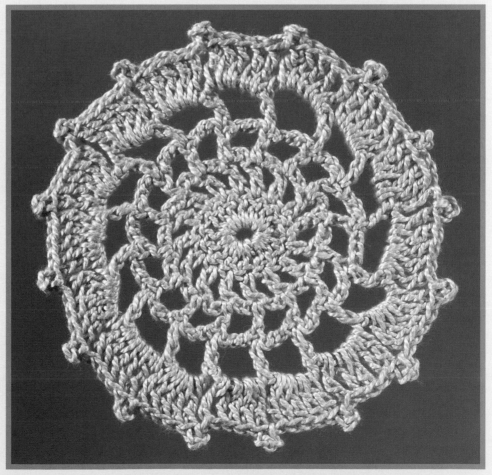

.15.
Hexagons

215 **Ch** 6 and sl st in first ch to form a ring.

Rnd 1: Ch 6 (counts as tr, ch 2), (tr, ch 2) 11 times in ring, sl st in 4th ch of beg ch to join.

Rnd 2: Sl st in next ch-2 space, ch 3 (counts as dc), (dc, ch 2, 2 dc) in first ch-2 space, *3 dc in next ch-2 space**, (2 dc, ch 2, 2 dc) in next ch-2 space; rep from * around, ending last rep at **, sl st in 3rd ch of beg ch to join. Fasten off.

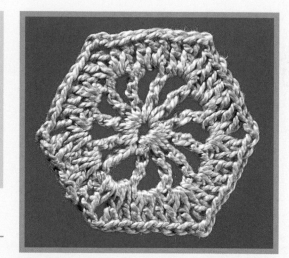

216 **Ch** 6 and sl st in first ch to form a ring.

Rnd 1: Ch 3 (counts as dc), 17 dc in ring, sl st in 3rd ch of beg ch to join.

Rnd 2: Ch 1, *sc in dc, ch 5, skip next 2 dc; rep from * around, sl st in first sc to join.

Rnd 3: Sl st in next ch-5 loop, ch 3 (counts as dc), (dc, ch 3, 2 dc) in first ch-5 loop, *2-dc cluster, working first half-closed dc in same ch-5 loop, work 2nd half-closed dc in next ch-5 loop, yo, complete cluster**, (2 dc, ch 3, 2 dc) in same ch-5 loop; rep from * around, ending last rep at **, sl st in 3rd ch of beg ch to join. Fasten off.

217

Ch 6 and sl st in first ch to form a ring.

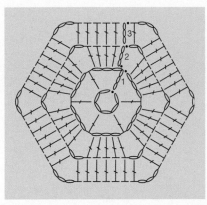

Rnd 1: Ch 6 (counts as dc, ch 3), (dc, ch 3) 5 times in ring, sl st in 3rd ch of beg ch to join.

Rnd 2: Sl st in next ch-3 loop, ch 3 (counts as dc), 4 dc in first ch-3 loop, ch 2, (5 dc, ch 2) in each ch-3 loop around, sl st in 3rd ch of beg ch to join.

Rnd 3: Ch 3 (counts as dc), dc in each of next 4 dc, *(dc, ch 3, dc) in next ch-2 space**, dc in each of next 5 dc; rep from * around, ending last rep at **, sl st in 3rd ch of beg ch to join. Fasten off.

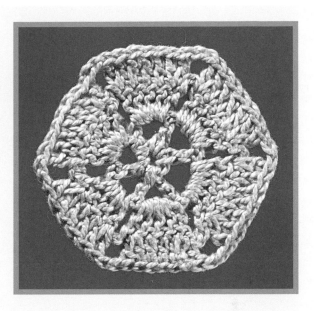

218

Ch 6 and sl st in first ch to form a ring.

Rnd 1: Ch 3 (counts as dc), 2 dc in ring, ch 1, (3 dc, ch 1) 5 times in ring, sl st in 3rd ch of beg ch to join.

Rnd 2: Sl st to next ch-1 space, ch 3 (counts as dc), (2 dc, ch 1, 3 dc) in first ch-1 space, (3 dc, ch 1, 3 dc) in each ch-1 space around, sl st in 3rd ch of beg ch to join.

Rnd 3: Sl st to next ch-1 space, ch 3 (counts as dc), (2 dc, ch 1, 3 dc) in first ch-1 space, *skip next 3 dc, 2 dc bet last skipped and next dc**, (3 dc, ch 1, 3 dc) in next ch-1 space; rep from * around, ending last rep at **, sl st in 3rd ch of beg ch to join. Fasten off.

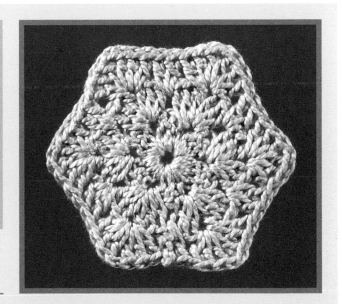

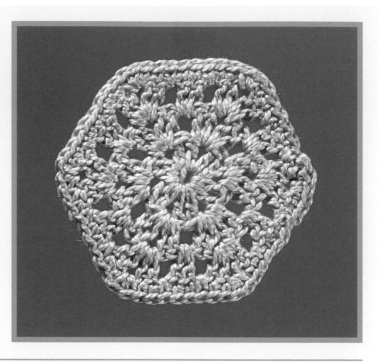

219

Ch 6 and sl st in first ch to form a ring.

Rnd 1: Ch 3 (counts as dc), dc in ring, ch 1, (2 dc, ch 1) 5 times in ring, sl st in 3rd ch of beg ch to join.

Rnd 2: Sl st to next ch-1 space, ch 3 (counts as dc), (dc, ch 1, 2 dc) in first ch-1 space, ch 1, (3 dc, ch 1, 3 dc, ch 1) in each ch-1 space around, sl st in 3rd ch of beg ch to join.

Rnd 3: Sl st to next ch-1 space, ch 3 (counts as dc), (dc, ch 1, 2 dc) in first ch-1 space, *ch 1, 2 dc in next ch-1 space, ch 1**, (2 dc, ch 1, 2 dc) in next ch-1 space; rep from * around, ending last rep at **, sl st in 3rd ch of beg ch to join.

Rnd 4: Ch 1, *sc in each of next 2 dc, 2 sc in next ch-2 space, (sc in each of next 2 dc, sc in next ch-1 space) twice; rep from * around, sl st in first sc to join. Fasten off.

220

Ch 5 and sl st in first ch to form a ring.

Rnd 1: Ch 3 (counts as dc), 11 dc in ring, sl st in 3rd ch of beg ch to join.

Rnd 2: Ch 3 (counts as dc), dc in first st, *2 dc in next dc, ch 1**, 2 dc in next dc; rep from * around, ending last rep at **, sl st in 3rd ch of beg ch to join.

Rnd 3: Ch 3 (counts as dc), dc in first st, *dc in each of next 2 dc, 2 dc in next dc, ch 2, skip next ch-1 space**, 2 dc in next dc; rep from * around, ending last rep at **, sl st in 3rd ch of beg ch to join.

Rnd 4: Ch 3 (counts as dc), dc in first st, *dc in each of next 4 dc, 2 dc in next dc, ch 3, skip next ch-2 space**, 2 dc in next dc; rep from * around, ending last rep at **, sl st in 3rd ch of beg ch to join.

Rnd 5: Ch 3 (counts as dc), dc in first st, *dc in each of next 6 dc, 2 dc in next dc, ch 4, skip next ch-3 loop**, 2 dc in next dc; rep from * around, ending last rep at **, sl st in 3rd ch of beg ch to join. Fasten off.

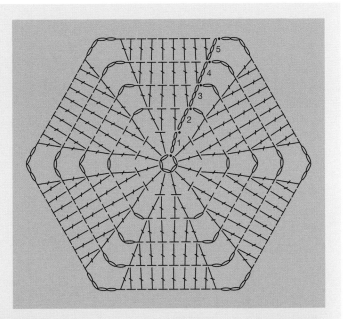

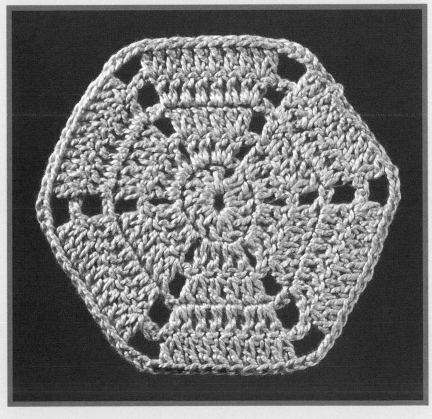

221

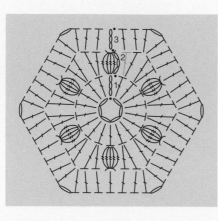

Beginning pop-corn (beg pop): Ch 4 (counts as tr), 4 tr in same st, drop loop from hook, insert hook from front to back in 4th ch of beg ch, place dropped loop on hook, draw loop through st.

Popcorn (pop): 5 tr in same st, drop loop from hook, insert hook from front to back in first dc of 5-tr group, place dropped loop on hook, draw loop through st.

Ch 6 and sl st in first ch to form a ring.

Rnd 1: Ch 3 (counts as dc), 17 dc in ring, sl st in 3rd ch of beg ch to join.

Rnd 2: Beg pop in first st, *2 dc in each of next 2 dc**, pop in next dc; rep from * around, ending last rep at **, sl st in 3rd ch of beg ch to join.

Rnd 3: Ch 3 (counts as dc), *dc in each of next 2 dc, (dc, ch 1, dc) bet same dc and next dc, dc in each of next 2 dc**, dc in next pop; rep from * around, ending last rep at **, sl st in 3rd ch of beg ch to join. Fasten off.

222

Y-stitch (Y-st): *Tr in space, 2 dc in middle of last tr made.*

Ch 6 and sl st in first ch to form a ring.

Rnd 1: Ch 4 (counts as tr), 2 dc in 3rd ch from hook (counts as Y-st), ch 1, (Y-st, ch 1) 5 times in ring, sl st in 4th ch of beg ch to join.

Rnd 2: Ch 3 (counts as dc), dc in next dc, *ch 3, 2-dc cluster, working first half-closed dc in same dc as last dc made, work 2nd half-closed dc in next dc, yo, complete cluster, ch 3, skip next ch-1 space**, 2-dc cluster worked across next 2 dc; rep from * around, ending last rep at **, sl st in 3rd ch of beg ch to join.

Rnd 3: Sl st in next ch-3 loop, ch 3 (counts as dc), 2 dc in first ch-3 loop, *ch 3, working over next ch-3 loop, dc in next corresponding ch-1 space 2 rnds below, ch 3**, 3 dc in next ch-3 loop; rep from * around, ending last rep at **, sl st in 3rd ch of beg ch to join.

Rnd 4: Ch 3 (counts as dc), *(dc, ch 3, dc) in next dc, dc in next dc, 3 dc in each of next 2 ch-3 loops**, dc in next dc; rep from * around, ending last rep at **, sl st in 3rd ch of beg ch to join. Fasten off.

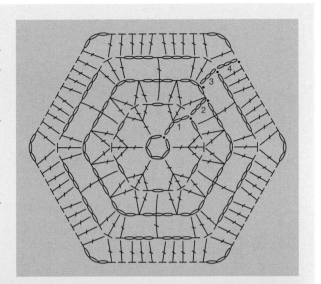

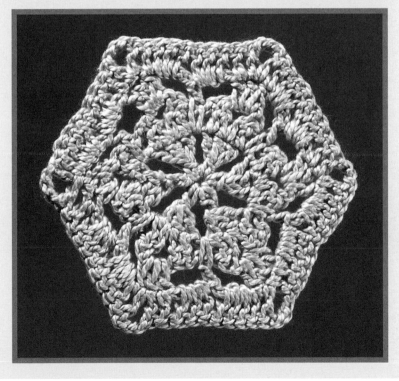

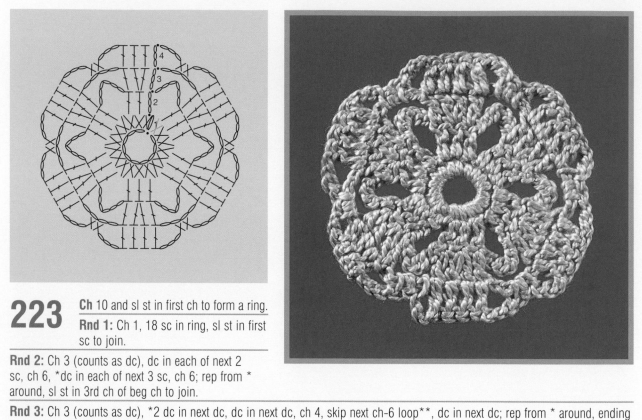

223

Ch 10 and sl st in first ch to form a ring.

Rnd 1: Ch 1, 18 sc in ring, sl st in first sc to join.

Rnd 2: Ch 3 (counts as dc), dc in each of next 2 sc, ch 6, *dc in each of next 3 sc, ch 6; rep from * around, sl st in 3rd ch of beg ch to join.

Rnd 3: Ch 3 (counts as dc), *2 dc in next dc, dc in next dc, ch 4, skip next ch-6 loop**, dc in next dc; rep from * around, ending last rep at **, sl st in 3rd ch of beg ch to join.

Rnd 4: Ch 3 (counts as dc), *dc in each of next 3 dc, ch 3, 2 sc in next ch-4 loop, ch 3**, dc in next dc; rep from * around, ending last rep at **, sl st in 3rd ch of beg ch to join. Fasten off.

224

Ch 8 and sl st in first ch to form a ring.

Rnd 1: Ch 7 (counts as dc, ch 4), (dc, ch 4) 5 times in ring, sl st in 3rd ch of beg ch to join.

Rnd 2: Ch 4 (counts as tr), *(2 tr, ch 3, 2 tr) in next ch-4 loop, tr in next dc; rep from * around, omitting last tr, sl st in 4th ch of beg ch to join.

Rnd 3: Sl st to next ch-3 loop, ch 4 (counts as tr), 4 tr in first ch-3 loop, ch 8, (5 tr, ch 8) in each ch-3 loop around, sl st in 4th ch of beg ch to join.

Rnd 4: Ch 4 (counts as tr), tr in each of next 4 tr, *ch 5, sc in next ch-8 loop, ch 5**, tr in each of next 5 tr; rep from * around, ending last rep at **, sl st in 4th ch of beg ch to join. Fasten off.

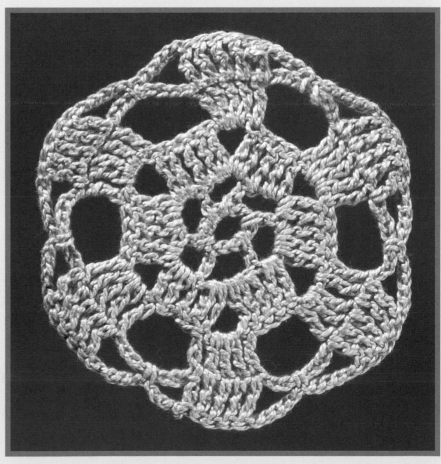

225

Ch 6 and sl st in first ch to form a ring.

Rnd 1: Ch 3 (counts as dc), 2 dc in ring, ch 1, (3 dc, ch 1) 5 times in ring, sl st in 3rd ch of beg ch to join.

Rnd 2: Sl st to next ch-1 space, ch 3 (counts as dc), 2 dc in first ch-1 space, ch 3, (3 dc, ch 3) in each ch-1 space around, sl st in 3rd ch of beg ch to join.

Rnd 3: Ch 3 (counts as dc), dc in first st, *dc in next dc, 2 dc in next dc, ch 5, skip next ch-3 loop**, 2 dc in next dc; rep from * around, ending last rep at **, sl st in 3rd ch of beg ch to join.

Rnd 4: Ch 3 (counts as dc), dc in first st, *dc in each of next 3 dc, 2 dc in next dc, ch 3, sc in next ch-5 loop, ch 3**, 2 dc in next dc; rep from * around, ending last rep at **, sl st in 3rd ch of beg ch to join.

Rnd 5: Ch 3 (counts as dc), dc in first st, *dc in each of next 5 dc, 2 dc in next dc, ch 3, (sc, ch 3) in each of next 2 ch-3 loops**, 2 dc in next dc; rep from * around, ending last rep at **, sl st in 3rd ch of beg ch to join. Fasten off.

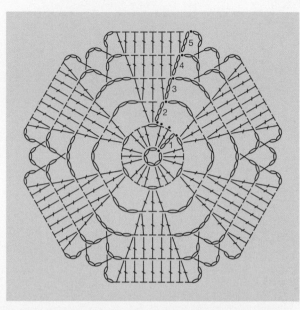

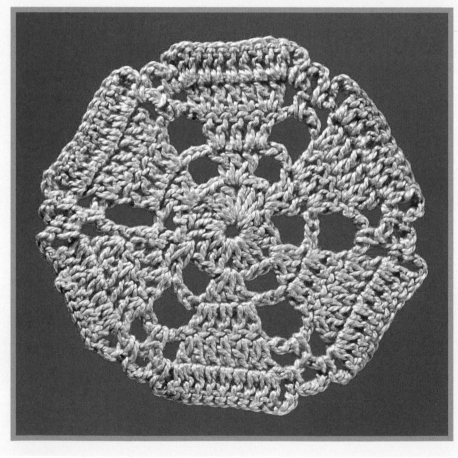

226

Ch 6 and sl st in first ch to form a ring.

Rnd 1: Ch 3 (counts as dc), 17 dc in ring, sl st in 3rd ch of beg ch to join.

Rnd 2: Ch 3 (counts as dc), 2 dc in first st, *ch 3, sc in each of next 2 dc, ch 3**, 3 dc in next dc; rep from * around, ending last rep at **, sl st in 3rd ch of beg ch to join.

Rnd 3: Sl st in next dc, ch 3 (counts as dc), (dc, ch 1, 2 dc) in same dc, *ch 2, sc in next ch-3 loop, ch 1, sc in next ch-3 loop, ch 2, skip next dc**, (2 dc, ch 1, 2 dc) in next dc; rep from * around, ending last rep at **, sl st in 3rd ch of beg ch to join.

Rnd 4: Sl st to next ch-1 space, ch 1, *sc in ch-1 space, ch 3, skip next ch-2 space, 3 dc in next ch-1 space, ch 3, skip next ch-2 space; rep from * around, sl st in first sc to join.

Rnd 5: Ch 3 (counts as dc), (dc, ch 2, 2 dc) in first sc, *ch 2, sc in next ch-3 loop, dc in each of next 3 dc, ch 2, sc in next ch-3 loop, ch 2**, (2 dc, ch 2, 2 dc) in next sc; rep from * around, ending last rep at **, sl st in 3rd ch of beg ch to join. Fasten off.

227

2-dc puff st: *(Yo, insert hook in next space, yo, draw yarn through space, draw yarn through 2 loops on hook) twice in same space, yo, draw yarn through 3 loops on hook.*

3-dc puff st: *(Yo, insert hook in next space, yo, draw yarn through space, draw yarn through 2 loops on hook) 3 times in same space, yo, draw yarn through 4 loops on hook.*

Ch 6 and sl st in first ch to form a ring.

Rnd 1: Ch 3 (counts as dc), 2-dc puff st in ring, ch 3, (3-dc puff st, ch 3) 5 times in ring, sl st in first puff st to join.

Rnd 2: Sl st in next ch-3 loop, ch 3 (counts as dc), (2-dc puff st, ch 3, 3-dc puff st) in first ch-3 loop, ch 3, *(3-dc puff st, ch 3, 3-dc puff st) in next ch-3 loop, ch 3; rep from * around, sl st in 3rd ch of beg ch to join.

Rnd 3: Sl st to center of next ch-3 loop, ch 3 (counts as dc), 2-dc puff st in first ch-3 loop, *ch 3, (3-dc puff st, ch 3, 3-dc puff st) in next ch-3 loop, ch 3**, 3-dc puff st in next ch-3 loop; rep from * around, ending last rep at **, sl st in 3rd ch of beg ch to join.

Rnd 4: Sl st in next ch-3 loop, ch 3 (counts as dc), 2 dc in first ch-3 loop, *(3 dc, ch 2, 3 dc) in next ch-3 loop**, 3 dc in each of next 2 ch-3 loops; rep from * around, ending last rep at **, 3 dc in next ch-3 loop, sl st in 3rd ch of beg ch to join.

Rnd 5: Ch 1, *sc in each of next 6 dc, 2 sc in next ch-2 space, dc in each of next 6 dc; rep from * around, sl st in first sc to join. Fasten off.

228

Puff st: *(Yo, insert hook in next st, yo, draw yarn through st, draw yarn through 2 loops on hook) twice in same st, yo, draw yarn through 3 loops on hook.*

Beginning popcorn (beg pop): *Ch 3 (counts as dc), 4 dc in same space, drop loop from hook, insert hook from front to back in 3rd ch of beg ch, place dropped loop on hook, draw loop through st.*

Popcorn (pop): *5 dc in same space, drop loop from hook, insert hook from front to back in first dc of 5-dc group, place dropped loop on hook, draw loop through st.*

Ch 6 and sl st in first ch to form a ring.

Rnd 1: Ch 1, 12 sc in ring, sl st in first sc to join.

Rnd 2: Ch 3 (counts as dc), dc in first sc, ch 3, skip next sc, *puff st in next sc, ch 3, skip next sc; rep from * around, sl st in 3rd ch of beg ch to join.

Rnd 3: Ch 1, sc in next dc, *(2 sc, ch 3, 2 sc) in next ch-3 loop**, sc in next puff st; rep from * around, ending last rep at **, sl st in first sc to join.

Rnd 4: Sl st to next ch-3 loop, beg pop in first ch-3 loop, ch 8, (pop, ch 8) in each ch-3 loop around, sl st in first pop to join.

Rnd 5: Sl st in next ch-8 loop, ch 3 (counts as dc), (4 dc, ch 3, 5 dc) in first ch-8 loop, (5 dc, ch 3, 5 dc) in each ch-8 loop around, sl st in 3rd ch of beg ch to join. Fasten off.

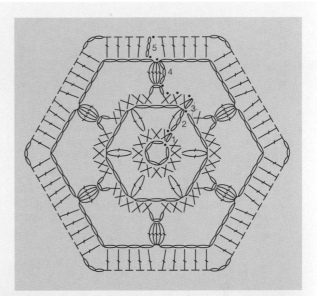

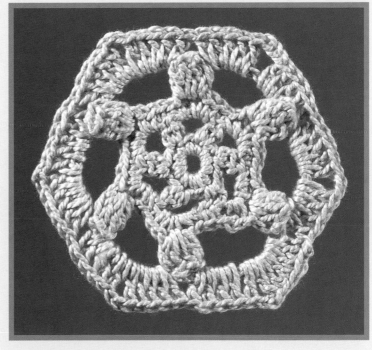

229

Beginning popcorn (beg pop): *Ch 3 (counts as dc), 3 dc in same space, drop loop from hook, insert hook from front to back in 3rd ch of beg ch, place dropped loop on hook, draw loop through st.*

Popcorn (pop): *4 dc in same space, drop loop from hook, insert hook from front to back in first dc of 4-dc group, place dropped loop on hook, draw loop through st.*

Ch 6 and sl st in first ch to form a ring.

Rnd 1: Ch 1, 12 sc in ring, sl st in first sc to join.

Rnd 2: Ch 5 (counts as dc, ch 2), (dc, ch 2) in each sc around, sl st in 3rd ch of beg ch to join.

Rnd 3: Sl st in next ch-2 space, beg pop in first ch-2 space, ch 3, (pop, ch 3) in each ch-2 space around, sl st in first pop to join.

Rnd 4: Sl st in next ch-3 loop, ch 3 (counts as dc), 3 dc in first ch-3 loop, ch 1, (4 dc, ch 1) in each ch-3 loop around, sl st in 3rd ch of beg ch to join.

Rnd 5: Sl st to next ch-1 space, ch 3 (counts as dc), (2 dc, ch 2, 3 dc) in first ch-1 space, *ch 2, 4 dc in next ch-1 space, ch 2**, (3 dc, ch 2, 3 dc) in next ch-1 space; rep from * around, ending last rep at **, sl st in 3rd ch of beg ch to join. Fasten off.

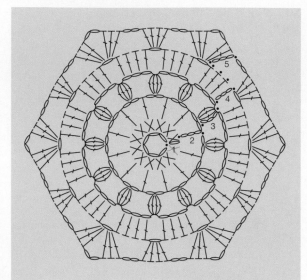

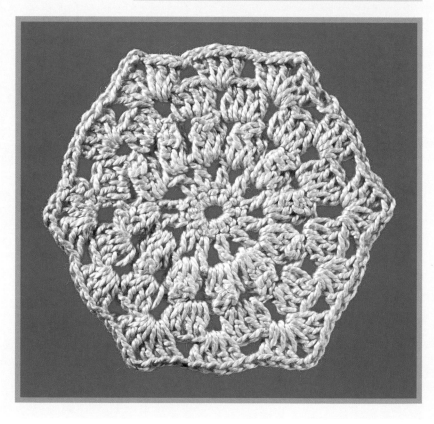

230

3-looped bobble: *(Yo, insert hook in next st, yo, draw yarn through st and up to level of work) 3 times in same st, yo, draw yarn through 7 loops on hook.*

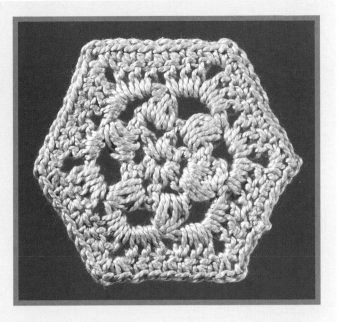

4-looped bobble: *(Yo, insert hook in next st, yo, draw yarn through st and up to level of work) 4 times in same st, yo, draw yarn through 9 loops on hook.*

Ch 6 and sl st in first ch to form a ring.

Rnd 1: Ch 6 (counts as dc, ch 3), (dc, ch 3) 5 times in ring, sl st in 3rd ch of beg ch to join.

Rnd 2: Sl st to center of next ch-3 loop, ch 3 (counts as dc), 3-looped bobble in first ch-3 loop, ch 5, (4-looped bobble, ch 5) in each ch-3 loop around, sl st in first bobble to join.

Rnd 3: Sl st in next ch-5 loop, ch 3 (counts as dc), (2 dc, ch 3, 3 dc) in first ch-5 loop, (3 dc, ch 3, 3 dc) in each ch-5 loop around, sl st in 3rd ch of beg ch to join.

Rnd 4: Ch 1, *sc in each of next 3 dc, (sc, ch 2, sc) in next ch-2 space, sc in each of next 3 dc; rep from * around, sl st in first sc to join. Fasten off.

231

Ch 6 and sl st in first ch to form a ring.

Rnd 1: Ch 3 (counts as dc), 2 dc in ring, ch 3, (3 dc, ch 3) 5 times in ring, sl st in 3rd ch of beg ch to join.

Rnd 2: Sl st to next ch-3 loop, ch 5 (counts as dtr), (2 dtr, ch 2, 3 dtr) in first ch-2 space, (3 dtr, ch 2, 3 dtr) in each ch-3 loop around, sl st in 5th ch of beg ch to join.

Rnd 3: Ch 3 (counts as dc), *dc in each of next 2 dtr, (2 dc, ch 2, 2 dc) in next ch-2 space, dc in each of next 4 dtr; rep from * around, omitting last dc, sl st in 3rd ch of beg ch to join.

Rnd 4: Sl st in next dc, ch 3 (counts as dc), working behind beg ch-3 just made, dc in beg ch-3 of Rnd 3 (crossed dc made), *skip next st, dc in next st, working behind last dc made, dc in last skipped st (crossed dc made); rep from * around, sl st in 3rd ch of beg ch to join. Fasten off.

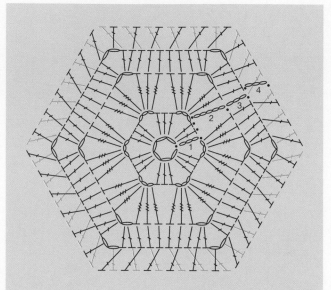

.16.
Floral Patterns

232 Ch 8 and sl st in first ch to form a ring.

Rnd 1: Ch 1, *sc in ring, ch 4, sc in 2nd ch from hook, hdc in each of next 2 ch, sc in ring, ch 6, sc in 2nd ch from hook, hdc in each of next 4 ch; rep from * 3 times, sl st in first sc to join. Fasten off.

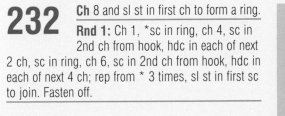

233

Ch 10.

Row 1: Sc in 2nd ch from hook, dc in each of next 7 ch, sc in last ch.

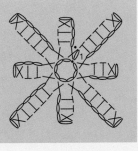

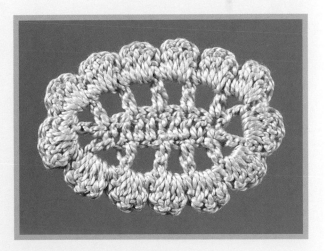

Work now progresses in rnds.

Rnd 1: Ch 5 (counts as dc, ch 2), dc in end sc, working across opposite side of foundation ch, (ch 2, skip next ch, dc in next ch) 4 times, ch 2, (dc, ch 2, dc) in end ch, (ch 2, skip next st, dc in next st) 4 times, ch 2, sl st in 3rd ch of beg ch to join.

Rnd 2: Ch 1, *sc in dc, 3 dc in next ch-2 space; rep from * around, sl st in first sc to join. Fasten off.

234

Puff st: (Yo [twice], insert hook in next space, yo, draw yarn through space, [yo, draw yarn through 2 loops on hook] twice) twice in same space, yo, draw yarn through 3 loops on hook.

Ch 8 and sl st in first ch to form a ring.

Rnd 1: Ch 1, *sc in ring, ch 4, puff st in ring, ch 4; rep from * 4 times, sl st in first sc to join.

Rnd 2: Ch 1, *sc in sc, ch 11, skip next 2 ch-4 loops; rep from * around, sl st in first sc to join. Fasten off.

235

Ch 13 and sl st in first ch to form a ring.

Rnd 1: Ch 1, *sc in ring, ch 5, dtr in ring, ch 5, sc in ring, ch 3; rep from * ; rep from * 7 times, sl st in first sc to join. Fasten off.

236

Puff st: (Yo, insert hook in next space, yo, draw yarn through space, draw yarn through 2 loops on hook) twice in same space, yo, draw yarn through 3 loops on hook.

Picot: Ch 3, sl st in 3rd ch from hook.

Ch 6 and sl st in first ch to form a ring.

Rnd 1: Ch 3 (counts as dc), dc in ring, *ch 11, puff st in ring, ch 1, picot, ch 1, puff st in ring; rep from * 4 times, ch 11, puff st in ring, ch 1, picot, ch 1, sl st in 3rd ch of beg ch to join. Fasten off.

237

Ch 6 and sl st in first ch to form a ring.

Rnd 1: Ch 6 (counts as dc, ch 3), (dc, ch 3) 7 times in ring, sl st in 3rd ch of beg ch to join.

Rnd 2: Ch 3 (counts as dc), *4 dc in next ch-3 loop**, dc in next dc; rep from * around, ending last rep at **, sl st in 3rd ch of beg ch to join.

Rnd 3: Ch 1, *sc in dc, ch 6, sc in 2nd ch from hook, hdc in next ch, dc in next ch, tr in next ch, dtr in next ch, skip next 4 dc; rep from * around, sl st in first sc to join. Fasten off.

238

Ch 6 and sl st in first ch to form a ring.

Rnd 1: Ch 3 (counts as dc), 15 dc in ring, sl st in 3rd ch of beg ch to join.

Rnd 2: *Ch 3, skip next dc, sl st in next dc; rep from * around, ending with last sl st in first sl st to join.

Rnd 3: Sl st in next ch-3 loop, ch 3 (counts as dc), 5 dc in first ch-3 loop, 6 dc in each ch-3 loop around, sl st in 3rd ch of beg ch to join. Fasten off.

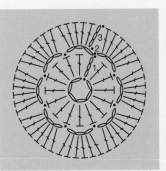

239

2-dc puff st: *(Yo, insert hook in next st, yo, draw yarn through st, draw yarn through 2 loops on hook) twice in same st, yo, draw yarn through 3 loops on hook.*

3-dc puff st: *(Yo, insert hook in next st, yo, draw yarn through st, draw yarn through 2 loops on hook) 3 times in same st, yo, draw yarn through 4 loops on hook.*

Ch 6 and sl st in first ch to form a ring.

Rnd 1: Ch 1, 8 sc in ring, sl st in first sc to join.

Rnd 2: Ch 3 (counts as dc), 2-dc puff st in first sc, ch 3, (3-dc puff st, ch 3) in each sc around, sl st in 3rd ch of beg ch to join.

Rnd 3: Ch 6 (counts as dc, ch 3), *sc in next ch-3 loop, ch 3**, dc in next puff st, ch 3; rep from * around, ending last rep at **, sl st in 3rd ch of beg ch to join.

Rnd 4: Ch 1, *sc in dc, ch 1, skip next ch-3 loop, tr in next sc, ch 2, tr in middle of last tr made, ch 2, (dc, ch 2, dc) in middle of last tr made, ch 2, dc in middle of first tr made, ch 1, skip next ch-3 loop; rep from * around, sl st in first sc to join. Fasten off.

240

Ch 10 and sl st in first ch to form a ring.

Rnd 1: Ch 3 (counts as dc), 23 dc in ring, sl st in 3rd ch of beg ch to join.

Rnd 2: Ch 6 (counts as dc, ch 3), skip next 2 dc, *dc in next dc, ch 3, skip next 2 dc; rep from * around, sl st in 3rd ch of beg ch to join.

Rnd 3: *Ch 9, sc in 2nd ch from hook, hdc in next ch, dc in next ch, tr in each of next 5 ch, skip next ch-3 loop, sl st in next dc; rep from * around, ending with last sl st in first sl st to join.

Rnd 4: Skip next ch, sc in each of next 7 ch, 3 sc in end ch, sc in each of next 7 sts, skip next tr, sl st in next sl st; rep from * around. Fasten off.

241

Puff st: (Yo, insert hook in next space, yo, draw yarn through space, draw yarn through 2 loops on hook) twice in same space, yo, draw yarn through 3 loops on hook.

Ch 6 and sl st in first ch to form a ring.

Rnd 1: Ch 3 (counts as dc), dc in ring, ch 5, (puff st, ch 5) 5 times in ring, sl st in 3rd ch of beg ch to join.

Rnd 2: Sl st in first ch-5 loop, ch 1, (sc, hdc, 5 dc, hdc, sc) in each ch-5 loop around, sl st in first sc to join. Fasten off.

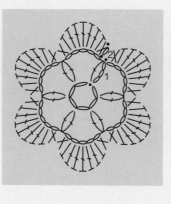

242

2-dc puff st: (Yo, insert hook in next space, yo, draw yarn through st, draw yarn through 2 loops on hook) twice in same space, yo, draw yarn through 3 loops on hook.

3-dc puff st: (Yo, insert hook in next space, yo, draw yarn through st, draw yarn through 2 loops on hook) 3 times in same space, yo, draw yarn through 4 loops on hook.

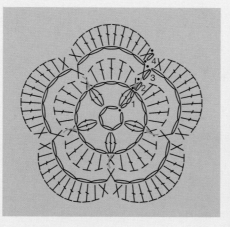

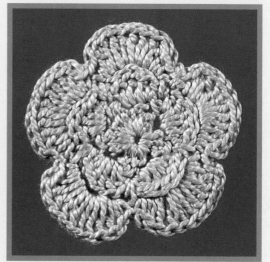

Ch 6 and sl st in first ch to form a ring.

Rnd 1: Ch 3 (counts as dc), 2-dc puff st in ring, ch 3, (3-dc puff st, ch 3) 4 times in ring, sl st in first puff st to join.

Rnd 2: Ch 1, *sc in puff st, (hdc, 3 dc, hdc) in next ch-3 loop; rep from * around, sl st in first sc to join.

Rnd 3: Ch 1, *sc in sc, ch 5, skip next 5 sts; rep from * around, sl st in first sc to join.

Rnd 4: Sl st in next ch-5 loop, ch 1, (sc, hdc, 8 dc, hdc, sc) in each ch-5 loop around, sl st in first sc to join. Fasten off.

243

Ch 8 and sl st in first ch to form a ring.

Rnd 1: Ch 4 (counts as dc, ch 1), (dc, ch 1) 11 times in ring, sl st in 3rd ch of beg ch to join.

Rnd 2: Sl st in next ch-1 space, ch 1, *sc in ch-1 space, ch 4, skip next ch-1 space; rep from * around, sl st in first sc to join.

Rnd 3: Ch 1, *sc in sc, ch 1, 4 dc in next ch-4 loop, ch 1; rep from * around, sl st in first sc to join.

Rnd 4: Ch 5 (counts as tr, ch 1), (tr, ch 1) 3 times in first sc, skip next 2 dc, sc bet last skipped and next dc, ch 1, skip next 3 sts**, (tr, ch 1) 4 times in next sc; rep from * around, ending last rep at **, sl st in first sc to join. Fasten off.

244

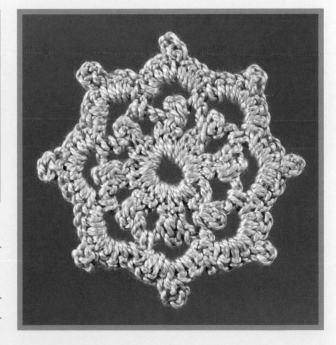

Picot: *Ch 3, sl st in 3rd ch from hook.*

2-dc puff st: *(Yo, insert hook in next space, yo, draw yarn through space, draw yarn through 2 loops on hook) twice in same space, yo, draw yarn through 3 loops on hook.*

3-dc puff st: *(Yo, insert hook in next space, yo, draw yarn through space, draw yarn through 2 loops on hook) 3 times in same space, yo, draw yarn through 4 loops on hook.*

Ch 8 and sl st in first ch to form a ring.

Rnd 1: Ch 3 (counts as dc), 2-dc puff st in ring, picot, ch 5, (3-dc puff st, picot, ch 5) 7 times in ring, sl st in first puff st to join.

Rnd 2: Sl st to center of next ch-5 loop, ch 1, (sc, ch 7) in each ch-5 loop around, sl st in first sc to join. Fasten off.

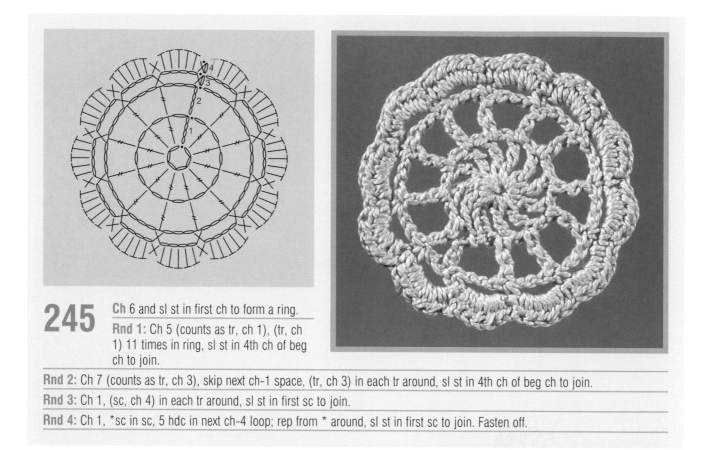

245

Ch 6 and sl st in first ch to form a ring.

Rnd 1: Ch 5 (counts as tr, ch 1), (tr, ch 1) 11 times in ring, sl st in 4th ch of beg ch to join.

Rnd 2: Ch 7 (counts as tr, ch 3), skip next ch-1 space, (tr, ch 3) in each tr around, sl st in 4th ch of beg ch to join.

Rnd 3: Ch 1, (sc, ch 4) in each tr around, sl st in first sc to join.

Rnd 4: Ch 1, *sc in sc, 5 hdc in next ch-4 loop; rep from * around, sl st in first sc to join. Fasten off.

246

Beginning popcorn (beg pop): Ch 3 (counts as dc), 4 dc in same st, drop loop from hook, insert hook from front to back in 3rd ch of beg ch, place dropped loop on hook, draw loop through st.

Popcorn (pop): 5 dc in same st, drop loop from hook, insert hook from front to back in first dc of 5-dc group, place dropped loop on hook, draw loop through st.

Ch 6 and sl st in first ch to form a ring.

Rnd 1: Ch 3 (counts as dc), 15 dc in ring, sl st in 3rd ch of beg ch to join.

Rnd 2: Beg pop in first sl, ch 3, skip next dc, *pop in next dc, ch 3, skip next dc; rep from * around, sl st in first pop to join.

Rnd 3: Sl st in next ch-3 loop, ch 1, (sc, hdc, 3 dc, hdc, sc) in each ch-3 loop around, sl st in first sc to join. Fasten off.

247

2-dtr puff st: (Yo [3 times], insert hook in next space, yo, draw yarn through space, [yo, draw yarn through 2 loops on hook] 3 times) twice in same space, yo, draw yarn through 3 loops on hook.

3-dtr puff st: (Yo [3 times], insert hook in next space, yo, draw yarn through space, [yo, draw yarn through 2 loops on hook] 3 times) 3 times in same space, yo, draw yarn through 4 loops on hook.

Ch 6 and sl st in first ch to form a ring.

Rnd 1: Ch 5 (counts as dtr), 2-dtr puff st in ring, ch 7, (3-dtr puff st, ch 7) 7 times in ring, sl st in first puff st to join. Fasten off.

248

Ch 6 and sl st in first ch to form a ring.

Rnd 1: Ch 3 (counts as dc), 11 dc in ring, sl st in 3rd ch of beg ch to join.

Rnd 2: Ch 3 (counts as dc), dc in first st, 2 dc in each dc around, sl st in 3rd ch of beg ch to join.

Rnd 3: Ch 5 (counts as dc, ch 2), skip next dc, *dc in next dc, ch 2, skip next dc; rep from * around, sl st in 3rd ch of beg ch to join.

Rnd 4: Sl st in first ch-2 space, ch 3, (tr, 2 dtr, tr, dc) in first ch-2 space, (dc, tr, 2 dtr, tr, dc) in each ch-2 space around, sl st in 3rd ch of beg ch to join. Fasten off.

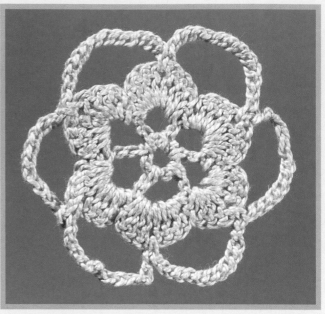

249

Ch 8 and sl st in first ch to form a ring.

Rnd 1: Ch 7 (counts as dc, ch 4), (dc, ch 4) 5 times in ring, sl st in 3rd ch of beg ch to join.

Rnd 2: Sl st in next ch-4 loop, ch 1, (sc, ch 1, 3 dc, ch 1, 3 dc, ch 1, sc) in each ch-4 loop around, sl st in first sc to join.

Rnd 3: Sl st in each of next 5 sts to ch-1 space, ch 1, *sc in ch-1 space, ch 13, skip next 10 sts; rep from * around, sl st in first sc to join. Fasten off.

250

Puff st: *(Yo [twice], insert hook in next space, yo, draw yarn through space, [yo, draw yarn through 2 loops on hook] twice) 4 times in same space, yo, draw yarn through 5 loops on hook.*

Ch 6 and sl st in first ch to form a ring.

Rnd 1: Ch 4 (counts as tr), 19 tr in ring, sl st in 4th ch of beg ch to join.

Rnd 2: Ch 1, *sc in tr, ch 4, skip next tr; rep from * around, sl st in first sc to join.

Rnd 3: Sl st in next ch-4 loop, ch 1, (sc, ch 4, puff st, ch 4, sc) in each ch-4 loop around, sl st in first sc to join. Fasten off.

251

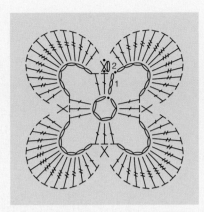

Ch 6 and sl st in first ch to form a ring.

Rnd 1: Ch 3 (counts as dc), 2 dc in ring, ch 7, (3 dc, ch 7) 3 times in ring, sl st in 3rd ch of beg ch to join.

Rnd 2: Sl st in next dc, ch 1, *sc in dc, (2 dc, 3 tr, 5 dtr, 3 tr, 2 dc) in next ch-7 loop, skip next dc; rep from * around, sl st in first sc to join. Fasten off.

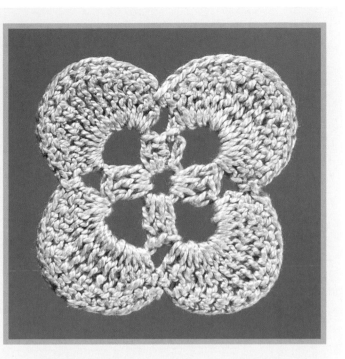

252

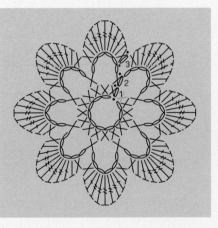

Ch 10 and sl st in first ch to form a ring.

Rnd 1: Ch 1, 16 sc in ring, sl st in first sc to join.

Rnd 2: Ch 1, *sc in sc, ch 6, skip next sc; rep from * around, sl st in first sc to join.

Rnd 3: Sl st in next ch-6 loop, ch 1, (sc, hdc, dc, 5 tr, dc, hdc, sc) in each ch-6 loop around, sl st in first sc to join. Fasten off.

253

Ch 8 and sl st in first ch to form a ring.

Rnd 1: Ch 3 (counts as dc), 2 dc in ring, ch 6, (3 dc, ch 6) 5 times in ring, sl st in 3rd ch of beg ch to join.

Rnd 2: Sl st in next dc, *11 dc in next ch-6 loop, skip next dc, sl st in next dc; rep from * around, ending with last sl st in first sl st to join. Fasten off.

254

Picot: Ch 4, sl st in 4th ch from hook.

Ch 6 and sl st in first ch to form a ring.

Rnd 1: Ch 1, (sc, ch 3) 12 times in ring, sl st in first sc to join.

Rnd 2: Sl st in next ch-3 loop, ch 1, (sc, ch 3) in each ch-3 loop around, sl st in first sc to join.

Rnd 3: Sl st in next ch-3 loop, ch 1, *(sc in ch-3 loop, ch 6, sc in next ch-3 loop, ch 3; rep from * around, sl st in first sc to join.

Rnd 4: Sl st in next ch-6 loop, ch 3 (counts as dc), (4 dc, picot, 5 dc) in first ch-6 loop, sc in next ch-3 loop, *(5 dc, picot, 5 dc) in next ch-6 loop, sc in next ch-3 loop; rep from * around, sl st in 3rd ch of beg ch to join. Fasten off.

255

Ch 6 and sl st in first ch to form a ring.

Rnd 1: Ch 12 (counts as tr, ch 8), (tr, ch 8) 7 times in ring, sl st in 4th ch of beg ch to join.

Rnd 2: Sl st in next ch-8 loop, ch 1, (sc, hdc, dc, 3 tr, ch 5, 3 tr, dc, hdc, sc) in each ch-8 loop around, sl st in first sc to join. Fasten off.

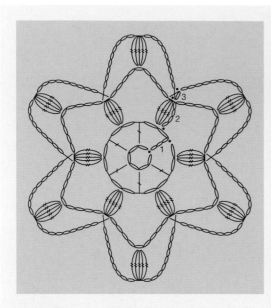

256

4-tr puff st: (Yo [twice], insert hook in next space, yo, draw yarn through space, [yo, draw yarn through 2 loops on hook] twice) 4 times in same space, yo, draw yarn through 5 loops on hook.

5-tr puff st: (Yo [twice], insert hook in next space, yo, draw yarn through space, [yo, draw yarn through 2 loops on hook] twice) 5 times in same space, yo, draw yarn through 6 loops on hook.

Ch 6 and sl st in first ch to form a ring.

Rnd 1: Ch 5 (counts as dc, ch 2), (dc, ch 2) 5 times in ring, sl st in 3rd ch of beg ch to join.

Rnd 2: Sl st in next ch-2 space, ch 4 (counts as tr), 4-tr puff st in first ch-2 space, ch 9, (5-tr puff st, ch 9) in each ch-2 space around, sl st in first puff st to join.

Rnd 3: Ch 1, *sc in puff st, ch 9, 5-tr puff st in next ch-9 loop, ch 9; rep from * around, sl st in first sc to join. Fasten off.

257

Picot: Ch 4, sl st in 4th ch from hook.

Ch 6 and sl st in first ch to form a ring.

Rnd 1: Ch 1, 16 sc in ring, sl st in first sc to join.

Rnd 2: Ch 1, *sc in each of next 2 sc, (sc, ch 10, sc) in next sc, sc in next sc; rep from * around, sl st in first sc to join.

Rnd 3: Ch 1, *sc in sc, skip next 2 sc, (2 hdc, 17 dc, 2 hdc) in next ch-10 loop, skip next 2 sc; rep from * around, sl st in first sc to join.

Rnd 4: Ch 1, *sc in sc, ch 5, skip next 5 sts, (sc in next dc, picot, ch 5, skip next 4 dc) twice, sc in next dc, picot, ch 5, skip next 5 sts; rep from * around, sl st in first sc to join. Fasten off.

258

Ch 6 and sl st in first ch to form a ring.

Rnd 1: Ch 3 (counts as dc), 15 dc in ring, sl st in 3rd ch of beg ch to join.

Rnd 2: Ch 3 (counts as dc), dc in next dc, ch 11, *dc in each of next 2 dc, ch 11; rep from * around, sl st in 3rd ch of beg ch to join.

Rnd 3: Sl st to center of next ch-11 loop, ch 3 (counts as dc), (3 dc, ch 3, 4 dc) in first ch-11 loop, (4 dc, ch 3, 4 dc) in each ch-11 loop around, sl st in 3rd ch of beg ch to join. Fasten off.

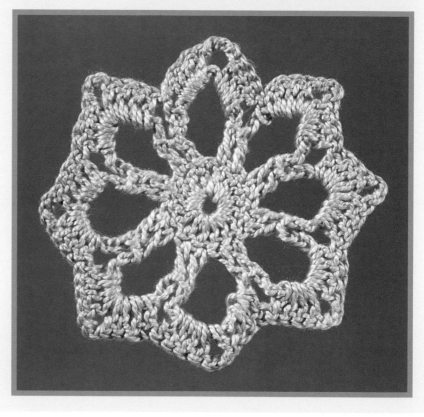

259

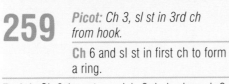

Picot: Ch 3, sl st in 3rd ch from hook.

Ch 6 and sl st in first ch to form a ring.

Rnd 1: Ch 3 (counts as dc), 2 dc in ring, ch 2, (3 dc, ch 2) 4 times in ring, sl st in 3rd ch of beg ch to join.

Rnd 2: Sl st to next ch-2 space, ch 1, (sc, ch 6) in each ch-2 space around, sl st in first sc to join.

Rnd 3: Ch 4 (counts as tr), *9 tr in next ch 6 loop**, tr in next sc; rep from * around, ending last rep at **, sl st in 4th ch of beg ch to join.

Rnd 4: Ch 1, *sc in each of next 2 tr, picot; rep from * around, sl st in first sc to join. Fasten off.

260

Picot: Ch 3, sl st in 3rd ch from hook.

Ch 6 and sl st in first ch to form a ring.

Rnd 1: Ch 6 (counts as dc, ch 3), (dc, ch 3) 4 times in ring, sl st in 3rd ch of beg ch to join.

Rnd 2: Sl st in next ch-3 loop, ch 3 (counts as dc), 4 dc in first ch-3 loop, ch 2, (5 dc, ch 2) in each ch-3 loop around, sl st in 3rd ch of beg ch to join.

Rnd 3: Turn, sl st in next ch-2 space, turn, ch 1, (sc, ch 10) in each ch-2 space around, sl st in first sc to join.

Rnd 4: Sl st in next ch-10 loop, ch 5 (counts as dc, ch 2), (dc, ch 2) 4 times in first ch-10 loop, (dc, ch 2) 5 times in each ch-10 loop around, sl st in 3rd ch of beg ch to join.

Rnd 5: Sl st in next ch-2 space, ch 1, (sc, picot, sc) in each ch-2 space around, sl st in first sc to join. Fasten off.

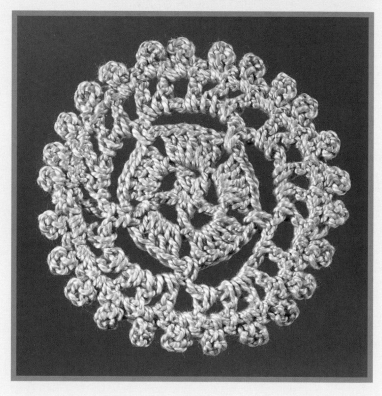

261

Ch 6 and sl st in first ch to form a ring.

Rnd 1: Ch 3 (counts as dc), 15 dc in ring, sl st in 3rd ch of beg ch to join.

Rnd 2: Ch 10 (counts as tr, ch 6), skip next dc, *tr in next dc, ch 6, skip next dc; rep from * around, sl st in 4th ch of beg ch to join.

Rnd 3: Sl st in next ch-6 loop, ch 1, (3 sc, ch 1, 3 sc, ch 1) in each ch-6 loop around, sl st in first sc to join.

Rnd 4: Sl st to next ch-1 space, ch 3 (counts as dc), (2 dc, ch 3, 3 dc) in first ch-1 space, *skip next 3 sc, sc in next ch-1 space, skip next 3 sc**, (3 dc, ch 3, 3 dc) in next ch-1 space; rep from * around, ending last rep at **, sl st in 3rd ch of beg ch to join. Fasten off.

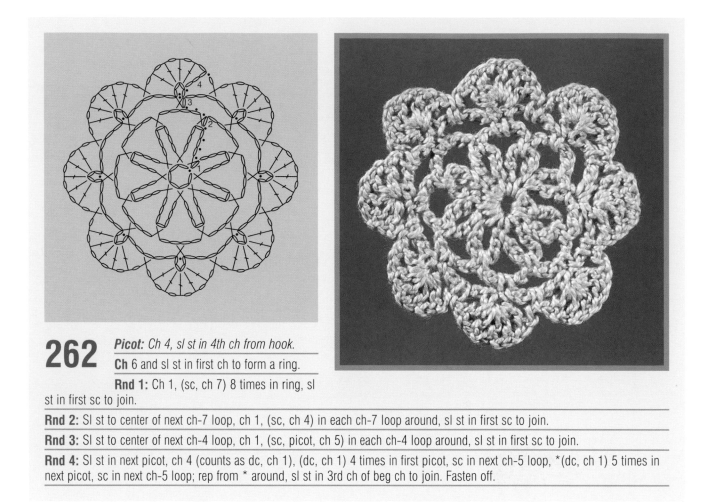

262

Picot: Ch 4, sl st in 4th ch from hook.

Ch 6 and sl st in first ch to form a ring.

Rnd 1: Ch 1, (sc, ch 7) 8 times in ring, sl st in first sc to join.

Rnd 2: Sl st to center of next ch-7 loop, ch 1, (sc, ch 4) in each ch-7 loop around, sl st in first sc to join.

Rnd 3: Sl st to center of next ch-4 loop, ch 1, (sc, picot, ch 5) in each ch-4 loop around, sl st in first sc to join.

Rnd 4: Sl st in next picot, ch 4 (counts as dc, ch 1), (dc, ch 1) 4 times in first picot, sc in next ch-5 loop, *(dc, ch 1) 5 times in next picot, sc in next ch-5 loop; rep from * around, sl st in 3rd ch of beg ch to join. Fasten off.

263

Ch 6 and sl st in first ch to form a ring.

Rnd 1: Ch 1, 8 sc in ring, sl st in first sc to join.

Rnd 2: Ch 5 (counts as dc, ch 2), (dc, ch 2) in each sc around, sl st in 3rd ch of beg ch to join.

Rnd 3: Ch 3 (counts as dc), *3 dc in next ch-2 space**, dc in next dc; rep from * around, ending last rep at **, sl st in 3rd ch of beg ch to join.

Rnd 4: Ch 1, *sc in dc, ch 11, skip next 3 dc; rep from * around, sl st in first sc to join.

Rnd 5: Sl st to center of next ch-11 loop, ch 1, (sc, ch 9) in each ch-11 loop around, sl st in first sc to join.

Rnd 6: Ch 1, *sc in sc, 9 tr in center ch of next ch-9 loop; rep from * around, sl st in first sc to join. Fasten off.

264

Ch 10 and sl st in first ch to form a ring.

Rnd 1: Ch 1, (sc, ch 10) 8 times in ring, sl st in first sc to join.

Rnd 2: Sl st to center of next ch-10 loop, ch 4 (counts as dc, ch 1), dc in first ch-10 loop, ch 5, (dc, ch 1, dc, ch 5) in each ch-10 loop around, sl st in 3rd ch of beg ch to join.

Rnd 3: Sl st in next ch-1 space, ch 3 (counts as dc), (dc, ch 2, 2 dc) in first ch-1 space, *ch 2, sc in next ch-5 loop, ch 2**, (2 dc, ch 2, 2 dc) in next ch-1 space; rep from * around, ending last rep at **, sl st in 3rd ch of beg ch to join.

Rnd 4: Sl st to next ch-2 space, ch 3 (counts as dc), (2 dc, ch 3, 3 dc) in first ch-2 space, *ch 3, skip next ch-2 space, sc in next sc, ch 3, skip next ch-2 space**, (3 dc, ch 3, 3 dc) in next ch-2 space; rep from * around, ending last rep at **, sl st in 3rd ch of beg ch to join.

Rnd 5: Sl st to next ch-3 loop, ch 3 (counts as dc), (2 dc, ch 3, 3 dc) in first ch-3 loop, *ch 4, skip next ch-3 loop, sc in next sc, ch 4, skip next ch-3 loop**, (3 dc, ch 3, 3 dc) in next ch-3 loop; rep from * around, ending last rep at **, sl st in 3rd ch of beg ch to join. Fasten off.

265

Ch 6 and sl st in first ch to form a ring.

Rnd 1: Ch 6 (counts as dc, ch 3), (dc, ch 3) 4 times in ring, sl st in 3rd ch of beg ch to join.

Rnd 2: Ch 1, (sc, hdc, 3 dc, hdc, sc) in each ch-5 loop around, sl st in first sc to join.

Rnd 3: Ch 1, *sc bet 2 sc, ch 5, skip next 7 sts; rep from * around, sl st in first sc to join.

Rnd 4: Ch 1, (sc, hdc, 5 dc, hdc, sc) in each ch-5 loop around, sl st in first sc to join.

Rnd 5: Ch 1, *sc bet 2 sc, ch 7, skip next 9 sts; rep from * around, sl st in first sc to join.

Rnd 6: Ch 1, (sc, hdc, 7 dc, hdc, sc) in each ch-7 loop around, sl st in first sc to join.

Rnd 7: Ch 1, *sc bet 2 sc, ch 9, skip next 11 sts; rep from * around, sl st in first sc to join.

Rnd 8: Ch 1, (sc, hdc, 9 dc, hdc, sc) in each ch-9 loop around, sl st in first sc to join. Fasten off.

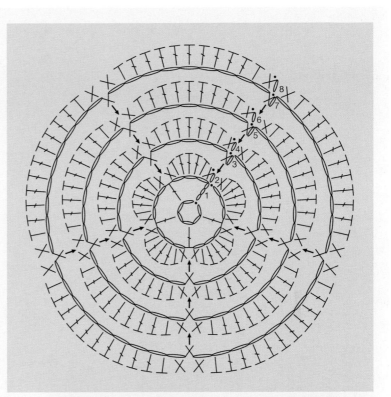

.17.
Sculptured Blocks

266 **Ch** 6 and sl st in first ch to form a ring.

Rnd 1: Ch 1, (sc, ch 2, 4 dc, ch 2) 4 times in ring, sl st in first sc to join.

Rnd 2: Ch 1, *sc in sc, ch 5, skip next 2 ch-2 spaces; rep from * around, sl st in first sc to join.

Rnd 3: Sl st in next ch-5 loop, ch 3 (counts as dc), (3 dc, ch 3, 4 dc) in first ch-5 loop, ch 2, (4 dc, ch 3, 4 dc, ch 2) in each ch-5 loop around, sl st in 3rd ch of beg ch to join.

Rnd 4: Sl st to next ch-3 loop, ch 3 (counts as dc), (3 dc, ch 3, 4 dc) in first ch-3 loop, *ch 1, 4 dc in next ch-2 space, ch 1**, (4 dc, ch 3, 4 dc) in next ch-3 loop; rep from * around, ending last rep at **, sl st in 3rd ch of beg ch to join. Fasten off.

267

Ch 8 and sl st in first ch to form a ring.

Rnd 1: Ch 1, (sc, ch 2, 5 dc, ch 2) 4 times in ring, sl st in first sc to join.

Rnd 2: Ch 1, *sc in sc, ch 5, skip next 2 ch-2 spaces; rep from * around, sl st in first sc to join.

Rnd 3: Sl st in next ch-5 loop, ch 3 (counts as dc), (3 dc, ch 2, 4 dc) in first ch-5 loop, ch 2, (4 dc, ch 2, 4 dc, ch 2) in each ch-5 loop around, sl st in 3rd ch of beg ch to join.

Rnd 4: Sl st to next ch-2 space, ch 3 (counts as dc), (3 dc, ch 3, 4 dc) in first ch-2 space, *ch 1, 4 dc in next ch-2 space, ch 1**, (4 dc, ch 3, 4 dc) in next ch-2 space; rep from * around, ending last rep at **, sl st in 3rd ch of beg ch to join. Fasten off.

268

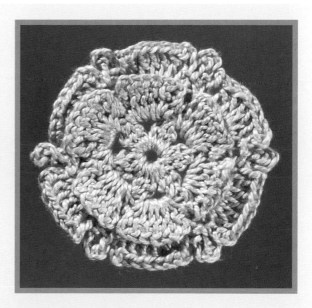

2-dc puff st:
(Yo, insert hook in next space, yo, draw yarn through space, draw yarn through 2 loops on hook) twice in same space, yo, draw yarn through 3 loops on hook.

3-dc puff st: *(Yo, insert hook in next space, yo, draw yarn through space, draw yarn through 2 loops on hook) 3 times in same space, yo, draw yarn through 4 loops on hook.*

Ch 6 and sl st in first ch to form a ring.

Rnd 1: Ch 3 (counts as dc), 2-dc puff st in ring, ch 3, (3-dc puff st, ch 3) 5 times in ring, sl st in first puff st to join.

Rnd 2: Ch 1, (sc, ch 3, 4 dc, ch 3, sc) in each ch-3 loop around, sl st in first sc to join.

Rnd 3: Ch 1, *sc bet 2 sc, ch 5, skip next 2 ch-3 loops; rep from * around, sl st in first sc to join.

Rnd 4: Sl st in next ch-5 loop, ch 1, (sc, ch 3, 5 dc, ch 3, sc, ch 5) in each ch-5 loop around, sl st in first sc to join. Fasten off.

269

Ch 6 and sl st in first ch to form a ring.

Rnd 1: Ch 3 (counts as dc), 17 dc in ring, sl st in 3rd ch of beg ch to join.

Rnd 2: Ch 1, *sc in dc, ch 3, skip next 2 dc; rep from * around, sl st in first sc to join.

Rnd 3: *Ch 3, (dc, 3 tr, dc) in next ch-3 loop, ch 3, sl st in next sc; rep from * around, ending with last sl st in first sl st to join.

Rnd 4: Sl st in each of next 6 sts, *ch 9, skip next 2 ch-3 loops, skip next 2 sts, sl st in next tr; rep from * around, ending with last sl st in first sl st to join.

Rnd 5: Sl st in next ch-9 loop, ch 2 (counts as hdc), 11 hdc in first ch-9 loop, 12 hdc in each ch-9 loop around, sl st in 2nd ch of beg ch to join. Fasten off.

270

Picot: Ch 3, sl st in 3rd ch from hook.

Ch 6 and sl st in first ch to form a ring.

Rnd 1: Ch 3 (counts as dc), 15 dc in ring, sl st in 3rd ch of beg ch to join.

Rnd 2: Ch 1, *sc in dc, ch 5, skip next dc; rep from * around, sl st in first sc to join.

Rnd 3: Sl st in next ch-5 loop, ch 3 (counts as dc), (6 dc, picot, 7 dc) in first ch-5 loop, (7 dc, picot, 7 dc) in each ch-5 loop around, sl st in 3rd ch of beg ch to join.

Rnd 4: Ch 1, *working over last rnd, sc in next corresponding sc 2 rnds below, ch 5, skip next shell; rep from * around, sl st in first sc to join.

Rnd 5: Sl st in ncxt ch-5 loop, ch 3 (counts as dc), 5 dc in first ch-5 loop, 6 dc in each ch-5 loop around, sl st in 3rd ch of beg ch to join.

Rnd 6: Sl st in next dc, ch 3 (counts as dc), (dc, ch 1, 2 dc) in first dc, skip next 2 dc, *(2 dc, ch 1, 2 dc) in next dc, skip next 2 dc; rep from * around, sl st in 3rd ch of beg ch to join. Fasten off.

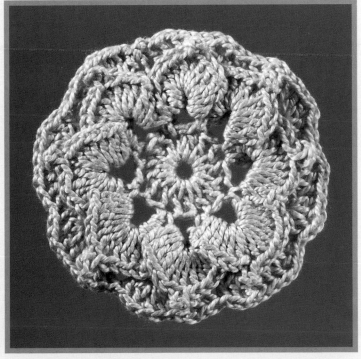

271

Ch 6 and sl st in first ch to form a ring.

Rnd 1: Ch 1, 16 sc in ring, sl st in first sc to join.

Rnd 2: Ch 6 (counts as dc, ch 3), skip next sc, *dc in next sc, ch 3, skip next sc; rep from * around, sl st in 3rd ch of beg ch to join.

Rnd 3: Ch 1, (sc, hdc, 5 dc, hdc, sc) in each ch-3 loop around, sl st in first sc to join.

Rnd 4: Ch 1, *sc bet 2 sc, ch 5, skip next 9 sts; rep from * around, sl st in first sc to join.

Rnd 5: Ch 1, (sc, hdc, 6 dc, hdc, sc) in each ch-5 loop around, sl st in first sc to join.

Rnd 6: Sl st in each of next 3 sts, ch 1, *sc in dc, ch 6, skip next 2 dc, sc in next dc, ch 6, skip next 6 sts; rep from * around, sl st in first sc to join.

Rnd 7: Sl st to center of next ch-6 loop, ch 1, *sc in ch-6 loop, (ch 6, sc) in each of next 2 ch-6 loops, ch 4, (4 dc, ch 4, 4 dc) in next ch-6 loop, ch 4; rep from * around, sl st in first sc to join. Fasten off.

272

Ch 6 and sl st in first ch to form a ring.

Rnd 1: Ch 1, 10 sc in ring, sl st in first sc to join.

Rnd 2: Ch 1, 2 sc in each sc around, sl st in first sc to join.

Rnd 3: Ch 6 (counts as tr, ch 2), (tr, ch 2) in each sc around, sl st in 4th ch of beg ch to join.

Rnd 4: Ch 1, (sc, ch 2, dc, ch 2, sc) in each ch-2 space around, sl st in first sc to join.

Rnd 5: Ch 1, *sc bet 2 sc, ch 3, skip next 2 ch-2 space; rep from * around, sl st in first sc to join.

Rnd 6: Ch 1, (sc, 3 dc, sc) in each ch-3 loop around, sl st in first sc to join.

Rnd 7: Sl st in each of next 2 sts, *ch 3, skip next 4 sts, sl st in next dc, ch 3, skip next 4 sts, (dc, ch 3, dc) in next dc, (ch 3, skip next 4 sts, sl st in next dc) twice; rep from * around, ending with last sl st in first sl st to join. Fasten off.

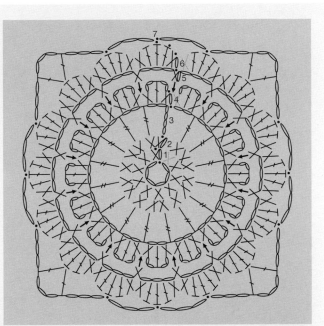

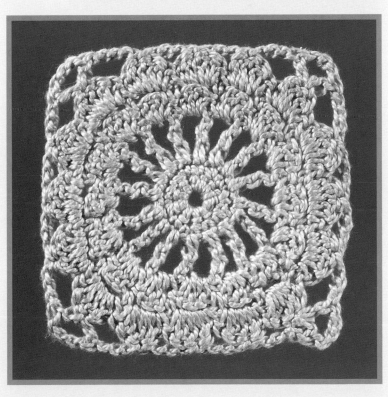

.18.
Small Blocks

273 **Ch** 20.

Row 1: Dc in 8th ch from hook, ch 2, skip next 2 ch, dc in each of next 4 ch, (ch 2, skip next 2 ch, dc in next ch) twice, turn.

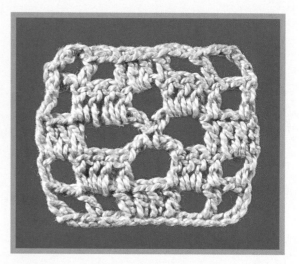

Row 2: Ch 5 (counts as dc, ch 2), skip next ch-2 space, dc in next dc, 2 dc in next ch-2 space, dc in next dc, ch 5, skip next 2 dc, dc in next dc, 2 dc in next ch-2 space, dc in next dc, ch 2, skip next 2 ch of turning ch, dc in next ch of turning ch, turn.

Row 3: Ch 3 (counts as dc), 2 dc in next ch-2 space, dc in next dc, ch 5, sc in next ch-5 loop, ch 5, skip next 3 dc, dc in next dc, 2 dc in next ch-2 space of turning ch, dc in 3rd ch of turning ch, turn.

Row 4: Ch 5 (counts as dc, ch 2), skip first 3 dc, dc in next dc, 3 dc in next ch-5 loop, ch 2, 3 dc in next ch-5 loop, dc in next dc, ch 2, skip next 2 dc, dc in 3rd ch of turning ch, turn.

Row 5: Ch 5 (counts as dc, ch 2), skip next ch-2 space, dc in next dc, ch 2, skip next 2 dc, dc in next dc, 2 dc in next ch-2 space, dc in next dc, ch 2, skip next 2 dc, dc in next dc, ch 2, skip next 2 ch of turning ch, dc in 3rd ch of turning ch. Fasten off.

274

Bobble: *(Yo, insert hook in next st, yo, draw yarn through st and up to level of work) 4 times in same st, yo, draw yarn through 9 loops on hook.*

Ch 24.

Row 1: Dc in 4th ch from hook, dc in each ch across, turn.

Row 2: Ch 3 (counts as dc), dc in each of next 3 dc, *skip next dc, bobble in next dc, ch 2, skip next dc*, dc in each of next 8 dc; rep from * to * once, dc in each of next 3 dc, dc in 3rd ch of turning ch, turn.

Row 3: Ch 3 (counts as dc), dc in each of next 3 dc, *skip next ch-2 space, bobble in next bobble, ch 2*, dc in each of next 8 dc; rep from * to * once, dc in each of next 3 dc, dc in 3rd ch of turning ch, turn.

Rep Row 3 until block is 1 row less than desired depth.

Last Row: Ch 3 (counts as dc), dc in each st across, working 2 dc in each ch-2 space, ending with dc in 3rd ch of turning ch. Fasten off.

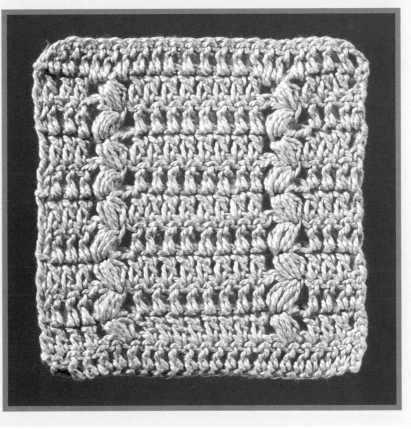

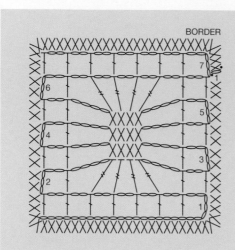

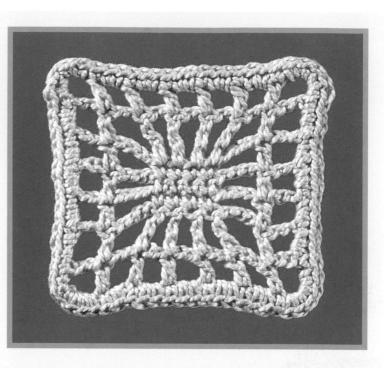

275

Ch 26.

Row 1 (RS): Dc in 8th ch from hook, *ch 2, skip next 2 ch, dc in next ch; rep from * across, turn.

Row 2: Ch 5 (counts as dc, ch 2), skip next ch-2 space, dc in next dc, ch 4, tr in each of next 4 dc, ch 4, skip next ch-2 space, dc in next dc, ch 2, skip next 2 ch of turning ch, dc in 5th ch ch of turning ch, turn.

Row 3: Ch 5 (counts as dc, ch 2), skip next ch-2 space, dc in next dc, ch 4, skip next ch-4 loop, sc in each of next 4 tr, ch 4, skip next ch-4 loop, dc in next dc, ch 2, skip next 2 ch of turning ch, dc in 3rd ch ch of turning ch, turn.

Rows 4-5: Ch 5 (counts as dc, ch 2), skip next ch-2 space, dc in next dc, ch 4, skip next ch-4 loop, sc in each of next 4 sc, ch 4, skip next ch-4 loop, dc in next dc, ch 2, skip next 2 ch of turning ch, dc in 3rd ch ch of turning ch, turn.

Row 6: Ch 5 (counts as dc, ch 2), skip next ch-2 space, dc in next dc, skip next ch-4 loop, (ch 2, tr) in each of next 4 sc, ch 2, skip next ch-4 loop, dc in next dc, ch 2, skip next 2 ch of turning ch, dc in 3rd ch ch of turning ch, turn. Fasten off.

Border

Rnd 1: With RS facing, join yarn in top right-hand corner loop, ch 1, 7 sc in corner, (sc in next dc, 2 sc in next ch-2 space) 6 times, 5 more sc in corner loop, working across side edge, work 2 sc in each row-end st across, 7 sc in next corner loop, working across bottom edge, (sc in next ch at base of dc, 2 sc in next ch-2 space) 6 times, 5 more sc in corner loop, working across side edge, work 2 sc in each row-end st across, sl st in first sc to join. Fasten off.

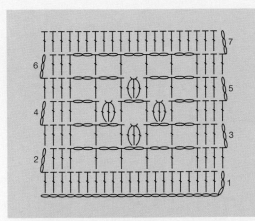

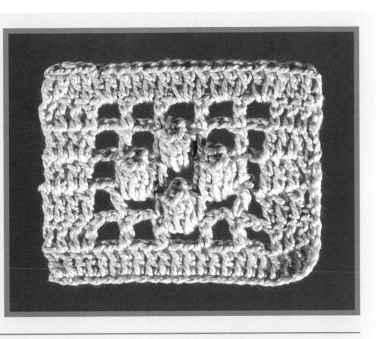

276

Popcorn (pop): 3 dc in same st, drop loop from hook, insert hook from front to back in first dc of 3-dc group, place dropped loop on hook, draw loop through st.

Ch 24.

Row 1: Dc in 4th ch from hook, dc in each ch across, turn.

Row 2: Ch 3 (counts as dc), dc in each of next 3 dc, (ch 2, skip next 2 dc, dc in next dc) 5 times, dc in each of next 2 dc, dc in 3rd ch of turning ch, turn.

Row 3: Ch 3 (counts as dc), dc in each of next 3 dc, (ch 2, skip next ch-2 space, dc in next dc) twice, pop in next next ch-2 space, dc in next dc, (ch 2, skip next ch-2 space, dc in next dc) twice, dc in each of next 2 dc, dc in 3rd ch of turning ch, turn.

Row 4: Ch 3 (counts as dc), dc in each of next 3 dc, ch 2, skip next ch-2 space, dc in next dc, pop in next next ch-2 space, dc in next dc, ch 2, skip next pop, dc in next dc, pop in next next ch-2 space, dc in next dc, ch 2, skip next ch-2 space, dc in each of next 3 dc, dc in 3rd ch of turning ch, turn.

Row 5: Ch 3 (counts as dc), dc in each of next 3 dc, ch 2, skip next ch-2 space, dc in next dc, ch 2, skip next pop, dc in next dc, pop in next next ch-2 space, dc in next dc, ch 2, skip next pop, dc in next dc, ch 2, skip next ch-2 space, dc in each of next 3 dc, dc in 3rd ch of turning ch, turn.

Row 6: Ch 3 (counts as dc), dc in each of next 3 dc, (ch 2, skip next ch-2 space or pop, dc in next dc) 5 times, dc in each of next 2 dc, dc in 3rd ch of turning ch, turn.

Row 7: Ch 3 (counts as dc), dc in each of next 3 dc, (2 dc in next ch-2 space, dc in next dc) 5 times, dc in each of next 2 dc, dc in 3rd ch of turning ch. Fasten off.

.19.
Sampler Blocks

277 **Ch** any number of sts for desired width.

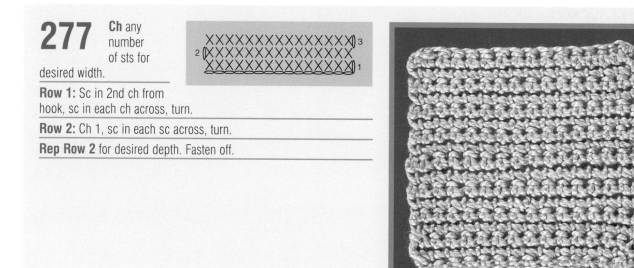

Row 1: Sc in 2nd ch from hook, sc in each ch across, turn.

Row 2: Ch 1, sc in each sc across, turn.

Rep Row 2 for desired depth. Fasten off.

278

Ch any number of sts for desired width.

Row 1 (RS): Sc in 2nd ch from hook, sc in each ch across, turn.

Row 2: Ch 1, sc in each sc across, turn.

Rep Row 2 for desired depth. Fasten off.

Border:

Rnd 1: With RS facing, join yarn in top right-hand corner sc, ch 1, *(sc, ch 5, sc) in corner st, (ch 5, skip next st, sc in next st) across to within 2 sts of next corner, ch 5, (sc, ch 5, sc) in next corner sc, working across side edge, (ch 5, skip next row-end sc, sc in next row-end sc) across to within 2 rows of next corner; rep from * around, sl st in first sc to join. Fasten off.

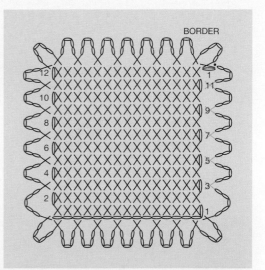

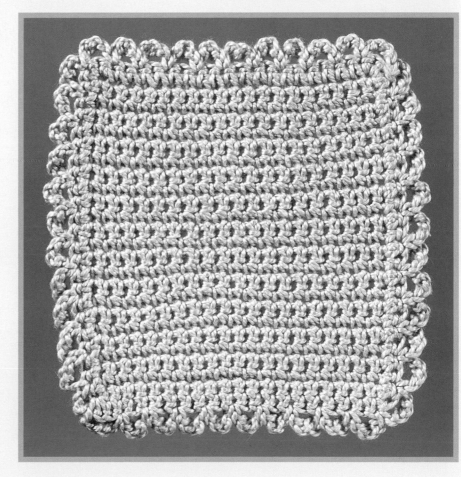

279

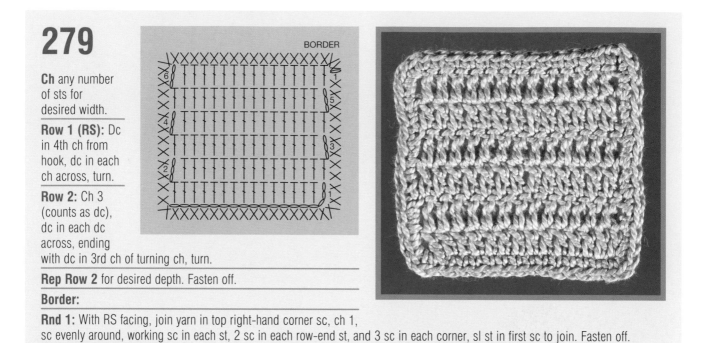

BORDER

Ch any number of sts for desired width.

Row 1 (RS): Dc in 4th ch from hook, dc in each ch across, turn.

Row 2: Ch 3 (counts as dc), dc in each dc across, ending with dc in 3rd ch of turning ch, turn.

Rep Row 2 for desired depth. Fasten off.

Border:

Rnd 1: With RS facing, join yarn in top right-hand corner sc, ch 1, sc evenly around, working sc in each st, 2 sc in each row-end st, and 3 sc in each corner, sl st in first sc to join. Fasten off.

280

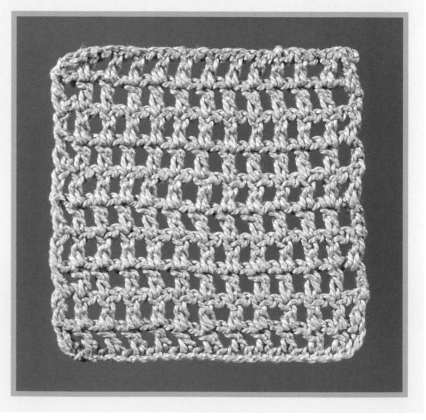

Ch a multiple of 2 for desired width.

Row 1: Dc in 6th ch from hook, *ch 1, skip next ch, dc in next ch; rep from * across, turn.

Row 2: Ch 4 (counts as dc, ch 1), skip next ch-1 space, *dc in next dc, ch 1, skip next ch-1 space; rep from * across to turning ch, dc in next ch of turning ch, turn.

Rep Row 2 for desired depth. Fasten off.

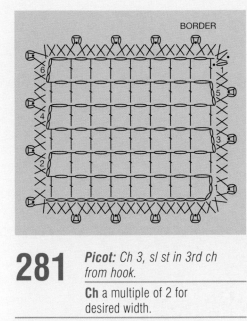

BORDER

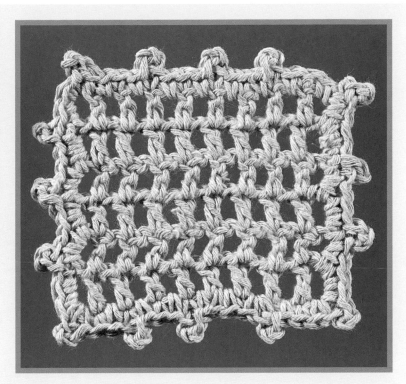

281

Picot: Ch 3, sl st in 3rd ch from hook.

Ch a multiple of 2 for desired width.

Row 1 (RS): Dc in 6th ch from hook, *ch 1, skip next ch, dc in next ch; rep from * across, turn.

Row 2: Ch 4 (counts as dc, ch 1), skip next ch-1 space, *dc in next dc, ch 1, skip next ch-1 space; rep from * across to turning ch, dc in next ch of turning ch, turn.

Rep Row 2 for desired depth. Fasten off.

Border:

Rnd 1: With RS facing, join yarn in top right-hand corner loop, ch 1, 3 sc in corner, sc in next ch-1 space, picot, *sc in each of next 4 sts, picot; rep from * around working 2 sc in each row-end st across side edges, maintaining picot pattern, sl st in first sc to join. Fasten off.

282

Ch a multiple of 4 plus 1 for desired width.

Row 1: Dc in 4th ch from hook, dc in next ch, *ch 1, skip next ch, dc in each of next 3 ch; rep from * across, turn.

Row 2: Ch 3 (counts as dc), dc in each of next 2 dc, *ch 1, skip next ch-1 space, dc in each of next 3 dc; rep from * across, ending with last dc in 3rd ch of turning ch, turn.

Rep Row 2 for desired depth. Fasten off.

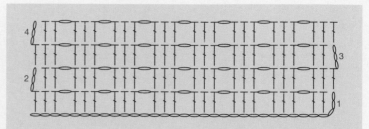

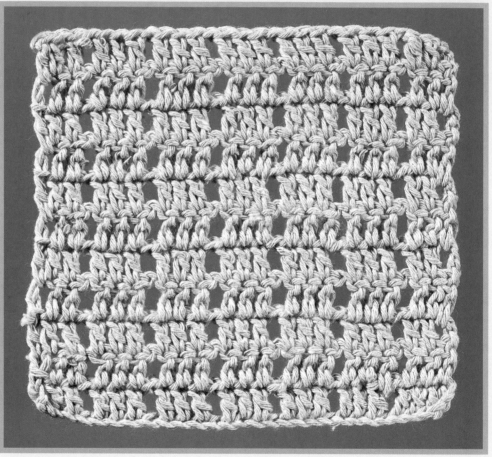

283

Ch a multiple of 4 plus 1 for desired width.

Row 1: Dc in 4th ch from hook, dc in next ch, *ch 1, skip next ch, dc in each of next 3 ch; rep from * across, turn.

Row 2: Ch 4 (counts as dc, ch 1), skip first 2 dc, *dc in next dc, dc in next ch-1 space, dc in next dc, ch 1, skip next dc; rep from * across to turning ch, dc in 3rd ch of turning ch, turn.

Rep Row 2 for desired depth. Fasten off.

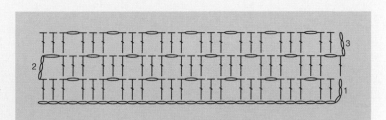

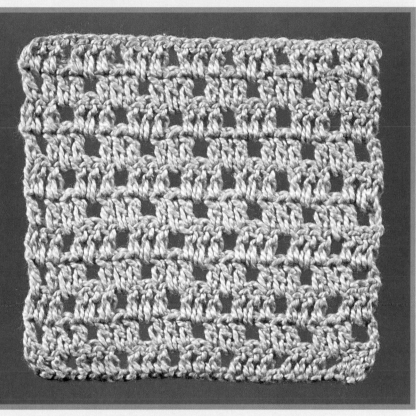

284

Ch a multiple of 2 for desired width.

Row 1: Dc in 6th ch from hook, *ch 1, skip next ch, dc in next ch; rep from * across, turn.

Row 2: Ch 3 (counts as dc), skip next ch-1 space, *2 dc in next dc, skip next ch-1 space; rep from * across to turning ch, 2 dc in next ch of turning ch, turn.

Row 3: Ch 4 (counts as dc, ch 1), skip next dc, *dc in next dc, ch 1, skip next dc; rep from * across to turning ch, dc in 3rd ch of turning ch, turn.

Rep Rows 2-3 for desired depth. Fasten off.

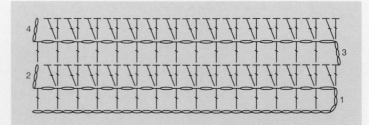

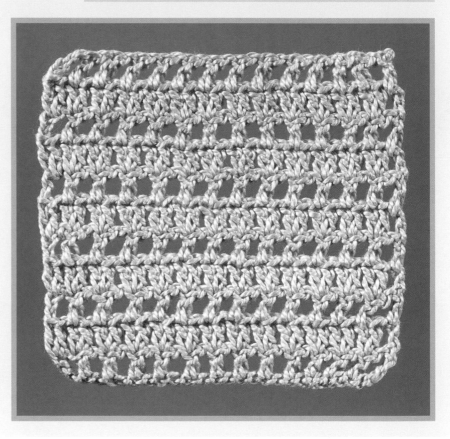

285

Ch a multiple of 8 plus 6 for desired width.

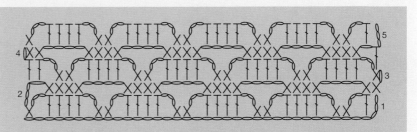

Row 1: Dc in 4th ch from hook, *ch 3, skip next ch, sc in each of next 2 ch, ch 3, skip next ch, dc in each of next 4 ch; rep from * across to within last 2 ch, ch 3, skip next ch, sc in last ch, turn.

Row 2: Ch 4 (counts as dc, ch 1), skip next ch-3 loop, *sc in each of next 4 dc, ch 4, skip next 2 ch-3 loops; rep from * across to within last 2 sts, sc in next dc, sc in 3rd ch of turning ch, turn.

Row 3: Ch 1, sc in first sc, ch 3, skip next sc, *4 dc in next ch-4 loop, ch 3, skip next sc, sc in each of next 2 sc, ch 3, skip ncxt sc; rep from * across to turning ch, dc in ch-1 space of turning ch, dc in 3rd ch of turning ch, turn.

Row 4: Ch 1, sc in first 2 dc, *ch 4, skip next 2 ch-3 loops, sc in each of next 4 dc; rep from * across to within last ch-3 loop, ch 1, skip next ch-3 loop, dc in last sc, turn.

Row 5: Ch 3, dc in next ch-1 space, *ch 3, skip next sc, sc in each of next 2 sc, ch 3, skip next sc, 4 dc in next ch-4 loop; rep from * across to within last 2 sc, ch 3, skip next sc, sc in last sc, turn.

Rep Rows 2-5 for desired depth. Fasten off.

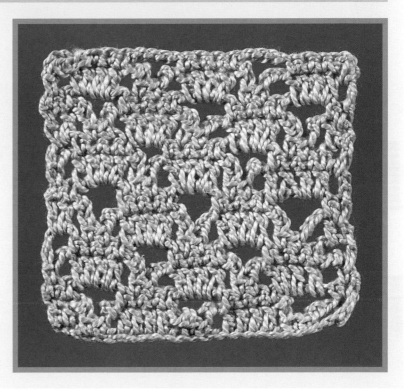

286

Ch a multiple of 10 plus 6 for desired width.

Row 1: Sc in 2nd ch from hook, sc in each of next 4 ch, *dc in each of next 5 ch, sc in each of next 5 ch; rep from * across, turn.

Row 2: Ch 3 (counts as dc), dc in each of next 4 sc, *sc in each of next 5 dc, dc in each of next 5 sc; rep from * across, turn.

Row 3: Ch 1, sc in each of first 5 dc, *dc in each of next 5 sc, sc in each of next 5 dc; rep from * across, ending with last sc in 3rd ch of turning ch, turn.

Rep Rows 2-3 for desired depth. Fasten off.

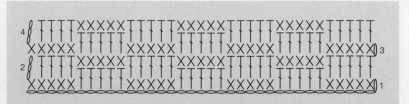

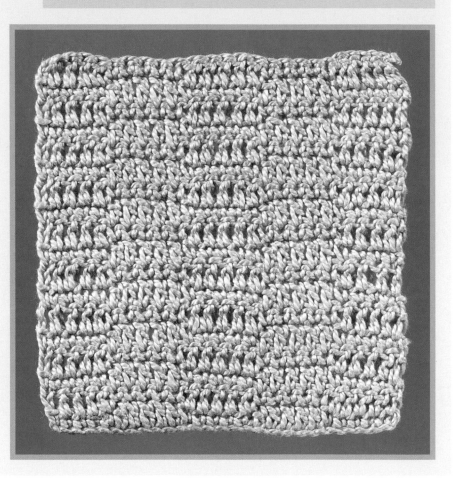

287

Ch a multiple of 2 plus 1 for desired width.

Row 1: Sc in 2nd ch from hook, sc in each ch across, turn.

Row 2: Ch 3 (counts as dc), 2 dc in next sc, *skip next sc, 2 dc in next sc; rep from * across, turn.

Row 3: Ch 3 (counts as dc), skip first 2 dc, *2 dc bet last skipped and next dc, skip next 2 dc; rep from * across to turning ch, 2 dc in 3rd ch of turning ch, turn.

Rep Row 3 for desired depth. Fasten off.

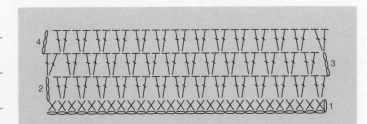

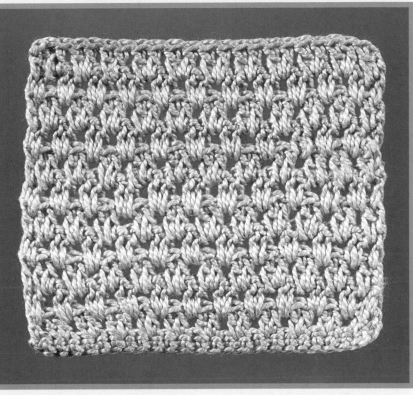

288

Ch a multiple of 4 plus 3 for desired width.

Row 1: Sc in 2nd ch from hook, sc in next ch, *ch 2, skip next 2 ch, sc in each of next 2 ch; rep from * across, turn.

Row 2: Ch 3 (counts as dc), dc in next sc, *ch 2, skip next ch-2 space, dc in each of next 2 sc; rep from * across, turn.

Row 3: Ch 1, sc in each of first 2 dc, *ch 2, skip next ch-2 space, sc in each of next 2 dc; rep from * across, ending with last sc in 3rd ch of turning ch, turn.

Rep Rows 2-3 for desired depth. Fasten off.

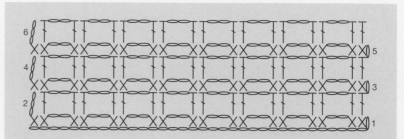

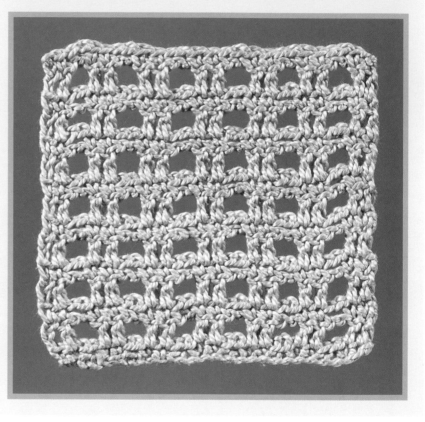

289

Ch a multiple of 6 plus 4 for desired width.

Row 1: Dc in 4th ch from hook, *ch 1, skip next 2 ch, dc in next ch, ch 1, skip next 2 ch, 3 dc in next ch; rep from * across, ending with 2 dc in last ch, turn.

Row 2: Ch 4 (counts as dc, ch 1), skip next ch-1 space, *3 dc in next dc, ch 1, skip next dc**, dc in next dc, ch 1, skip next ch-1 space; rep from * across, ending last rep at **, dc in 3rd ch of turning ch, turn.

Row 3: Ch 3, dc in first sc, *ch 1, skip next dc, dc in next dc, ch 1, skip next ch-1 space, 3 dc in next dc; rep from * across, ending with 2 dc in 3rd ch of turning ch, turn.

Rep Rows 2-3 for desired depth. Fasten off.

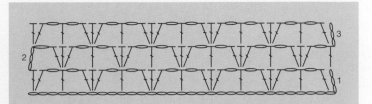

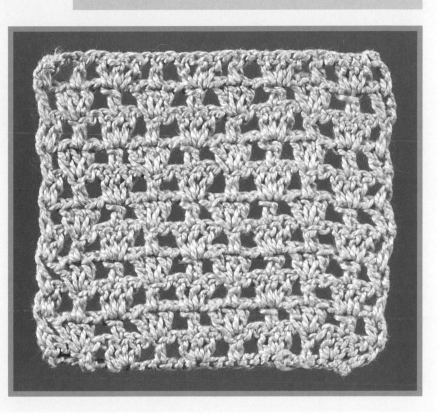

290

Ch a multiple of 3 plus 2 for desired width.

Row 1: Sc in 2nd ch from hook, *ch 2, skip next 2 ch, sc in next ch; rep from * across, turn.

Row 2: Ch 3 (counts as dc), dc in first sc, *skip next ch-2 space, 3 dc in next sc; rep from * across, ending with 2 dc in last sc, turn.

Row 3: Ch 1, sc in first dc, *ch 2, skip next 2 dc, sc in next dc; rep from * across, ending with last sc in 3rd ch of turning ch, turn.

Rep Rows 2-3 for desired depth. Fasten off.

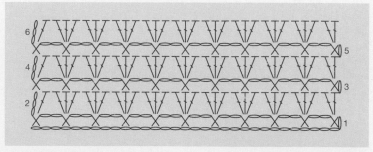

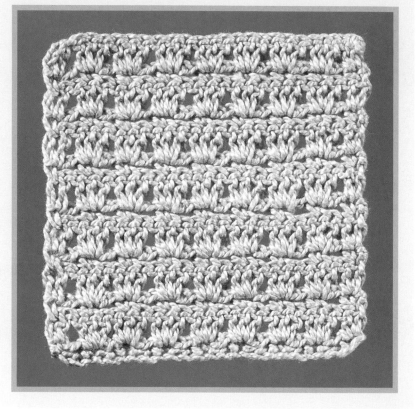

291

Ch a multiple of 8 plus 6 for desired width.

Row 1: Dc in 6th ch from hook, *skip next 2 ch, 5 dc in next ch, skip next 2 ch, dc in next ch, ch 1, skip next ch, dc in next ch; rep from * across, turn.

Row 2: Ch 4 (counts as dc, ch 1), skip next ch-1 space, *dc in next dc, skip next 2 dc, 5 dc in next dc, skip next 2 dc, dc in next dc, ch 1, skip next ch-1 space; rep from * across to turning ch, dc in next ch of turning ch, turn.

Rep Row 2 for desired depth. Fasten off.

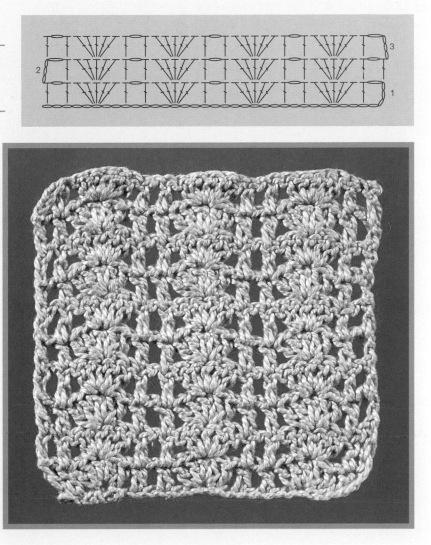

292

Ch a multiple of 4 plus 2 for desired width.

Row 1: 4 dc in 6th ch from hook, *skip next 3 ch, 4 dc in next ch; rep from * across, ending with 3 dc in last ch, turn.

Row 2: Ch 1, sc in each dc across, ending with last sc in top of turning ch, turn.

Row 3: Ch 3 (counts as dc), skip first sc, 2 dc in next sc, *skip next 3 sc, 4 dc in next sc; rep from * across to within last 2 sc, skip next sc, dc in last sc, turn.

Row 4: Ch 1, sc in each dc across, ending with last sc in 3rd ch of turning ch, turn.

Row 5: Ch 3 (counts as dc), skip first 3 sc, *4 dc in next sc, skip next 3 sc; rep from * across to within last sc, 3 dc in last sc, turn.

Rep Rows 2-5 for desired depth, ending with Row 2 of 4 of pattern. Fasten off.

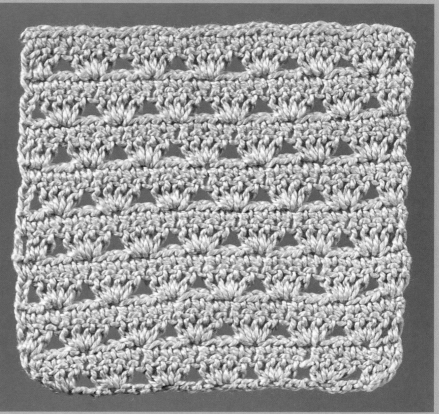

293

Ch a multiple of 6 plus 3 for desired width.

Row 1: Dc in 4th ch from hook, dc in each of next 4 ch, *ch 1, skip next ch, dc in each of next 5 ch; rep from * across to within last ch, dc in last ch, turn.

Row 2: Ch 3 (counts as dc), dc in first dc, *ch 2, skip next 2 dc, sc in next dc, ch 2, skip next 2 dc, 3 dc in next ch-1 space; rep from * across, ending with 2 dc in 3rd ch of turning ch, turn.

Row 3: Ch 3 (counts as dc), dc in next dc, *dc in next ch-2 space, ch 1, dc in next ch-2 space**, dc in each of next 3 dc; rep from * across, ending last rep at **, dc in next dc, dc in 3rd ch of turning ch, turn.

Row 4: Ch 1, sc in first dc, *ch 2, skip next 2 dc, 3 dc in next ch-1 space, ch 2, skip next 2 dc, sc in next dc; rep from * across, ending with last sc in 3rd ch of turning ch, turn.

Row 5: Ch 3 (counts as dc), *dc in next ch-2 space, dc in each of next 3 dc, dc in next ch-2 space**, ch 1; rep from * across, ending last rep at **, dc in last sc, turn.

Rep Rows 2-5 for desired depth. Fasten off.

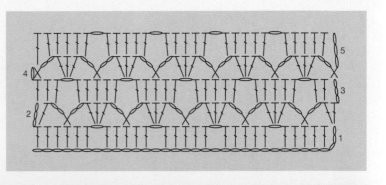

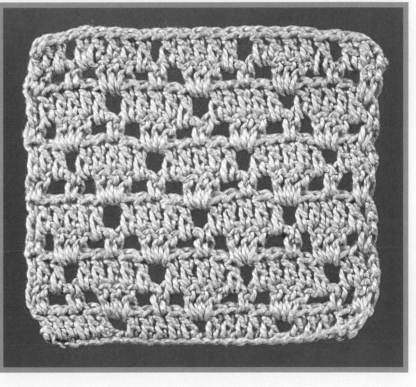

294

Ch a multiple of 5 plus 3 for desired width.

Row 1: (Dc, ch 2, dc, ch 2, dc) in 5th ch from hook, *skip next 4 ch, (dc, ch 2, dc, ch 2, dc) in next ch; rep from * across to within last 3 ch, skip next 2 ch, hdc in last ch, turn.

Row 2: Ch 4 (counts as hdc, ch 2), *sc in next ch-2 space, ch 3, sc in next ch-2 space**, ch 4; rep from * across, ending last rep at **, ch 2, hdc in top of turning ch, turn.

Row 3: Ch 2 (counts as hdc), skip next ch-2 space, *(dc, ch 2, dc, ch 2, dc) in next ch-3 loop**, skip next ch-4 loop; rep from * across, ending last rep at **, hdc in 3rd ch of turning ch, turn.

Rep Rows 2-3 for desired depth. Fasten off.

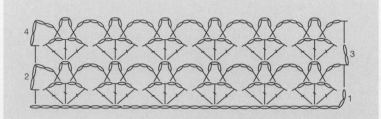

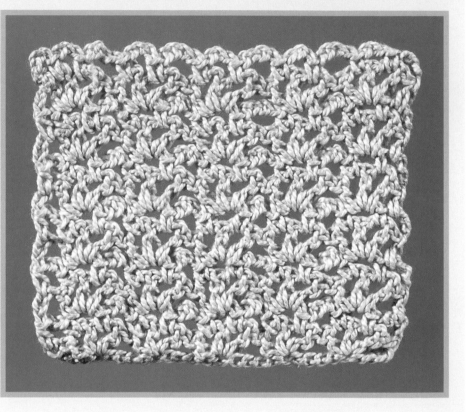

295

Ch a multiple of 8 plus 1 for desired width.

Row 1 (WS): Dc in 4th ch from hook, dc in each ch across, turn.

Row 2: Ch 3 (counts as dc), dc in each of next 2 dc, *FPdc in next dc, dc in each of next 3 dc**, ch 1, skip next dc, dc in each of next 3 dc; rep from * across, ending last rep at **, with last dc in 3rd ch of turning ch, turn.

Row 3: Ch 3 (counts as dc), dc in each of next 2 dc, *BPdc in next dc, dc in each of next 3 dc**, ch 1, skip next ch-1 space, dc in each of next 3 dc; rep from * across, ending last rep at **, with last dc in 3rd ch of turning ch, turn.

Rep Rows 2-3 for desired depth. Fasten off.

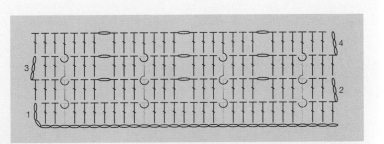

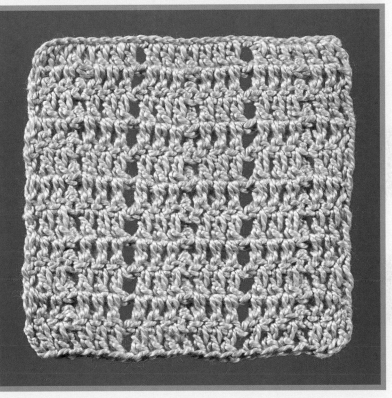

296

Ch a multiple of 12 plus 17 for desired width.

Row 1 (WS): Dc in 4th ch from hook, dc in each ch across, turn.

Row 2: Ch 3 (counts as dc), dc in each of next 2 dc, *(skip next dc, [dc, ch 1, dc] in next dc, skip next dc) 3 times**, FPdc in each of next 3 dc; rep from * across, ending last rep at **, dc in each of next 2 dc, dc in 3rd ch of turning ch, turn.

Row 3: Ch 3 (counts as dc), dc in each of next 2 dc, *(dc, ch 1, dc) in each of next 3 ch-1 spaces, skip next dc**, BPdc in each of next 3 dc; rep from * across, ending last rep at **, dc in each of next 2 dc, dc in 3rd ch of turning ch, turn.

Rep Rows 2-3 for desired depth. Fasten off.

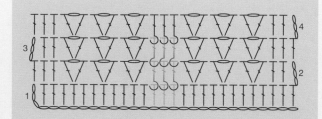

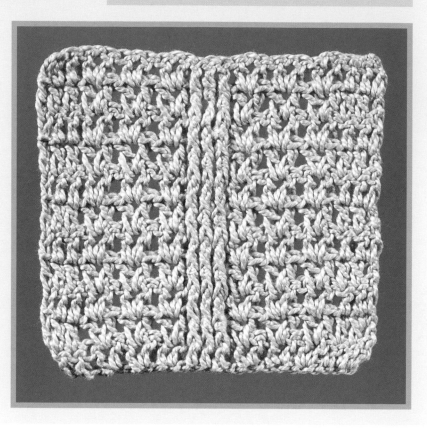

297

Ch a multiple of 3 plus 1 for desired width.

Row 1: Sc in 2nd ch from hook, sc in each ch across, turn.

Row 2: Ch 3 (counts as dc), skip first sc, *(dc, ch 1, dc) in next sc, skip next 2 sc; rep from * across to within last 2 sc, dc in next sc, ch 1, 2-dc cluster, working first half-closed dc in same sc holding last dc, work 2nd half-closed dc in last sc, yo, complete cluster, turn.

Row 3: Ch 3 (counts as dc), puff st in next ch-1 space, (ch 2, puff st) in each ch-1 space across to turning ch, dc in 3rd ch of turning ch turn.

Row 4: Ch 1, sc in first dc, sc in next puff st, *2 sc in next ch-2 space, sc in next puff st; rep from * across to turning ch, sc in 3rd ch of turning ch, turn.

Row 5: Ch 1, sc in each sc across, turn.

Rep Rows 2-5 for desired depth. Fasten off.

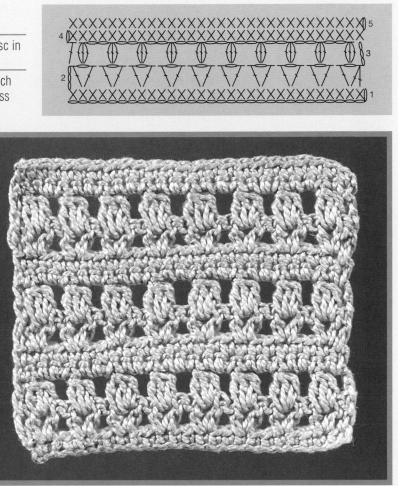

298

Ch a multiple of 4 plus 2 for desired width.

Row 1: (Sc, ch 2, 4 dc) in 2nd ch from hook, *skip next 3 ch, (sc, ch 2, 4 dc) in next ch; rep from * across to within last 4 ch, skip next 3 ch, sc in last ch, turn.

Row 2: Ch 3 (counts as dc), 2 dc in first sc, *skip next 4 dc, (sc, ch 2, 4 dc) in next ch-2 space; rep from * across to within last ch-2 space, sc in last ch-2 space, turn.

Row 3: Ch 3 (counts as dc), 2 dc in first sc, *skip next 4 dc, (sc, ch 2, 4 dc) in next ch-2 space; rep from * across to within last 3 sts, skip next 2 dc, sc in 3rd ch of turning ch, turn.

Rep Row 3 for desired depth. Fasten off.

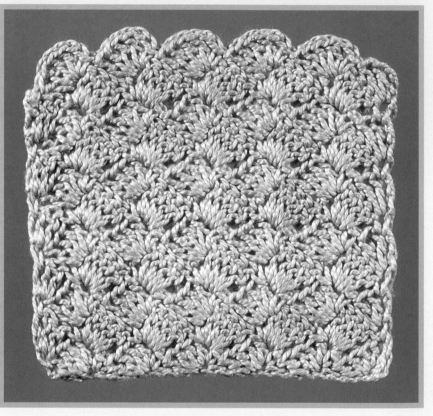

299 **Ch** a multiple of 4 plus 2 for desired width.

Row 1: Sc in 2nd ch from hook, *ch 3, skip next 3 ch, sc in next ch; rep from * across, turn.

Row 2: Ch 1, (sc, ch 3, 2 dc, hdc, sc) in each ch-3 loop across, turn.

Row 3: Ch 6 (counts as dc, ch 3), skip first 4 sts, sc in next ch-3 loop, (ch 3, sc) in each ch-3 loop across, turn.

Rep Rows 2-3 for desired depth. Fasten off.

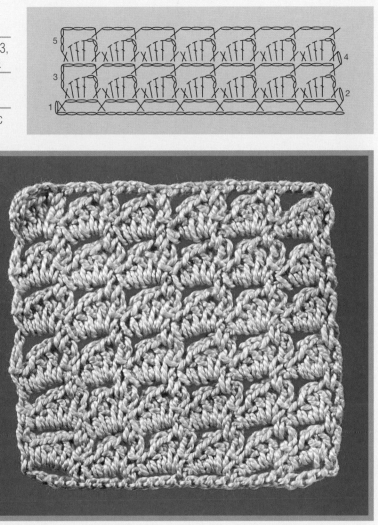

300

Popcorn (pop): 4 dc in same st, drop loop from hook, insert hook from front to back in first dc of 4-dc group, place dropped loop on hook, draw loop through st.

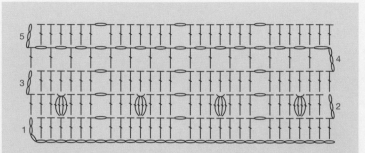

Ch a multiple of 8 plus 1 for desired width.

Row 1: Dc in 4th ch from hook, dc in each of next 5 ch, *ch 1, skip next ch, dc in each of next 7 ch; rep from * across, turn.

Row 2: Ch 3 (counts as dc), dc in each of next 2 dc, *pop in next dc, dc in each of next 3 dc**, ch 1, skip next ch-1 space, dc in each of next 3 dc; rep from * across, ending last rep at **, with last dc in 3rd ch of turning ch, turn.

Row 3: Ch 3 (counts as dc), dc in each of next 6 sts, *ch 1, skip next ch-1 space, dc in each of next 7 sts; rep from * across, ending with last dc in 3rd ch of turning ch, turn.

Row 4: Ch 4 (counts as dc, ch 1), skip first 2 dc, *dc in next dc, ch 1, skip next st; rep from * across to turning ch, dc in 3rd ch of turning ch, turn.

Row 5: Ch 3 (counts as dc), *(dc in next ch-1 space, dc in next dc) 3 times**, ch 1, skip next ch-1 space, dc in next dc; rep from * across, ending last rep at **, with last dc in 3rd ch of turning ch, turn.

Rep Rows 2-5 for desired depth. Fasten off.

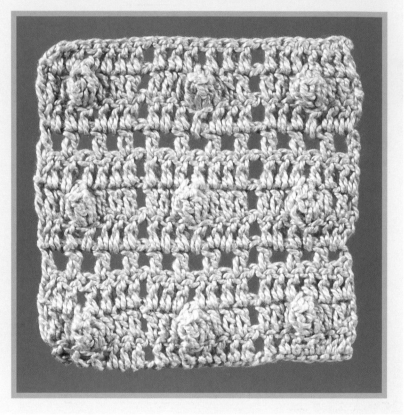

Crochet Terms and Abbreviations

Abbreviations

beg	begin, beginning		RS	right side
BPdc	back post double crochet		rnd(s)	round(s)
			sc	single crochet
ch	chain		sl st	slip stitch
dc	double crochet		st(s)	stitch(es)
dtr	double treble crochet		tr	treble crochet
FPdc	front post double crochet		trtr	triple treble crochet
			WS	wrong side
hdc	half double crochet		V-st	V-stitch
pop	popcorn		yo	yarn over
rep	repeat			

* Repeat directions following * as many times as indicated
() Repeat directions inside parentheses as many times as indicated
() Work directions inside parentheses into stitch indicated

U.S. Term	U.K./AUS Term
sl st slip st	**sc** single crochet
sc single crochet	**dc** double crochet
hdc half double crochet	**htr** half treble crochet
dc double crochet	**tr** treble crochet
tr treble crochet	**dtr** double treble crochet
dtr double treble crochet	**trip tr or trtr** triple treble crochet
trtr triple treble crochet	**qtr** quadruple treble crochet
rev sc reverse single crochet	**rev dc** reverse double crochet
yo yarn over	**yoh** yarn over hook

■ Acknowledgments ■

I'd like to thank Charles Nurnberg, president of Sterling Publishing Company in New York, who very kindly remembered me from 20 years ago, when I wrote my first crochet books, and gave me the wonderful opportunity of reprising them with Lark Books and passing on again these timeless techniques and my own love of crochet.

Thanks also to the Lark team who helped me through the revision of this book and who brought the entire project together—my editor Susan Kieffer, technical editor Karen Manthey, and art director Shannon Yokeley. I appreciate your dedication and vision. And, thanks to the following for their assistance with editorial details: Amanda Carestio, Dawn Dillingham, Rosemary Kast, and intern Halley Lawrence, and to the following for their assistance with production details: Jeff Hamilton, Avery Johnson, and intern Eva Reitzel.

■ About the Author ■

Linda Schapper's artistic vision is expressed in a wide range of media, from patchwork quilts and crochet, to painting and liturgical textiles, all of which are characterized by a folk-art style. She has traveled and taught extensively around the world in more than 30 countries, speaks four languages, and has had some 100 exhibits of her patchwork quilts. She has written eight books, four of them on crochet. She now divides her time between painting and writing, primarily about her liturgical work.

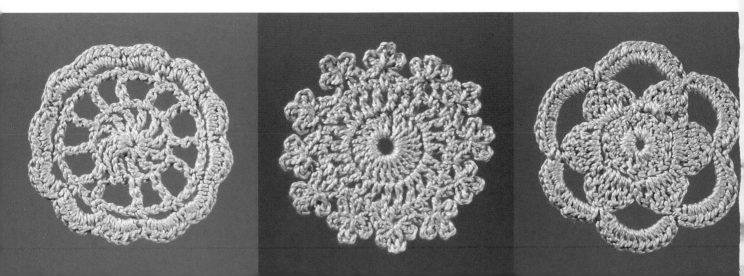